CONTENTS
EDINBURGH REVIEW ISSUE 93

TWICE YEARLY: SPRING 1995

Editorial	5
Fiction	
Gavin Bowd: The Grey Brother	11
Janice Galloway: not flu	16
W. N. Herbert: Dead Picts	24
Margery Metzstein: Family Fugue	31
Gary Allen: Strange Fruit	34
Interviews	
Glenn Patterson & Niall McGrath	41
Margaret Elphinstone & Lisa Babinec	51
Ciaran Carson & Niall McGrath	61
Poetry from the Six Counties	67

John Brown   Martin Mooney   James Simmons
Pat Ramsay   Medbh McGuckian   Gerald Dawe
Fred Johnston   Frank Ormsby   John Hewitt

Allusion, Theft and Free Translation	
R. A. Jamieson & Murdo Macdonald: An Ossianic Miscellany	91
Murray Pittock: Forging North Britain in the Age of Macpherson	125
Frank Kuppner: Extracts from Tartan Wisdom	140
Edwin Morgan: Recycling, Mosaic and Collage	149
Macdonald Daly: Concplags and Totplag: *Lanark* Exposed	167
Thom Nairn: Two Poems	201
Reviews & Shortleet	209

Edinburgh Review, 22 George Square, Edinburgh EH8 9LF
tel 0131-650 6206
fax 0131-662 0053

editors	Robert Alan Jamieson
	Gavin Wallace
advisory editors	Jackie Jones, Murdo Macdonald
cover	Ann Ross Paterson
production	Pam O'Connor
publicity	Kathryn MacLean
logo	Alasdair Gray
©	the contributors 1995

ISSN 0267 6672   ISBN 0 7486 6198 0

distributed in the UK by Edinburgh University Press
typeset in Sabon by Koinonia Ltd, Bury
printed and bound in Great Britain by
by Page Bros Limited, Norwich

subsidised by the Scottish Arts Council

back issues available
from Polygon,
22 George Square,
Edinburgh EH8 9LF
tel 0131-650 6206

EDITORIAL

Crossing the Divide

ALL TEXTS are forgeries, and all those who produce them are forgers. When James Joyce launched his hero Stephen Daedulus' flight into 'silence, exile and cunning' to 'forge in the smithy of my soul the uncreated consciousness of my race', he encapsulated in the powerful ambiguity of a single word a paradox which has become even more appropriate to a postmodern age. For as Murray Pittock points out in this issue, to 'forge' is both to create, and to counterfeit; to innovate and imitate; to temper the heat of imaginative daring with the cold cunning of deceit to produce that which is both original and fake. In Norman MacCaig's words, 'the lie of art/ Telling its great truth'.

And as for texts, so for races and nations: they too can be forgeries, both true and false. Filtered through the theoretical movements which succeeded modernism, the Joycean forgery has become the concept of the nation as the 'imagined community', in Benedict Anderson's influential coinage. Anderson's notion of nationality as determined by ideological constructs which are to differing degrees 'fictional', has, not surprisingly, been eagerly adopted in Scotland as a country which has repeatedly had to re-invent itself and its own history – or forge it, as Pittock suggests was the case in the 18th century. Scottish writers have, of course, for better or for worse, played a conspicuous role in such constructions. Some have felt burdened with the doom of their country's problematic 'identity'; others have gleefully subverted it to their own idiosyncratic purposes.

Many more are beginning to renounce that instinctive genuflection to the 'identity problem' as Scottish culture continues a process of far-reaching reconfiguration. The 'imagined community' which is 'Scotland' may, or may not, exist. What is undeniable is that a Scottish 'community of the imagination' is now a palpable and powerful force as a polyphonic chorus of voices and tongues. Perhaps this is why contemporary Scottish writing continues to show a generous and sensitive openness to engage in dialogue with other arts, other cultures, other worlds: an eagerness to translate, expropriate, assimilate: a desire to continue crossing the divide.

Such energetic heterogeneity is both promoted and welcomed by this journal. In **Edinburgh Review** No. 93 we devote a substantial feature to celebrations, subversions and interpretations of the continuing importance of 'allusion, theft and free translation' to the Scottish imagination, from Macpherson's *Ossian* to Gray's *Lanark*.

Whether it is Andrew Greig's adaptation of the new musical technique of sampling into narrative poetry in *Western Swing*, or Allan Massie pretending to be Sir Walter Scott in *The Ragged Lion* (both reviewed in this issue), or Frank Kuppner's deviant deconstruction of Wittgenstein, all testify to a creative and intellectual climate vibrantly alive to transformation. And as that inimitable boundary-crosser Edwin Morgan's catch-all account of the dictionary-delvers, acrostickers and copy-cats of literature confirms, such flights of co-operative and non-co-operative re-creation – or intertextuality and plagiarism, if you prefer – promise bewildering, sometimes maddening, but always worthwhile journeys.

The imagination which forges communities can link them too: in this issue we've made the imaginative journey to Ulster, to try to build a bridge between Scottish and Northern Irish writing. But producing a journal twice a year inevitably means that the world moves on in the time between planning an issue and its publication. It's hard to be topical when your production schedule stretches from one solstice to the other, and sometimes interim changes cause annoyance, if not outright embarrassment. In the case of this number, 1994 saw a shift that brought a quiet rejoicing and we sincerely hope that by the time this is published, the murmur will have become full grown joy. Forget topicality – twenty five years of folk living with dread of sudden loss, twenty five years of distrust – that makes the concerns of a journal like this seem unimportant. We are thinking, of course, of the announcement of the putative IRA ceasefire on August 31st 1994 – that Irish border-crosser Van Morrison's birthday, by some apt synchronistic twist – and the tentative withdrawal of British troops in January 1995.

When the planning for No. 93 began, peace in Northern Ireland seemed distant, even unreachable, and all the writing from Ulster in the following pages dates from a time before the prospect materialised. Having read through the contents closely preparing for publication, and in the knowledge of how swiftly the situation has changed, we find subtle prefigurations in certain pieces: the closing line of Pat Ramsay's poem *Overlooking Belfast Lough*: 'Like anywhere, *here* is a place to build'; the conclusion to Frank Ormsby's second *Cradle Song*: 'a new place and reason for love to begin'; Glenn Patterson talking to Niall McGrath about Belfast: 'So the city is constantly redefining itself, Which I think is an enormously liberating thought, because nothing is finalised. There is always the possibility of change.' Of course this is a selective reading. Had the change not taken place, we might have been highlighting John Brown's poem *The Singer's House*: 'High over Divis a tin bee hovers/ Dips its white proboscis tip/ Into the red brick flower of the city/ Sunshafts at midnight slant along the battlements'; or taking the description of the Orange march from Gary Allen's *Strange Fruit* as evidence of how little things have changed.

Yet the fact that we're able to find such seeds of hope in writing which predates August 31st 1994 is a sign that the new mood in Ulster wasn't without some forewarning, and proof perhaps of the importance of art as a potentially hope-inspiring, transformative force, reaching deep into the hearts and minds of folk to dredge up treasure from among the sludge of 'smear, sleaze and cynicism' that daubs so many public places with a gutter-based war-paint. These days, it seems that no one's free from taint. All are compromised to some degree, and 'compromise' in this contemporary usage has negative overtones, of 'giving in' to temptation or 'giving up' the fight. But 'compromise', literally, is a word essential in negotiation towards peace. In situations where we have to trade our own ideals off against those held by folk we've been conditioned into thinking of as 'them', compromise is about 'giving' – without preposition – something substantial, like credence to another set of beliefs. Where both sides are prepared to give ground, to admit to their own shortcomings and tolerate the hopes of the other, a settlement may be established.

Those of us who've only watched the news, read the books and papers, have only the vaguest notion of what the last twenty-five years in Ulster have been like. Images gathered from brief field trips assume symbolic significance – walking through Belfast as an armoured car trundles past, the soldier up-top with his gun levelled at the pavement, and that instant when the barrel points at you; crossing the border into Donegal, your driver pointing out the fresh wreath at the roadside by the checkpoint, where a car and its driver blew up the week before. Filled up with such random data, and lacking an awareness of the ordinary in Ulster life, we compute solutions to problems that we've never been confronted with, and confuse the chronic with the acute. Whereas the truth is, as Glenn Patterson says, that 'at any one time it's not one story, it's at least a million and a half. And these stories are changing all the time and you've got to keep up with that.' There's no 'one true story' to prove the others false.

The tale of James Macpherson, here told in *An Ossianic Miscellany*, is a salutary example of what can happen when one man claims to be the translator of the true. When we feel ourselves to be one of the defeated, the disenfranchised other, as Murray Pittock suggests the young Jacobite Macpherson did, it's natural enough to seek some means of dignifying the culture we belong to. Like the young Daedulus, Macpherson may have seen his mission as a calling, to 'forge in the smithy of my soul the uncreated consciousness of my race'. But too extravagant claims can jeopardise a just appreciation of the situation – the weight becomes too great and the centre cannot hold. The virtues of Macpherson's work, and the sources he made use of, were disregarded by many because of the subsequent scandal. He and those who encouraged him were dicing with the pride of a nation. Today, as ever, politicians and religious leaders like those contemporary 'self-styled prophets' who have led their cults to mass suicide, risk even more by their dogmatic intransigence.

But those seeds of hope inspire the faith that, ultimately, scores are settled fairly. Elsewhere in this issue, James Macpherson is compared to Burns on the grounds that their careers had certain connections and parallels, though their lives took very different courses. The diverse circumstances of their deaths make the difference clear. Burns on his death bed, despite all his traumas, was not the poor man downcast as popular sentiment portrays him, nor the turncoat regretful of his conduct as the more radical school would want. He was able to joke, telling Dr Maxwell when he came to see him that he was 'only a poor craw, no worth the pluckin'.

Macpherson, by contrast, was consumed with guilt at the end – 'From the minute he was confined to bed, till a little before he expired, he never ceased imploring Divine mercy in the most earnest and exemplary way', according to one Mrs Grant of Laggan who was present. Afterwards, as he had instructed in his will, his body was carried by coach to London, where he was buried in Westminster Abbey at his own expense. The journey took eighteen days. As Angus, the retired train-driver who is keeper of the Clan Macpherson Museum in Newtonmore phrased it, perhaps alluding to the scandal of 'Ossian': 'Eighteen days! Man, he must have been rank-rotten by the time they got him there'.

Better for what remained of him, maybe, had Macpherson taken a plot in the humble kirkyard in Kingussie rather than create a stink in pursuit of a place in the eternal hall of fame; or, as Murdo Macdonald writes in his poem *A Glen for John Hewitt*, dedicated to the Ulster poet for whom atheism and the semi-mythic Ossian were both bridges crossing the divide, better to have: 'endured each question and defeat/ and held with understanding to your lack of faith', rather than fabricate a tale of ancient glories and hold it up unflinchingly as true – better, perhaps, for James Macpherson to have clung to his northern home, and not his Northern Homer.

FICTION

GAVIN BOWD

JANICE GALLOWAY

W. N. HERBERT

MARGERY METZSTEIN

GARY ALLEN

The Grey Brother

Gavin Bowd

THERE LIES the pond, dark and still. Above it, the midges bite and the bats will flit. Tadpoles turn from commas into scribbles. Skaters beam on beer-dark water. Children have whipped toads there. A young boy was drowned there. You have to wait for hours for the occasional ripple. There stands the heron, grey as ashes. At times, it cranes its neck or shafts its legs into the waters. It is a naked solitude, preferring the mist.

It was at a time when the pond was frozen white. The ferns and the grass were starched with frost. Sheep limped in the hard furrows, by the turnip-heads.
  And the cold had free rein to occupy the houses. Wood was thrown on the fires. But the coal that had kissed the children with its lingering flame was gone. The pits of Lothian were empty, or had been closed down, or had not been sunk. The monks, their owners, would not give the people access. They gathered in their abbey to send prayers to the beyond. So much love was promised when the body was taken by the worms.
  Heron stood aimlessly in Gilmerton Grange. He had been an engineer in Tranent. He had designed the arrangement of pulleys that sent the men and buckets up and down the shaft. He had told them how to combat the floods. He had smelt out the richest seams. He had supervised the sifting of coal from the rock. It was thanks to his intelligence that, at Sunday Mass, the begging children would go home with the black stones of Lothian.
  But now the pits were exhausted. Or they were sealed. Heron felt beneath the turf the sea of coal that extended out beneath the Firth. Combustible fossil. Fire and warmth for everyone. But the grass was left to sway in the wind, mocking his idle hands.
  The cold rasped the pale skins of the people. When the wind came charging in from Fife, it augmented the torture. Cats had once come in from the cold, to wrap up their hypocrisy in laps. Now they shifted restlessly across the land, wailing and wailing about historic injustice.

Heron had one beautiful daughter. She lived with him in Gilmerton Grange. They had become very close after the death of his wife. She spent the day with her book and drawings. She walked the hounds and inspected the grounds.

Her womanhood had perturbed Heron, who had seen again beside him a beautiful woman. The arresting gaze of her face. The blatant curves of her body. Once he had surprised her bathing. She had simply turned round and laughed, unabashed of her large, pink nipples and the ample triangle of her cunt.

There was not much here for a beautiful young lady. Stretches of rough grass and copse, pockmarked with quarrying, until the Pentlands rose sternly above them. There was beauty here, but one to be strolled upon. Not one to be touched, or that can touch. There were the buffoonish sophisticates of Edinburgh, strutting their pretensions down the Royal Mile. And there were the whistles of the miners, sinewy and stooped, who broke their backs for their bloodless children and the massacred bellies of their wives.

Her region was one long winter, to whose biting air her sobbing breast rose and her thighs opened in helpless spasms.

The trees stood petrified in the air. The owl joined the frost with its screech. The foxes tore apart with gusto the pathetic stump of the child that a family had left there to rot.

Gouged, brown, wounded earth. That once was trampled by miners for hours on end. From which the Lothians drew their heat. Which now was rock-hard with inertia. It was owned by the Abbot of Newbattle, a richly-endowed abbey upon the banks of the South Esk.

The Abbot did not need the pits. He sat among his ornaments and artworks, drinking ales, wines and spirits. His rooms were warm with coal that the monks chipped from open seams. He prepared his next sermon, knowing that his idle and suffering brethren would come unto him. That they would flail themselves with guilt and puff themselves up with pride about the beyond.

He knew both chastity and the world. He knew the adventures with the Sisters, the delicious anguish of being human. He knew the torment of the feminine boys who passed through the seminary. And he knew the passion with which brethren kissed the crucifix and railed against all fleshly sins. How he despised them.

The cold was out there, crushing Scotland. The horses stood whinnying head to toe. The comfort of the Abbey was a shallow distraction. A tepid, watery boredom.

The Abbot resolved to ride to Gilmerton Grange. To see his engineer, Heron, with a view to meeting his daughter. He had once seen her naked at baptism. And now he mused upon the miracle that exploded in her garments.

Down along the river. The hoofs clattering on the path. The harsh krarak of the crows. The endless complaint of the seagulls, pining for the North Sea. Until the clean, solid features of the Grange, and the nurse standing at its door.

Heron was out in the woods, looking for fuel. He found a seam of coal that jutted out of the ground in a humpback curve. Heron took his pick and chopped away at it, releasing rough nuggets of coal. He chopped up branches from dead trees. And he ripped up thorn bushes.

Hours of labour made him sweat. Until the cold made droplets freeze on his back, and his hands were numb on the handle of the pick. Then he turned back for the Grange, past the frozen pond, the cacophonic rookery, and the cowering sheep.

It would be wrong to say that the Abbot of Newbattle was an unattractive man. His charisma had merited his promotion. His booming voice gave resonance to the holy texts. Nuns and miners bowed to him, winced delightfully to his arrows of scorn. Listening to him, and chanting his words, the monks knew that they had obeyed their calling: that these long, wretched days in Scotland aimed for a higher purity.

He was corpulent, as befits a man who gorges on the tributes of his congregation. But it was a healthy, worldly corpulence, well-suited to ceremonial robes. His flesh was shiny, and his gestures were sure. What he took in his hands lent itself gladly to his control.

He was glad to find himself alone with Heron's daughter. Her astonishing beauty was plain to see. And the darting of his eyes from head to toe left her in no doubt about his approval. How did this flower bloom in such a season?

There followed a stilted, cough-punctuated talk about Church finances, the weather, and the misfortunes of virtue. But both telegraphed to one another their insincerity, their ardent adherence to the beyond. Longing looks that became detached from their chattering lips. Until the lips were joined, like the looks were joined, and they found themselves on the floor, the Abbot scrabbling for her underwear, then releasing himself upon her. Fear, joy, confusion, a suddenly acquired addiction.

The nurse had heard the amorous struggle in the girl's room. But she did not intervene. It is not right for a beautiful girl to while away her youth in such a desert. No dignity in her tossing around at night, alone, her fingers writhing between her thighs. And there is reason to be happy about the worldliness of a priest, like the arctic flowers that spring out from the cracks in limestone.

She would shoot at the Abbot a knowing stare. And, as he left the Grange in a welter of platitudes, she would whisper to him that she would gladly aid them in their illicit intercourse.

Cold gripped Scotland. Waves of pain rushed down from the Arctic. The sun rose feebly to light up the coal-bings. The old were hastening their exit for the beyond. Children shivered in their cots. Life was reduced to a glacial pace. And people thought of the coal that would be found yards beneath the crunching turf. In your delirium, you could see the black waves crashing on the distant magma.

Heron pursued his solitary quest for fuel. He applied his engineer's hands to cutting up the thorn bushes, then carrying them along the path to Gilmerton Grange, where he stacked them against the wall. Stack upon stack of thorns, until a massive pile began to grow, to the amazement of the nurse.

The nurse would inform the Abbot of Heron's comings and goings. Then he would mount his horse and make haste for the Grange, whipping its haunch as he thought of the delights to come. And, with a brief speech to God about his inner torment, he would mount Heron's daughter and nuzzle his face in her eager breasts. How the sweat poured and the heat brought the blood to their cheeks!

Icicles had established themselves in the eaves of the houses. The woodwork was warped. Mist would not clear. Joints became stiff. Dreams were of May and the bursting of foliage.

Heron gathered his stacks of thorns, dreaming of pit-shafts. But he puzzled at the sudden gaiety of his daughter: her relaxed gait, her impatient staring through the window. How could she bloom in such a desert?

Until, one day, while carrying thorns back to the Grange, he espied the Abbot in conversation with the nurse. He then entered, throwing his arms around his daughter, who ran to greet him. Heron put down his bundle and stealthily made his way around the walls of the Grange. From behind a tree, he craned his neck, so as to see into his daughter's room.

There was the bulging figure of the Abbot, naked except for his hat, upon the splayed and yelping body of his daughter. Faster and faster, they rocked together, shouting all forms of cries to heaven.

Heron turned and hit his head upon the tree-trunk. Sobbing, mourning the lost honour of his daughter. He made curses on the Abbot like a jilted lover. At dinner, that evening, he adopted a glacial stillness, and spent hours standing by his study's window, oblivious to the nervous giggles of the daughter and the nurse.

The cold wrung its hands upon the land. Could it really be colder on the moon that hung glinting in the sky? The seam in the forest choked its last fragments. The foxes scuttled around, whining for the corpses of children.

Heron brought more stacks of thorns. The pile grew up until it covered windows and spilt over onto the roof of the Grange. A strange fervour drove Heron to tear up and down the path, emptying the land of its bushes.

Then, one day, Heron announced that he was going to Edinburgh. He would petition the King to reopen the mines. A rational plan for investment in the coal industry of the Lothians would permit the warming of hands and the employment of wasted labour.

And he left. And that night the Abbot and the daughter met, like lovers should. The night would be for lovemaking, passionate confusion of limbs and sheets. The nurse cooked for them a fitting repast, which they devoured with what remained of the cellar. There was a brief but joyful conversation. Then they retired to the bed that the nurse had freshly made.

Heron watched this from the ridge of the hill. They could not see him, for by now it was dark. But he could see the candle-light which lit up the cheery faces of the Abbot and his daughter. Heron wretched a long gob of hatred. The billowing wind that wrecked the Pentlands was a friend to his wretched heart.

He descended the path to the Grange. Then, with a tinderbox, protected by his cloak, he added sparks to the mountain of thorns. After several attempts, the branches took fire. More and more of the thorns joined the flame, and Heron willed them to burn faster and faster. How could they hear the ascending roar as the wind threatened to blow away the world?

The thorns revealed their violence. One massive bonfire dined on the Grange. While Heron stood back smiling, his neck trembling with emotion. Inside, they were taking fright: the fat-headed Abbot, that silly bitch of a daughter. Scrabbling and choking, they were prisoners of the smoke and the timbers that had adhered to the catastrophe. Abbot, daughter and nurse collapsed together as the fire trampled throughout the house.

It was a goodly sight. The Grange blazed beautifully in the stormy night. Long and warm, like a ton of coal. Men, women and children would come to join Heron, stretching out their palms and the soles of their feet. The cold had left Lothian for the Firth of Forth. It was easy to forget the morning's ashes.

Gavin Bowd, poet and short story writer, was born in 1966. He studied under Kenneth White at the Sorbonne from 1989-90, and now teaches French in Ireland.

not flu

Janice Galloway

A whisper.

Shuffling.
Peter's voice, muffled through the layer of hollowfill, a word in the unknown tongue. Bloody Dutch.
Rachel peeled her face out the pillow, turning towards more light than was bearable. A magnesium flare on the dressing table mirror. Christ. He'd opened the bloody curtains again. The duvet was too close, one stiff corner shoving against her lip. She shifted to avoid it, making one hand an eyeshade against the closed lids. It didn't help much. Tiny silver-red beams, cloud linings the colour of fresh blood, filtered through the spaces between her fingers, the tang of overnight sweat from her open palm tracing nippy threadveins over the soft-boiled whites. The sounds went on as before, worming uninvited into the aural cavities. She could hear them quite distinctly. A polythene bag opening and closing, taking surreptitious ages, then muttering. Trying to be so bloody careful and not wake her up. That they didn't know she was lying awake listening made it worse somehow: the dark magnified things, somehow, made it impossible to blank them out. That was no excuse though. It didn't make it ok. Listening to folk behind their backs for heavensake. It wasn't nice. It was worse. It was morally objectionable and untrustworthy. Eavesdropping, you called it. Well, that's what Enid Blyton books called it. She couldn't think of any other word. Eavesdropping. Bloody disgraceful. Rachel closed her eyes, shifting the hand that had covered them over an ear instead, trying to behave. The other hand had surfaced from beneath the sheet, reaching to rub a sore place just behind the hairline. The roots there thick, greasy. Needing washed. Slattern. That was a funny word as well but it fitted. It fitted no problem. An eavesdropping slattern, lying in bed till godknew what time. One eye opened, found the clock. Five to five. It was always five to five. Over a week now and she still hadn't

replaced the fucking batteries. Rachel moaned, was about to sink her face back into the pillow again when another sound made her stop short. Knife noise, the scrape of stainless steel off cheap china. Her cups, her knives being passed hand to male hand in the kitchen. Under the fond impression they were undetected, the bastards were making breakfast.

The flash of anger was sudden. More to the point it was uncalled for. It was distinctly unpleasant. Rachel opened her eyes, making them water like hell to serve her right. The man was a guest for godsakes. A foreign guest. He was here because he'd been asked, because he'd been invited and what's more it was her had done the bloody inviting. And what was wrong with people making breakfast, people speaking Dutch, come to that? Even if she didn't understand it. It was his bloody language – what else was he supposed to speak? On top of everything else, that was meant to be the point. Peter, back only six months and virtually having to relearn English, he'd been away for so long. Eight years, spinning out one grant after another, getting a radical education or something. Being formed. That beautiful, choked way he spoke, accent so overlaid with another tongue it was hard to tell where he belonged. Motherwell born and bred and that affected cow in the delicatessen over the road thought he was South African. Sud Afrique? twisting the pitch up on the last syllable like a parrot. She said it every time he went in there. He just laughed. Mary he called her. First name terms. He was never out that shop. Other ways, though, other ways he just wasn't settling back at all. And the way he fretted about his Dutch going to waste, that his pass-for-the-real-thing idioms would rust. So it was *her* that said it, her idea. Ask one of your mates over, on you go, it's your place too and he smiled that way that made her stomach slide like sand. A carnal sensation. Less than a week after, when he said Sebastian was coming, the feeling came again only this time closer to the lower intestine. Someone she didn't know would be sharing their living space for a fortnight. More food and electricity, having to put a camp bed up in the living room every night, whether he would leave his stuff lying all over the place, whether it was rude or bourgeois to care. And Dutch christ Dutch. Thinking about it made her dizzy. Peter just laughed when she said she was scared. Once. Then he'd gone back to his blueprints, his notes in the margins. She didn't mention it again: no-one to blame but herself.

By the time they were standing at the airport, though, clutching bunches of tulips she wasn't sure weren't a joke, it seemed better. It seemed better because of Peter's face. She'd never seen him look so something. Radiant, maybe. Happy. Helping to look for someone she'd seen only one bad photo of; relieved, for some reason, when he looked less like Peter than she'd thought he might. Even if she hadn't managed to shake his hand more than awkwardly, aware of blocking the aisle a whole planeload of other people were trying to walk down, even if she had felt surplus to requirements, it didn't matter. Watching Peter exchange kisses with the other man, his face lit like the sun, made all the apprehensions petty and mean-minded. She knew, when Peter gathered her in too, making a three-sided embrace, she knew it would all work out fine. Nomatter what the guy was like. Sebastian. Nomatter what Sebastian was like. Everything would be just fine.

Laughter.
Rachel's back stiffened, her ears pricking. In the other room, the toaster popped, ejecting both barrels: a single word emerging from a blur of giggles. There was no other word for it. Thirty-year-old men, giggling like children. Her eyes were closing again, one hand rising to her temple. She pressed the warm skin there, feeling the skull beneath push back. Bone under flesh, resisting like eggshell.
It might have been 4am.
She had woken with his breath in her ear. A half voice, not making words she could turn into meanings yet. Peter saying something. I don't know what to do. She had thought it an intimacy, the depth of dark and the heavy scent of him next to her, maybe a tenderness, and she had turned, expecting the weight of his hand to fall on her breast. A kiss, perhaps. Her nipples had tensed, waiting. But he didn't reach. He didn't touch her at all. The sheets were cold, he said. He whispered. The sheets were cold. The hand fumbled towards him, finding something cloying, clammy. The sheet on his side. Under his back, damp enough almost to be called wet. Something was wrong and there was no going back to sleep now, no embrace. I don't know what to do. There was a moment of nothing before he repeated it. He didn't know what to do. It was happening again.
Thinking about moving jesus. Trying to open her eyes.
The air inside the room was thick as raw meat. Just breathing it in was an effort. This was the fourth night of this bloody thing, this flu or whatever. That one day in bed she'd talked him into, they thought he might be on the mend. She heard him sigh again, the sound vast in the stale blackness. If she'd forced him to take those bloody vitamin things this might not be happening. He'd not liked her going on about them but she should have forced him all the

same. This was partly her fault then, another night of broken sleep and this sweating, not ordinary sweating but rivers of the bloody stuff, his skin in spate. She dragged her hand back from the sheet and lifted her head. Christ, the dizziness, a kind of spiralling soreness behind the eye sockets. It got worse as she hauled into a sit then pushed off the mattress to stand. The blackout curtains up for winter left no light to see by, none at all. She found the door anyway, banging her shin on something hard, falling over her own feet in an attempt to ignore it and keep going, not able to keep her eyes open for longer than seconds at a time. But it didn't matter. It didn't matter. Stumbling over the hall carpet to the cupboard. Peter was sick again. Somebody had to do something. Somebody had to get clean sheets.

The hall was cooler, the press unproblematic. The two sheets were right at the front: the same ones they'd put through the machine yesterday, the smell of that fabric stuff rising from traps in the fibres. A smell like peaches, almost soothing. Not ironed though. Now back through, the sheets trailing behind like wedding drag, the bedside light was on and Peter was standing up. Trying to stand up. She could see him, through half-shut lids and a mesh of eyelash, pulling something on over his chest, tugging it down, hardly able to keep his balance for christsake. She dropped the fresh sheets where she stood and started work on the bed, hauling. It wasn't easy. She'd probably tucked them in too tight making the thing up this morning, thinking it would be nice for him: hospital corners, wee games of nursemaid. Now it was a bastard to dismantle. The undersheet had to come off as well: sticky as the topsheets, maybe worse. He was beside her then, reaching one arm to help, veins visible through a ghostly wrist. She squinted sideways, trying to see his face but it hurt so she stopped and assumed instead. He'd exactly the same as the other nights. Terrible. Eyes heavy and skin taut over the high cheekbones, his lips chalked out. He shouldn't be trying to do this. He shouldn't be standing up, never mind anything else. But she said nothing. Trying to tell him how to look after himself always caused more problems than it was worth. The sheet was virtually off anyway. She let him tug the last bit free and dump it with the other two already on the carpet. She'd need to get another one now, take the dirty ones through to the washing pile, fetch a third from somewhere and start making the bloody thing up again. Peter was sighing. He didn't sit down though. He was looking at her. It wasn't till Peter sighed again that Rachel realised it wasn't the tired kind of sighing at all but another kind that had something to do with her and looked down. She was naked. Hauling the bed apart like a thing possessed stark, seal-belly naked.

I've no dressing gown.

The first thing that came into her head. It hung there, not explaining anything. She wasn't sure why she said it, why it sounded so much like apology. Looking down again for clues didn't help. She often slept naked, at least often in summer. Other times when there was a likelihood of sex. A wish for sex. And this wasn't summer. A confused embarrassment was spreading over her skin, some kind of shame she couldn't place. What was sure was that she wanted to cover herself. She remembered seeing his bathrobe somewhere, a heap on the floor before she had put the light out. Now she looked it was still there, behind the wicker chair leg. She stopped to pick it up, trying not to wonder whether it was right side out, whether he would mind. Whether it was even sanitary: with Peter like this, the bloody thing could be hoaching with disease, germs, bacteria and microbes. It didn't matter though. It didn't matter a damn. She wanted to get the bloody thing on before he sighed again, before she caught another glimpse of herself, and after all it was thoughtless: barging about naked with somebody in the house. Another man. Not that Sebastian looked at her much but that was beside the point. Other people's sensitivities and so on: it might have offended him to hell. Her toes dug into the carpet pile even thinking about it. The belt was in a knot now, a solid knot. When she looked back up, Peter was angled against the bedside, exactly where she had left him. Shaking. His whole body shaking, the clean teeshirt he'd put on already patched with dark under the arms.

Jesus Peter. Are you ok?

He said nothing.

Put the heater on or something. Sit in front of the heater and get warm for godsake.

He didn't look at her or say anything. Just crouched down on his hunkers, reaching for the socket. Rachel watched him feel for the switch, press it once, his neck sheeny with drying sweat and knew she couldn't think of a bloody thing to do. Except maybe make up the bed again, hope he got some sleep. They both got some sleep. And wait for the thing to pass off. Maybe that was all it needed: a decent night's kip and they'd be right as rain. She turned away from the sound of the fan, the soft billowing of overheated air, heading back to the press.

The shelves were empty. Nearly empty. Just one whole sheet and a torn thing like a sleeping bag liner crushed at the back. They'd have to do. The stuff on the pulley wouldn't be anything like dry yet. The torn thing would pass for a pillowcase: he only used the one. Ends tucked under and he'd never know the difference. Anyway, it was all there was. Rachel gathered up the cloth and went back through. Too fast. She knew even before the pain registered, a dry sharpness shooting from the ankle, she knew it was her own fault. If she hadn't been rushing, if she hadn't been so preoccupied, breenging about and so on. But she had and this was what happened. The bedside cabinet again, the same shin, exactly the same fucking place. The kind of pain that hugged the bone, that got worse after the initial impact. She tried not to react and failed. Jesus. Peter wheeled, looking anxious. She made a sharp intake of breath. Fuck fuck jesus. Then another noise, slow hissing.

Shhh. Peter saying Shhh.

She looked at him, still clutching the ankle, not sure.

Sshhhh. He looked desperate. For crying out loud, Rachel. All that noise, banging into things. You're so bloody clumsy. So bloody. He waved an arm limply. I don't know. I don't. I haven't got the bloody words any more. Can you not just be at peace for godsake? Be a bit less obvious or something? Do everybody a favour and just. His voice died back. Just calm down.

Neither of them moved.

People are sleeping. His shoulders slumped. Sleeping. Fading to nothing. Shh.

She kept looking at him. He didn't say anything else. Just clasped the rim of his teeshirt, hands cupped where his genitals were beneath the cloth before his gaze broke and he looked away.

Out of sight, Rachel straightened, giving herself time. Her eyes were wide open. They didn't hurt any more. On the other side of the bed, Peter sighed again, face the colour of separated milk. Terrible. He wasn't well, he was missing sleep. They both were. It wasn't the right time to start asking questions now, to be angry or anything else. It wasn't the time to mention the way the two of them blocked her out all the time, the way they were always together doing things she had no say in and it wasn't just the language. There were other things, lots of other things. The house didn't feel like her own. They way they kept different mealtimes, shut doors behind them when they stayed up in the evenings or worked together, heads close over blueprints and drawings. He was there between them all day even now, in the middle of the night changing the sheets in her own bedroom, the bastard wouldn't go away. Peter was embarrassed by her, scared she would wake him up by being too – what was it? Being too obvious. By being too fucking *there*, was that what he meant? The way the two of them went out every evening, some pub he never said the name of, the way Sebastian smiled when she asked. She wouldn't like it there, it would bore her and she said how can you be sure and he smiled again. He just knew. Now Rachel thought she knew something too. The reason he hung around the house so much, why there was not a time when they were alone except when she and Peter were in bed and even then he was semi-fucking comatose with sleep or drink, too tired to talk, too tired for anything at all. They hadn't fucked since that man had been here. They hadn't even embraced for christsake. It dawned so clearly it seemed crazy she hadn't worked it out before.

Shhh.

The low insect drone of the fan heater stopped. Completely. Peter had slid back down onto his heels, still shaking, and switched the bloody thing off. In the bloom of silence, Rachel looked hard at his back, the skin tight over his spine. He wasn't well. He had woken her up saying as much, not knowing what to do. He'd been doing it for three nights and for three nights, she'd fetched more sheets and stripped the old ones. Because she didn't know what to do either. And still they soaked through. Because it wasn't flu. It wasn't that kind of sickness. It was something between the two of them, something between the two men. And she knew she was shaking too only it didn't show. A bead of sweat glistened on his jaw, melting into stubble as he stood up, facing her. Eye to eye. He looked like a fucking ironing board, braced for something. Against something. He would not understand if she touched him now, if she took his face in her hands and kissed him. Hard.

Sorry, he said. Almost inaudible. Sorry.

Rachel shrugged and looked down. It wasn't the right time. Not the right time at all.

The sheet in her hands. She took a pace back and snapped it wide, a white billow over the mattress. Peter stood up and moved to the other side. Their hands started smoothing then, putting the thing to rights. Elsewhere, the Dutchman moaned, turning in his sleep. It wouldn't be long now, though. They'd go back to bed. They'd go back to bed and not sleep. He would sweat. It would not be possible to touch him because of the burning, his burning up and needing peace and calm. Her touch would not allow him peace. It would make him worse. And she would lie next to him, trying not to come too close.

She must have slept, finally, on the edge of her side of the mattress. This cramping in her shoulders, stiffness up the back of her neck. Maybe not well, but she had slept. And still he'd managed to be up first, pulling the curtains, getting on with things. Making breakfast for godsake. He laughed then. She heard him laugh, through in the other room and imagined his head tilted, his neck bared. He'd have fixed something for him and Sebastian, the way he had every morning, not mentioned his waking in the night. When she went through, there would be general jollity and making light of things, gentle protests she was only fussing and over-protective. You know how women are. She heard him laugh again: Sebastian, his voice rising as he laughed too.

Rachel lay as still. As still as.

Keeping her eyes tight shut. There was nothing she wanted to see.

Before long she would tell herself not to be difficult. She would tell herself not to be paranoid and get out of bed. She would wash her face with cold water to make it look less hellish and smile when she opened the kitchen door. She wouldn't ask if he'd taken the vitamin C, at least not immediately. A couple of minutes though and she wouldn't be able to help herself. Very soon now, she would get up, defying lost sleep and godknew what else. Godknew. She would butter toast, make a joke of herself dosing him with fizzy health supplements from a wine glass, and smile some more. It was all she could think of to do. Her head crushing tighter. Knowing it wasn't flu. It wasn't

flu.

Janice Galloway has written two award-winning novels and one story collection. She was most recently honoured by the American Academy of Arts and Letters, and won the McVitie's Prize in 1994. She likes cities and lives in Glasgow.

Dead Picts

W. N. Herbert

YOU KNOW before you start that something horrible is going to happen, so that's why you do it. At some level, anyway. Most people have got an inkling of what I'm saying. It's your antenna of the weird, unless it's been snapped off, car aerial-style. It was exactly the sort of place I avoid like the proverbial bubonic, what I call a 'broon pub'. It was also in the centre of town, too near the railway station. That was my rationalisation: I need to kill time before the train so I'll pop into the 'Comb and Mirror'. Shite, of course; it was my antenna receiving its last broadcast from the planet Zog.

I'd been in there once with my old man – these places are safe enough with the old man because he's guaranteed to know fifty percent of the punters. So I was familiar with the layout. A big bar up against the back wall with mirrors and old whisky flasks, bulbous empty things hanging upside down. The mirrors carrying adverts for extinct pale ales. To the right of this, the door to the toilets, all copperplate engraved on glass; to the left another door, similarly engraved, that said 'Saloon', a word that always made me think of Westerns and therefore, presumably, helped prepare me for the increasing Americanisation of our culture.

'That's whaur the women sit, through there,' the old man had pointed out. 'This is one of thae bars that still pretty much segregate things. I mind when a wifie wad pit her heid through that door an call her man hame and they'd been sittin in separate rooms o the same pub aa nicht.'

'Like the men's house and the women's house in some tribal societies,' I replied, eager to make the conversation go with a swing. This was shortly before I nearly graduated in Anthropology.

'Almost exactly,' he said, with that look my mother calls 'the Powrie fiss – they've aa gote it'. I was getting, she had informed me recently, 'mair like it every day'.

So here I was again, waiting for a train to take me south as usual. Same barman, same copperplate, same brown. I couldn't have sworn any of the customers had moved, though some of them must surely have died. And of course I stand next to the wrong elbow entirely to put in my order.

'I hear the Velvet Underground huv reformed.'

'Whut?'

'You know, Andy Warhol's lot. Split up years ago because of that Taffy, whit's his name? Ye would've thocht they'd mair integrity than to reform noo.'

'*Whutt??*'

My reaction was melodramatic, granted, but this was from an old codger half my height who still sported his bunnet like a tweedy caul. Casual acquaintance with the doings of the New York avant-garde was not, I think, to be anticipated.

'See me, though, I approve. I think ye've gote tae flout integrity if ye're goannae shak up yir attitudes.'

'Flout?' I hadn't meant to say this out loud, and realised at once it was a tactical error. He looked up at me for the first time. His skin was coppery and his nose was beaked. The eyes looked almost completely black. The faint trace of an ancient tattoo peeked over his thin shirt collar. It looked like an elephant. What kind of man, I asked myself, has an elephant tattooed on his throat?

'Wid ye like tae see my licence tae use big wurds?' he asked, hissing slightly.

'Flout isnae a big word, it's just that … your topic took me by surprise.'

'As the actress said tae the wee man at the sweetie counter.'

'Okay, I'm sorry.'

'Acceptit. So, since you shy awa frae meh efforts at …' a polysyllabic flourish here, 'contemporaneity, why don't you pick a subject?'

'Uh, I've gote tae get a train,' I stalled, fearing he could yet turn into Malcolm Canbore, king of all pub 'characters'.

'An this is afore ye've feenished yir pint?' he queried, pointing a pipe stem at my glass, which the barman had chosen this moment to serve me.

'Okay, chaps, chaps,' I said, giving him some thought for the first time. He was wearing a see-through plastic raincoat with big flat rubbery buttons (it hadn't rained all day). Under this I could see a much slept-in check jacket, and brown trousers that had two creases running roughly in parallel down each leg. The situation called for a delicate mixture of bravado and diplomacy.

'Yes. How about you telling me about the men-only policy in this bar: how does an intelligent man like yirself feel about that?'

'Ah now. Fur that we must go back to the matriarchal society of the Picts.'

'Must we?' My worst fears were confirmed. He was actually filling his pipe as he spoke. Was it possible in the 1930s, I wondered, to contract rickets of the brain?

'Of course. Ye see this isn't actually a men-only bar; that ...' and here he jabbed the stem toward the Saloon door, 'is a weemen-only bar.'

The gesture was unnervingly reminiscent of a Samurai film I had seen once, in which an old man eating rice is threatened by a ruffian. Without looking up he stabs his chopsticks into the ruffian's eye, wipes them on the man's sleeve, and goes back to eating his rice.

'Oh come on granda. Are you tellin me they're stuck in there because they like it?'

'Well, I'm no sayin it's general, but that is how things used to be done in the four Pictish kingdoms.'

'Oh yeah?' I drawled, going into my amateur pedantics turn. 'I read there were six kingdoms and they're no too sure about that.' He gave me another black look and started making those pipe-sucking noises, like a child with a milkshake. He was clearly about to bluff some more.

'Fine,' I said, getting in first, 'suppose you tell me how a men-only policy is meant to be a remnant of Pictish society?'

'Point A,' he began, pressing a mustard-coloured finger into a bar-mat; 'when nae written traces of a culture survive it is impossible to tell whut is and whut isnae a remnant o thon culture. You could be a pure-blooded Pict of a royal line and how would you know? Unless yir mither's Irish, of course.'

'Would ye mind no jabbin that pipe at me. Ye'll huv someone's eye out with that,' I countered feebly, aware that I was echoing a long line of maternal ancestors.

'Point B ...' he continued, applying another yellow digit to the beer-mat.

'Jist a minute, jist a minute. This argument's useless. Onywan can say that the Casuals are a remnant o tribal divisions because we cannae prove that they're no.'

'Point B: we can make assumptions based oan still-existent matriarchal societies.'

'Right. I've got ye there. I did a study of that fur my degree. I've been to one in Greece. The culture of Olymbos on the island of Karpathos. All inheritance through the daughter, a council of women ...'

As I said this I became conscious, as always when I flash a bit of learning, of having exposed myself. I glanced around. The barman was studying the back of a matchbox. He could be trying to get the joke printed on it, but I got the impression he had just averted his gaze. There was one other possible witness, a man sitting with his anorak done up sweating. He had the same expression as piano players do in Westerns when the gunslinger walks in. If, however, I was packing a piece of anthropology, my coppery little companion was up to the challenge.

'Whit do the men in Olymbos actually dae, if ye don't mind me askin?'

'They don't do anythin, as a matter of fact. Most of them bugger aff to the mainland. The women do all the work.'

'An where is it ye're goin again?'

'Hang oan; that's anither false parallel. I'm part of the ... the brain-drain if ye must know, and that's caused by the structures of competitive capitalism, a patriarchal invention.'

'Sure, pal, sure. Jist tell me: whit dae the men in Olymbos actually dae.'

'Nuthin, I've told you, nuthin. There's nuthin for them to do ...'

'Exactly. And that is the curse of a proaper matriarchy like the Pictish system: whut do ye do wi the men?'

That was the clincher, the rhetorical question as K.O.: I had no option but to wait patiently for the next slab of information. The wee man had handled it well, though, I had to grant him that. Bore or not, I hadn't really stood a chance. He gave me a small smirk that was almost sympathetic.

'So, the weemen dae maist o the wurk, right?'

'Like in Africa,' I replied. This was meant to be sardonic, but to no avail.

'And they inherit the proaperty. Sae whit are men there fur anyway? There's anely twa things that men can dae that weemen hae nae time fur – fechtin and makin things weird.'

'Define weird.' (At least I was putting up a fight.)

'Weird is magic, art and goads.'

'What about fertility goddesses?'

'Exactly. Who worshipped those, I ask you? Weemen are aaready fertile, remember? Sae they slip the men a few wee dollies tae pley wi, keep them oot o mischief. Awa worship us, and get the hell oot fae under wir feet.'

'So there were no female artists.'

'There are now, but that's cause they dinnae huv tae huv bairns aa the time tae keep the species goin. Ye cannae write in atween the hoosework, ask ony wifie.'

'Right, I will,' I said, sensing an exit line, and put down my glass, ready to go to the Saloon. The barman tapped wetly at my forearm.

'Ye cannae go in there, son.'

I gaped at my companion, who merely spread his hands silently.

They must, I thought, be hatching this up between them. The barman was filling up my glass. This was getting decidedly – what was the word? – weird.

'Twa things,' the little man reiterated. 'Gee them somethin abstract thir heids can pley wi, or send them oot oan the rammy. Now I'm not blamin any of those weemen – that wiz smart stuff. But what they couldnae haunnil wiz hoo faur the men wad take things. Cause if there's wan thing a man diz that a wifie diznae it's get cerried awa wi himsel.'

'We arra boyz,' the barman said, in melancholy tones, putting another pint before me. 'Compliments of the manageress.' I clutched it for stability.

'So it's 'we need tae destroy the hames o wir enemies sae that thir weemen cannae breed mair enemies tae destroy the hames o oor weemen.' Laive aathin tae us. We'll sort it oot. It disnae matter that whit we're daein disnae matter really, because we're too stupid tae wurk that oot. It's like huving a car that gaes twa hunnert miles an hour when ye're only allowed tae go at seventy. An whit dae ye caa yir car?'

'Hur,' all three of us chorused, shaking our heads ruefully. So this was why I had come in to the 'Comb and Mirror': to hear about the ultimate futility of my gender from a miniature bigot who listened to the Velvet Underground. I put a dent in my latest pint.

'I know ye're askin yirself: what is the solution?'
'I'm askin maself: huv I missed ma train?'
'But don't concern yirself, son, the solution is at hand ...'
'Hang on a meenit,' I was feeling rather fuddled suddenly. 'Did we get roond tae the problem here?'

His response was extraordinary; his face seemed to inflate like one of those saveloy-shaped balloons. I suppose he just drew closer, but I swear he looked like a smoked sausage leering.

'What sort of woman dae you desire? In yir innermaist hert I mean?'

No-one had ever said 'innermost heart' to me in dialect before. I don't think I realised that it was possible till that moment. As I stared into his black, dog-like eyes I weighed the phrase; in Scots it had an almost diabolic flavour to it, as though that part of my cardiacal organ had to be a dark and dismal place.

'I don't know, someone Japanese perhaps? Can she be educated?'
'Get serious son, is it no a Scottish lassie? Wan o thae wans wi heavy features and strong dark hair. Someone whas sexuality is a complete mystery tae ye and they can knoack ye oot wi a single blow? A gurl wi eyebrows.'

'Strong girl is like an ocean,' I nodded, quoting Iggy Pop thickly.

Something peculiar was happening to my attention span; each of his clauses was presenting itself as a separate tableau in some sort of landscape. They formed a perspective in which I could no longer see my own last statement.

'In that bar, son, is the collected genius of hundreds of years of Pictish weemenhood. Is it ony wonder that nae man may profane that presence? The Foard Capri was inventit centuries before the 1970s; it was inventit in the minds o the men that took over from the Pictish matriarchs, the warriors that made Scotland as we ken it. But that doesnae mean the Mithers went awa. Na, na; realisin the social evolution they'd initiated was overwhelmin, they infiltratit.'

The landscape in which his statements were arranging themselves was, I had worked out, time. His words seemed to recede over decades. I knew by now that I had been drugged but it was as much as I could do to focus on his face, let alone cope with what was happening to me. The barman had abandoned his station and was lifting me up. They were both walking towards the Saloon bar, dragging me with them as the wee man spoke.

'Every man has his Helen, the wan woman he canna resist. The Mithers can gee you that, in excheenge for … well, I'm sure ye'll agree it's a small price for the maist complete relationship ye'll ever ken.'

We were through the door by now. Instead of another bar, however, we were in a small room with a red chaise-longue and a large mirror along the right wall. Ahead was a glass door inscribed 'The Mithers'. On the chaise-longue was a lemony chiffon thing, a horrible seventies-style dress.

'Whu … who are you peopul?' I slurred out, as the barman produced a Stanley knife and started to cut my clothes off me. The wee man smiled, again with a slight note of compassion.

'We're jist attendants, pal. Dinnae bathir aboot the knife. Ye're an intelligent kind of guy, anthropology degree an aa …'

'Nearly,' I interjected feebly, as the barman tugged the dress over my head.

'Sae ye'll recognise this as an initiation ceremony,' he continued imperturbably. 'Of course ye cannae gae intae the presence o the Mithers in a man's habiliments.'

'A man's *whutt*??' I cried as the barman opened the door and propelled me through. It swung shut on my backside and propelled me forward into the gloom.

The room was full of women, I could tell that much. Big women, sitting at small tables sipping something, rum and coke probably. None of them were looking at me, as if men in Pan's People cast-offs were regularly thrust into their dimly-lit presence. A single coal fire provided all the light there was. I knew that I was terrified, sweating with fear, at the same moment as I understood that if any of them paid me the least attention, something horrible would happen. This moment distended. Then a door at the back of the room swung open, and a young woman in a black waitress dress and white apron walked in carrying a tray.

Even in this darkness I could tell she was the one I'd been prepared for, my Helen. She was shorter than me, but broader, strongly-featured with heavy Montgomery Clift eyebrows. Silently, she served a table of the grim-faced women, then looked at me. She smiled, baring strong milky teeth, and pulled a small knife from her apron pocket. She began to approach me, stealthily, as though I was about to make a run for it. Still the women paid no heed to what was going on in their midst.

I was rigid with fear both in the sense that I couldn't retreat, and in the sense that I had a big cold hard on. This surprised me, as I wasn't aware of being at all aroused. The whole scene felt more like something that happened at primary school, one of those inexplicable humiliations of the young. My erection, I worked out laboriously, must be another side effect of whatever drug I'd been slipped.

The knife must have been incredibly sharp, or perhaps that was another side effect of the drug, because I never felt a thing as she gripped my penis in one hand and expertly sliced it and the rest of my genitalia off with the other. I watched my blood exploding over her little white apron at the same moment as all the women arose in a single movement and bore me to the ground, applying bandages and poultices in the same expert silence as had marked the whole action. One of them pressed a comb and mirror into my still sweating palm.

As I lay there three thoughts went through my head, none of which related directly to my emasculation. The first was the look in her eyes as she cut me was orgasmic, no doubt about it. The second was that the reason I recognised this was because that was no lady, that was or had been a man. And the third was the little man's comment on the cost of encountering my Helen: 'I'm sure ye'll agree it's a small price for the maist complete relationship ye'll ever ken.'

Family Fugue

Margery Metzstein

Daughter's Song: First Movement: andante

'This house is full of noise. I can hear the sound reaching towards a peak, then fade into the distance. Each time the peak moves closer. Soon they will be out of control. The voices become more staccato and I can see the gritted teeth, the saliva pushing through, moving towards the bottom lip, threatening to escape. But not yet. They still have a space for control. Each time the notes move towards a renewed frenzy my stomach becomes part of the cacophony. The tide of their anger breaks against the walls of my womb, crushing me, enveloping me in the sound of their fury. As the voices become calmer, I can feel the tension ooze from my body.

It begins again. By this time I am so much in tune with the rhythms that I anticipate the final out of control when the violence and saliva will burst free. As I do, as I'm waiting, I hear myself screaming. My voice pitches high. I hear it pleading for them to stop. I don't think they know what I'm saying, but my screaming bursts into their passion.

There is a pause which sounds as magnified and tenuous as the silence between a heartbeat. They reclaim their voices, gather their anger and fear up into a tight ball and suck back, swallowing hard.

The air echoes with remembered sounds.'

Mother's Life: Second Movement

first voice: 'Fireflies flash into the black cocoon where the close weave of the blanket has been stretched over the years. These intermittent pinpoints of light only begin to penetrate, afterwards. At first, there is the soothing, salving, embrace of darkness.'

second voice: 'If we enter the room and neglect to switch on the light, we might see, when our eyes have become accustomed to the dark, a sequence of recognizable shapes. Sweeping our eyes across the room, from right to left, we can discern a small rectangle, a large solid form planted in the middle of the room, followed by a larger rectangle, filling approximately one third of the space between floor and ceiling. Because of their familiarity we could name these objects effortlessly – a bedside cabinet, a bed and a tallboy. Continuing round the room our eyes might hesitate at a small mountain huddled against the far left hand corner of the room. The texture of the mountain looks soft and could be identified as a blanket but the shape is odd. The contours suggest that there is something underneath, filling it up. The blanket appears to be draped around a form. This could be an unusually shaped chair but it is difficult to imagine any chair fulfilling the necessary requirements. If we stood and listened hard we might think we could hear a soft pulsing ebb and flow of sound. However, that could be a trick of the silence.'

third voice: 'I wonder how long I've been here? My legs are stiff. He sounds as if he's asleep. I might be able to come out soon. I'll wait for a while longer. I don't want it to start up again. I can hear footsteps. Whose? They sound steady. Hold your breath. There is someone in the room. No light. Must be standing in the dark. Breathe out slowly. Quietly. Is it him?'

first voice: 'The boy turned abruptly and left the room. He knew she was there. He slumped against the wall in the hallway and felt the pain pushing through. He couldn't cry. He couldn't comfort her. She would be embarrassed. He was unable to expose himself or her to the knot of emotions which would follow if he revealed his knowledge. That is why he had left the room. While looking at the blanket in the corner – peering, thinking hard – a tableau of violence had appeared before his eyes. Voices raised, harsh guttural animal sounds, fists clenched, spit and blows raining down on a shape bent double. The shape escaping, stumbling, seeking refuge in a free space with no light. He closed his eyes. The boy-slumped-against-the-wall-in-the-hallway, clenched himself tight, trying to shake off the recognition. His mother, nearly sixty, without dignity, reduced to a small heap in her bedroom on a Monday night, after the pubs had closed.'

The Dream: Last Movement

dream narrator: 'I am in our house. I can see my mother, moving around the lounge. She is slowly picking up objects and carefully placing them in a different spot. I am in the bedroom with my father. He is pushing himself against me. I can still see my mother and I wonder why she is ignoring me. I am wordlessly trying to tell her that I'm being raped. She knows but does not interrupt her movements. She looks entranced. I open my mouth to scream for help as my father's unshaven face grazes my cheek. I am nauseated by the sour smell of tobacco, alcohol and sweat. I scream but there is no sound. I can't understand why my mother will not listen. Why won't she help me?

The scene changes. I am in a white room, filled with light. My mother is moving slowly around the room. She is gliding, not dancing. I am unwrapping a parcel, leaning over the bed. There are layers and layers of tissue swathing a dazzling white, finely crocheted, dress. I gasp at the intricacy of the pattern, which is formed by a series of interlocking webs of very soft, very thin wool. On the front, there are three pearl buttons which reflect the light and seem to burst into a myriad colours simultaneously. I walk over to my mother and hold out the dress. She takes it from me, in slow motion. We smile at each other and I stroke her arm.'

Strange Fruit

Gary Allen

She had us up and fed on toast and tea since early morning, scrubbed pink down at the kitchen, hair combed till it hurt. With undisguised pride she dressed us in our new clothes; jumpers, ties, shirts, trousers, shiny plastic shoes with buckles, and even new socks, pants and vests. I looked at Colin and was glad that I didn't have to wear short trousers. Then she tried to get us to stand at the door, said that she thought she heard one coming. We had heard nothing, protested that it was too early yet, but she persisted, looked out of the window and said that all the other children round the estate – even wee Sean Murphy – were standing on the green.

When she opened the door the warm sunshine streamed into the house. As she pushed us gently out to the step, told us not to be so odd, to go and show our new clothes off, she said hello to a middle-aged, red-faced man in a kilt who was struggling with a large drum past the house. Then leaving us she turned back into the hall, said that she was going to wake him up and get herself ready. Gingerly we moved a few steps up the path, under the watchful eyes of the other proud mothers standing by their windows, but when she was gone we retreated back to the step again. The other children, posted like sentries round that part of the estate, looked at us, their faces sullen, parading under duress, and in our own acute embarrassment we stared back.

When I reached into my pocket and felt the five-shillings that I had collected from them and various relations, I felt a little better, thought about the soldiers I would buy later. Then I heard several strains of music coming from a few streets away, and I hoped that it was a pipe-band.

I watched as the other children stirred, moved in a group to the top of the estate. The music grew in strength, began to sound like a tune, and a sedate, rather formal, brass-band came round the corner in rows three abreast – men, boys and girls – playing the slow strains of a hymn. Behind came several rows of Orange-men in suits and sashes, the older men wearing bowler hats, some carrying ceremonial swords or halberts, their handles decorated with ribbons or Sweet-William. They looped into the next street and were gone as quickly as they had came.

Just then the door opened slightly and he looked out, his hair tousled, dressed in vest and trousers, the crooked toes of his bare feet white in the sunlight. He pretended to scold, asked who was making all that bloody noise? but the joke was lost on us, so he coughed with embarrassment and went into the living room.

She frowned when we came back into the house and sat on the settee, said that she had wasted her money on new outfits, that we were so bloody odd. He was sitting in the armchair, hunched over the newspaper and eating a breakfast of boiled egg and soda. I told you not to go throwing your money away, he mumbled to her as he chewed, but she rolled her eyes behind his back, from where she stood with her arms folded in the kitchen doorway, and replied that we needed new clothes anyway, and besides, she couldn't send us out like tramps. He snorted, licked a glop of yolk that had fell from the spoon onto his hand, Don't ask me for a sub later in the week when you're broke.

She went down to the mirror in the kitchen and finished putting on her make-up, and he ate the rest of his breakfast, lifted himself up slightly from the chair and farted, then lay back and lit a cigarette. Another band came round the corner and entered our street. We turned onto our knees, leaned over the back of the settee and watched the flute-band march past. Some of the children from the estate ran after them.

She came up from the kitchen. adjusting her bra-strap, looked into the smaller mirror on the wall above the fire-place and drew on her lipstick – she looked different all done-up, in her make-up and cheap jewellery, the hair self-styled and cosseted with lacquer. You're looking well, he told her, before rising and going down to the kitchen to shave, then upstairs to put on his suit.

When he came down again she asked him if he was going out with us? He crinkled a Woodbine between his fingers before lighting it, then tugged at the stiff collar of his shirt, prising it out from the fat of his neck, then he shrugged, said that he would maybe go with us as far as Bridge Street, but that he was meeting Jimmy McAuly later for a drink. She frowned, mumbled that Jimmy McAuly was more a wife to him than she was, and his threatening look warned her not to start.

When she went upstairs to get her light, summer coat, he called us over and asked us had we pocket-money? We didn't know whether to answer him or not, for he wasn't beyond forcing us to lend it to him. Under his impatient gaze I answered yes, and he asked how much? When I told him he nodded and said that that was enough, that we wouldn't need anymore, when he was young five-shilling was a month's pay, then he spat on his hands and patted down our hair.

Wee Harry Sloan just went by, he told her when she came into the living-room, the kilt nearly down to his ankles, he laughed maliciously. And auld John Smith marching with the Orange-men, hardly able to keep in line with too much drink, and she frowned again and mumbled why had he to try and spoil everything?

He looked at his watch and told her that it was time that we made a move. Out into the blinding light we went. Other groups came out of their houses and marched along the pavement, exchanging greetings. The woman from next door came out with a basket, dressed in a heavy coat and headscarf. Jesus, you would think she was going to the North Pole, he mumbled. She told my mother that old Edna was too weak to come out. Lying up in bed with her rosary and praying for rain, he whispered and my mother elbowed him in the ribs. She had sent the weans sixpence apiece for ice-cream, then she handed us the coins and stroked our cheeks. Five-and-six, I mumbled to Colin with glee, the day was going to be profitable.

As the crowd grew he became more impatient, stepping out slightly in front of us, sometimes having to wait for us to catch-up. More than once a man with the smell of drink on his breath tried to entice him into a public-house for a drink, but he made the excuse that he had his wife and children with him, then they would make a great show of searching their pockets for money for the kids, but could never find change, and if looks could kill, the black looks that Colin and I gave them would have hurled them straight into hell.

When we came into the town proper the pavements were thronged with people so that we had to walk on the road. An uncle and his wife kept them talking for so long that the beginning of the parade could already be heard in the distance, and I had visions of us being trampled by its advancing, pulsing weight. We pocketed another shilling that soothed my nerves a bit then hurried on down towards the bridge at the bottom of the hill. Then we found a space and waited, staring across the road at the mirror-image of adults and children with Union Jacks and ice-cream. Sean Murphy pushed in beside us and we shared his bag of sweets.

It seemed as if the world grew suddenly silent, like the moment of quiet before thunder or the unleashing of flood-waters, when no sound seemed to carry from the pavements. Then it broke, the thunder of drums, the clatter of feet, and the myriad whistling of flutes.

My heart beat fast as I turned my head and looked back up the hill. The road was awash with black. Floating – as if suspended mysteriously – in the air above, the softly waving banners and flags. Slowly the tide rolled or down the hill till they reached us with a surge of noise that was deafening and the first marchers had already passed.

I gazed skyward, to the colourful, floating bunting painted with scenes from the bible – Daniel in the den of lions, Moses on the mount, Jesus and his disciples, a woman hugging a rugged cross, men in armour reclining before a brilliant light – so, that to me, time, the ancient and the present, became entwined, and I gazed upon it all with awe, while far above small clouds moved across the blue of the sky. There were other banners, King Billy and dignitaries long dead, neat moustaches and brown eyes like frightened animals, small chins and sashes memorials.

I stepped back with the first thundering of the lambegs, the willowy sticks almost motionless with speed – I prayed to God that the small, stout men with arched backs that were playing them would keep a firm grip on their sticks. Slowly they moved past, and I read the inscriptions on front, admired the paintwork and decorations, the bunches of lilies or Sweet-William. Then came the pipe-bands, the flute bands, the accordion and brass bands, the big drums with their strange-sounding town-lands painted on them, mysterious places that seemed as if they had came out of the very earth itself – like mutant seedlings.

Row upon row of Orange-men filed past, sombre in hardhats and sashes. With wonder I stared at the silver emblems, ladders and stars, numbers and open bibles – and I couldn't fathom the mystery that winded like a river before me. Some of the old men were bent and twisted like the trunks of ancient trees, their faces a patchwork of colours and lines, some travelled at a snail's pace in the back of black cars adorned with red, white and blue ribbons, hardly looking out at the people lining the route.

My father would nod or shout a greeting to some of the men who waved back with the gloves they carried. Familiar faces shone out from the ranks. Uncles and cousins, or the fathers of friends, all transformed by a unity that was strange to my years. Every so often a shout would go up as a bandleader threw the heavy-topped bandstick high above the crowd and the street, far up into the blue reaches of the sky, travelling on an unending course, as the crowd held its breath till the stick turned and plummeted back to be caught with a cheer.

When the last of the parade had finally passed I felt deafened, dazzled. My mother spoke to me, but I couldn't make out what was said. Then Jimmy McAuly came across from the other side of the street, cracked a joke with my mother who greeted him politely, but formally stiff. He brought his great dog's, red face down close to us and panted, mumbled something about King Billy and reached Colin, Sean, and myself a two-shilling piece each, but though I pocketed the money I would not be bribed – I didn't like him.

My father changed suddenly, slapped Jimmy McAuly on the back and smiled with affection, something that was rare beyond words. He promised my mother that he would be home for his tea, then him and Jimmy McAuly sauntered across the bridge and into the Royal Bar. She watched long after they had gone, then turned and took Colin by the hand, started back up the hill, through the milling crowd of people who were going in the opposite direction, following the parade out to the field to hear the political speeches. I came behind with Sean.

As we reached the top of the town all was strangely silent. The heat was all but bearable, shadows falling across the empty, littered streets. I felt cheated somehow, as though I had been had, though I couldn't say why, just an empty feeling that left me saddened.

She turned and asked Sean where his mother was, and he said that she was in the house, doing the week's washing. Then she asked him would she mind if he came home and had some supper with us? He assured her that she wouldn't. She pulled open her purse and reached me some money, told Sean and I to go and get some fish and chips for the tea. Then, holding Colin's hand, she walked towards the estate.

I looked back down the hill, now deserted. A gentle breeze had risen, though it didn't dispel the heat any, and gathered handfuls of dust from the gutter into the air, stinging the eyes. Chip-papers and sweet-wrappers were blown across the pavements, and the sun reflected from the shop-windows and made me narrow my eyes. A small bunch of Sweet-William was lying in against the kerb. Sean turned it over with the toe of his shoe. It was as if they had all been ghosts, had faded back into the ground.

I was glad it was over, turned the money in my pocket as I hurried along with Sean to the chip-shop, and imagined what I would buy the following day when the shops were open again.

Gary Allen was born in Ballymena, Northern Ireland, in 1959. His stories have been published in Britain, Holland and France, including *Edinburgh Review* No. 82 and *Paris Transcontinental*. His poetry has appeared in magazines throughout Europe and America.

INTERVIEWS

GLENN PATTERSON & NIALL MCGRATH

MARGARET ELPHINSTONE & LISA BABINEC

CIARRAN CARSON & NIALL MCGRATH

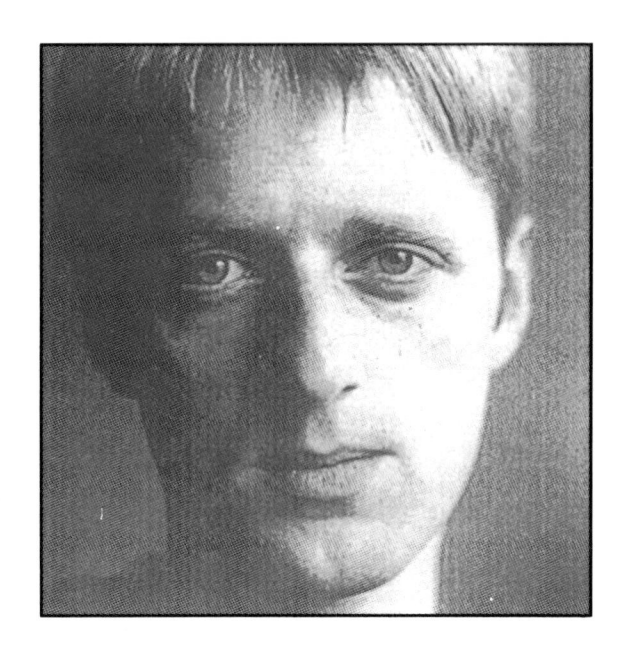

GLEN PATTERSON
Photo courtesy of Chatto & Windus

Glenn Patterson

interview with Niall McGrath

Born in Belfast in 1961, Patterson left Northern Ireland in 1982, living in Norwich and Manchester before returning in 1988 as writer in the community for Lisburn and Craigavon. His first novel Burning Your Own *(1988) was awarded a Betty Trask Prize and the Rooney Prize for Irish Literature. His second novel* Fat Lad *(1992) brought further acclaim. Niall McGrath met him in Belfast's famous Crown Bar in March 1994.*

NMc: *Can you tell me about your background and why you write?*
GP: I don't think there was ever a conscious decision made to write. I think it's more a question of wanting to tell stories. But you also learn to do that from the moment you hold anything in your hand. If you have a paintbrush or a pencil you start to make marks, you make narrative out of children talking about their paintings, there are stories in there. I started off wanting to be a poet. And that was largely for the lifestyle. For very bad reasons, like justifying smoking a lot of cigarettes and things and staying up late; Dylan Thomas was what my impression of what a poet was.

There's a very odd thing about schools in Northern Ireland – I have to say it might be about actually having a selection like an 11 Plus – that might benefit children from a working class background. I went to Methody [Methodist College, a grammar school], which people always consider to be a very middle class school. But from my estate in Finaghy there were at least a dozen of us joined the first year together. And we were all from very similar backgrounds; what you might characterize as skilled working-class families. These were people, like my own family, who moved out from round Woodvale and the Shankill, moved out in the early Sixties to the new housing estates. Methody seemed to be able to contain people from very well-to-do backgrounds as well as from working-class backgrounds in Belfast.

There was definitely a stage in my late teens when I was being pulled in various directions. On the one hand there was great pressure to, and I wanted to, conform to what was happening around the estate where I grew up – participate in what was happening there. This, increasingly as the Seventies progressed, was Loyalist, not infrequently overtly sectarian, behaviour. There was a lot of pull towards that. Yet there were people who were getting involved in music and things at school and who I was wanting to hang out with as well. Some of the interest in poetry came about through this interest in music, people like Bob Dylan – and Bob Dylan got his name from Dylan Thomas... There's a mistake some people make of tracing back some kind of coherent narrative thread through their lives – I think those things are fairly haphazard, at one time you could do one thing or the other. So I was being exposed to poetry and trying to write poetry at the same time as I was getting plastered and singing songs around the Orange bonfire. These things just went hand in hand.

Anyway, I was a terrible poet but I always had an interest in language and I think that's the one thing that sets apart people who are just interested in writing and writers is a deep fascination with how language can be used. I didn't go straight to university, I stayed on in Belfast for a couple of years, and then I went when I was twenty-one to university in England; some time around then I started thinking of myself as somebody who wrote. And then gradually you find yourself wanting to do this more and more. To the stage where I was getting...not published, but certainly getting a lot of encouragement from various people at the university. I started completing short stories that weren't bad but weren't good enough for publication. I just went on and found myself involved in writing something full-scale: there I was writing a novel. It was a very gradual process. And I think at no stage until I finished the first novel, which I think was a year after I finished my Masters, did I think of myself as being a writer. I was trying to find a way to deal with certain ideas and gradually hit upon the novel as the form that suited me best. And this particular story as a fit story for a first novel. At the age of twenty-six I found myself with a contract for a book – and you think 'that's it, I want to keep on doing this, I'm a writer'.

NMc: *Who do you perceive as your readership?*
GP: I think if I was being honest I'd say everybody.

NMc: *People in Northern Ireland in particular?*
GP: No, I had kind of a dual idea when I was writing *Burning Your Own*. I was living in England at the time, in Norwich. On the one hand, I was seeing things that were going on in England that to me made some kind of sense of things, or a different kind of sense of things, that had happened in Northern Ireland when I as a child.

People would come up to me in Norwich and say, 'You're Irish, from Belfast. God, isn't it terrible, why does it keep going on?' And yet at this time, the mid 1980s, the miners' strike was just over, with all the terrible violence that had been associated with that and the ructions there had been in communities, the tearing apart of and the polarisation of communities. And there also had been riots in inner cities: Toxteth, Mosside, Tottenham. So there were all these social pressures which to me, seeing how communities could be drawn into either violence against each other or into opposition against the Government, or violence against the police, or violence perpetrated on them by the police. So I thought if I could find a way of writing something about Northern Ireland, this made some kind of sense for me about Northern Ireland, it might be an interesting perspective on it. Perhaps what happened in Northern Ireland in 1969 could be approached by looking at how communities react under intense pressure, or when certain assumptions about **what that society is** are challenged from whatever source. Then how do they react? I thought writing something set in Northern Ireland, from the perspective of the mid-80s in England, might actually create some kind of interesting new angles on what happened in Northern Ireland in 1969. But it might also, by setting something there, be a way of saying something about what was happening there in the mid-80s. I was somebody living in a particular place thinking about another place and the two seemed to be involved in the same historical process. I refuse to look at anything happening in Northern Ireland out of its context; this is part of history.

NMc: *What writers would you say have influenced you?*
GP: Very few Irish ones really. I went to a school that could've been picked up by a whirlwind and set down somewhere in the southwest of England and you would never have known any difference, because our curriculum was really an English grammar school curriculum. The first Irish writer I ever read was Frank O'Connor but, big deal, that meant nothing to me. He might've been from England for all I knew. He just didn't speak to me of anything that made any sense, that I had experienced. I probably read Heaney before I read Louis MacNeice but Seamus Heaney, I mean, so he was Irish, but big deal again, it really meant nothing. Frank Ormsby actually was the first living Belfast writer I ever heard. I heard him

read in the museum when I was about in fifth year or sixth year at school. He was writing poems about Great Victoria Street and around here; and that really excited me, because that was the first time I'd heard anything that used the place where I lived as fit subject for literature. Literature, writing, could actually deal with the here and now. Any writing I'd done up to that stage had been in some kind of fictional nowhere. It existed in Storybookland. But here was somebody writing about here and now in the Belfast that I recognised. I could walk out from the reading and walk past Great Victoria Street.

NMc: *In* Burning Your Own *the gang around the bonfire deciding what to do after the centrepole is burned strike me as being like Golding's boys in* Lord of the Flies: *is this an influence?*

GP: This is terrible doing this kind of interview because you reveal just how ignorant you are. Do you know when I read *Lord of the Flies?* The year before last [1992]. Possibly because of what so many people had said about *Lord of the Flies*. I'd been aware of *Lord of the Flies* but I didn't really know very much about it.

As for the centrepole in *Burning Your Own* – first of all, I've been at bonfires so there was always this strong response to have the biggest centrepole. But my inspiration for that came from Yeats: 'things fall apart, the centre cannot hold'. I was gradually more and more aware of Irish writers and Irish literature, but they were certainly not formative influences on the work I was doing. Louis MacNeice I love; and *Snow*, in particular, was probably the poem that really interested me in writing. Because there was something about the use of language. Again, it's interesting how through this poet's capturing of this moment of epiphany I actually experienced the moment myself; I actually was **stunned** by this poem, for the first time ever not as an object of study but as a **poem**. I discovered that he had lived in Belfast, he had lived just up the Lisburn Road. That seemed much more immediate than Joyce, even living poets like Seamus Heaney.

The writers who were really important to me in terms of influence were American writers like Hemingway. In terms of style, when I wrote short stories that would have been my model, the early Hemingway short stories. And Dos Passos, his massive trilogy *USA*. This was somebody who thought a novel could encompass a nation and I liked some of that scope he gave the novel. And again something similar about the way he wrote about the relationship between characters and their countries, or countries as characters in people's lives. And so these were the writers who really interested me in terms of subject and who drew me towards the novel as a form. Irish writers were of interest belatedly I would say and certainly not centrally. I've become much more interested in it because I think the stuff that's coming out now, and especially in the north, like Robert McLiam Wilson, I think that there's been a certain amount of redefinition of what you can do and how you can write out of the north and about the north.

NMc: *In* Burning Your Own, *the Protestants are shown as believing in 'principle' yet fail to live up to their principles. Is this a thrusting criticism or merely a depiction of fact?*

GP: The things I always thought important in that book are, firstly, that I suspected that at times people were quite willing to criticize certain of the principles informing their lives and certain of the community beliefs, but at times of great tension they would actually take refuge in these things that they could otherwise see fault in because they were better than the other things. So at times of tension you get pulled back into these ... people retreat. So I wanted to show something like that happening. I thought there was a great moment lost, something terrible gets lost, which is subtlety, at times of great tension and at the centre of violence.

The other thing which I thought was that people are failed by these cliches really and these rules to live by. In particular, Mal's father in *Burning Your Own*: he is a man who repeats ad nauseum these empty phrases because he's been brought up so that these phrases together are what explain life. And when they fail and he then takes it out one, on himself, and two, on his family, because he would look for the fault anywhere than in the society itself or in the phrases themselves, but actually what has failed are these very things that he has always used to explain your life. And so there was that great crisis that happens; and people are afraid to look and see that perhaps this society is based on nothing, that it is in some ways empty.

NMc: *Do you agree that the most important image is the moon-landing, the 'enormity of distances'?*

GP: That was really important. It was something to do with perspective, again. The first section takes place exclusively on this housing estate and I wanted that to be really claustrophobic. It had to really build up this sense of enclosure. And increasingly to get that feeling that something was going to fall apart, it just couldn't hold. But I wanted to get some kind of context to this thing. I think the fault with a lot of writers from Northern Ireland, is that they write something that is written on to it instead of something that is written out of it, it doesn't grow out of it, it just approaches thinking that the story is about violence and that is the story, so you write that story on. So I'm very interested in showing always, in trying to get the context, this is the context in which these things are happening, this is the world in which these things are happening. So there were the Civil Rights marches in America, there was the Vietnam War. These things are important because there's also that idea of this very small territorial dispute. Increasingly, the tension in the novel is about a very small area of disputed land. And at the same time you've got somebody out there in space landing on the moon.

One of the things you do when you write, I'm convinced, is ensure that not everything has a one-to-one meaning: this does not mean that and does not explain something back, but you create juxtapositions, certain ideas and images…it's up to the reader, in a way, to create the meaning. But the writer might have certain ideas and hopes that through the arrangement of these images and these words the reader will take something, some particular meaning from it. You can't guarantee that that will happen. And often you're not even necessarily sure what this juxtaposition does or this combination of things except that you know that it creates something to you that is interesting and you might even change your mind about what exactly that does mean. Certainly it wasn't an accident that that was there. Writing is about selection as well, there are bits of news that you throw away, there are bits that are useful, in the same way that there are bits of your own life that you might use and there are bits that aren't useful. The moment that the moonlanding occurs is hemmed in by the two sections on the housing estate – and that claustrophobia.

NMc: *There is a sexual subtext, with teenagers like Mucker (with Sonia) trying to act hard and seem to be sexually active. Do you see this notion, of virility, in the characters' minds, in that kind of person's mind, as linking sex and 'power': that is social prestige within their peer group?*

GP: I've always been interested in that. I think there's a lot of peer group pressure. But also it's to do with this notion of conforming to your role, doing what is expected of you. For instance, macho violence against the girls by the young boys.

NMc: *Phallic images are important in* Burning Your Own: *the moonrocket, says Alex, is a 'giant cock'. Is the novel a criticism of Ulster's patriarchal society?*

GP: I think it's a society in which power and the abuse of power and the idea of, especially male, power is central. There are certain ways of acting out traditional roles that include a need of conflict, glamourisation of violence, glamourisation of **the hard man**. So I think there's something in that; these are the stages by which you become accepted and enter into this community. There are all kinds of rituals, from starting to drink and all this kind of thing about sex

– 'do you get it?' – this community of belonging. There's a lot of that, but again this is going hand-in-hand with the society in which actual real, serious violence is starting to break out. And the people who are involved in that violence are in many instances the children, the kids or these people who were...it's all a bit of banter and then suddenly it becomes very serious. This is real violence that's being talked about. So it's part of that sense of initiation into community; but also into those community values and what that actually means when you are being initiated into a community which is growing into violence or is slipping into violence.

NMc: *In* Fat Lad *it is recognised that Belfast is built on mud; the goldfish chases its own tail. The poet John Goodby tells me you said these depict the process of life. Can you elaborate?*

GP: I think there's been a movement: in *Burning Your Own* there was an interest in building, this idea of a housing estate being built on disputed territory. It was a made-up place; it was modelled loosely on the place where I grew up. I think it's very interesting that the Sixties Civil Rights campaigns were around the issue of housing. Therefore, the built environment has always been very closely connected with everything that's been going on in Northern Ireland in the last twenty-five years. A lot of it's about where you build, who you build for, what do you build in the city. In each society the buildings you build say something about how the society views itself. By the same taken, what is built projects onto future generations – who they are. So there's this kind of symbiotic relationship.

I became very interested in building. What changed for me was when I came back to Belfast in the late 1980s, a lot of work was going on around Laganside, and land reclamation. Suddenly, I saw that this wasn't something that was only going on in the last twenty-five years, but this was something that was always happening. That the way to understand the city was as something that was continually being built up and then falling down. Belfast has its own peculiar accelerated periods of building and demolition. Ciaran Carson writes about using the rubble from bombsites to reclaim more land: the bricks that were used to build some of those buildings in the first place were taken from local clays, so you have this sense in which you take from the earth, you build the buildings, those are destroyed or pulled down, and you dump it into the sea and you create more land and you rebuild. So the city is constantly redefining itself. Which I think is an enormously liberating thought, because nothing is finalised. There is always the possibility of change. In fact change is the only constant, and this is the urban oxymoron: the only thing that is constant is change.

This tends against traditionalist readings and anything that says

'We shall not be moved', 'not an inch', things like that. Things will change; inevitably, things will change. It might take centuries but things change all the time. I'm interested in that whole kind of process. But that doesn't mean that I think that all building that's going on in Belfast is good. I think that a lot of what has happened in Belfast in terms of the regeneration is dreadful. Nevertheless, there's the potential for change. If you start to accept that then it gives you a whole different reading of the place and what is possible. I think you can do that for any city; as I say, I just happen to be writing about Belfast, so far. You get the city you deserve: if you build a nice front, then you get all the things that you leave underneath or behind. Somebody told me about Blackstaff Square around the back here, which also features in *Fat Lad*, makes nonsense until you look at it from the top of the Europa Hotel – that there are certain things built for certain views. I think that's unduly cynical, but there are certain ways of building that can **exclude**.

At the end of *Fat Lad* the bookshop gets burned by a firebomb. There's even a bit in it about how the Europa used to be bombed all the time and how it isn't bombed anymore, and it was bombed again by the time the novel had come out! *Fat Lad* was set very specifically between February 1990 and 1991. In retrospect, it might be called 'the time between the carbombs', because the carbombs came back shortly thereafter. I wasn't sure they would start carbombing again, but I was pretty sure that it was only a matter of time before places like the Castle Court did get it, because none of this was dealing with what was really of importance in the city.

NMc: *In* Fat Lad *is Drew's being beaten by his father symbolic of a violent society?*

GP: Well again I think it's more this thing about how do people accommodate ... His father is another of these people who like Mal's father in *Burning Your Own* is outmanoeuvred, growing up with certain expectations of their society, of their position in society. Also, under certain pressures: there's this thing about Drew's father growing up in a nation of titanic men, these larger-than-life characters, but he can't live up to it. A lot of this becomes focussed on producing a son. Again, these great traditional male roles and what it is to be a man. The Troubles begin shortly thereafter; again, this feeling of being outmanoeuvred, so he focuses a lot of his anger on his son. He internalises all this and then projects it out onto his son. How do people cope with violence? The first thing that happens when the Troubles begins in the novel, the first treating of it, talks about them staying in the house, just always being in the house from when he came home in the evening until he went out in the morning; they didn't really answer the door. Again, as in *Burning Your Own*, there's this claustrophobic atmosphere and the public violence has ramifications in private lives.

NMc: *The relationship with Anna takes Drew to Dublin and shows the treatment by Catholic men of their women, for example, the tarring and feathering. The Catholic side is generally regarded as being even more conservative, the Catholic middle-class even more begrudging than the Protestant. Is Anna a foil to bring in this aspect to the bigger picture of Ulster society?*

GP: Anna is a character who is defined by a characteristic: she has a lot of hair and she is improbable. She was meant to have improbable hair that looked like it would just blow away. She was meant to be held very much in check all the time, as if trying to stop herself from flying apart. She was meant to be eccentric in certain ways and yet there had to be a background to that. Her hair in some ways, no matter how preposterous it was, was still some kind of defiance against people who had done this. I just wanted to write about a particular period when certain things happened and these certain things did happen. There is also a lot of Biblical stuff in that novel about gender roles and fertility, abortions, contraception and so on. There is a lot to do with hair and sexuality and over it the Old Testament; one of the ways in which you humiliated a woman was to cut off her hair. Tarring and feathering? Misogyny is over two thousand years old, we didn't invent it.

NMc: *And the* Fat Lad *motif itself?*

GP: The whole *Fat Lad* thing is simply a big joke from this thing written on Ellen's ruler as a child. So it's actually more to do with her. I like this whole thing that you can personify a country: *Fat Lad*, the initials of the Six Counties. And it's slightly ridiculous. I'm interested in the ridiculousness of our lives, in being informed by these structures that are completely arbitrary. *Fat Lad* could've been *A Lad* if they'd left out Fermanagh and Tyrone, it could've been *A Dad* if it had been Derry not Londonderry, it could've been all of these things, and yet I was brought up and taught at school: *Fat Lad*. I always thought of Northern Ireland, I looked at the map and I saw this little fat man... So I was interested in some ways in what these things become. I mean, his sister's **crush**, there are lots of puns in that. Nobody is really the fish in *Fat Lad*; nothing really is, except this overall...experience.

NMC: *Drew's bookshop job – what symbolic weight has it for you? Do you see it as a storehouse of knowledge?*

GP: Part of that. One of the things I was actually thinking was this kind of standardisation of British shops – Sock Shop and so on. I actually worked in a bookshop as well for a while. But I was very struck one day by the way that if you haven't sold your paperbacks how you return them: you rip the back off and you throw away the book and send back the cover and you get your refund. So there was something about the whole use of knowledge and writing as well coming into that.

And to use a shop it seemed to me was a good way to highlight what was happening in Belfast in the late 80s/early 90s because that was the retail boom really. I felt slightly cynical about certain practices, such as the strategy to expand as quickly as possible, then sell out and contract. So there were certain things there about Britain's retail boom in the 1980s, not just about Northern Ireland.

NMc: *Why does the Giant's Causeway appear?*

GP: People used to say, 'I'm sick of all these things about the violence and the trouble; this is a lovely place, why doesn't somebody write about the Giant's Causeway?'. What is interesting about Northern Ireland is exactly that Belfast is a modern European city – one in which people fire rockets at police landrovers within a quarter of a mile from where we're sitting. It's a modern European city, it has very attractive, beautiful countryside – it has the Giant's Causeway and landmines. So all these things exist side by side. So you don't write about one to the exclusion of the other. One of the reasons for writing *Fat Lad* was it seemed to me that the fictional representations of Northern Ireland got stuck about 1972; and it doesn't look like that anymore. It certainly wasn't the same story. It's **never** the same story; it's changing. At any one time it's not one story, it's at least a million and a half. And these stories are changing all the time and you've got to keep up with that. It's got to be updated. It seemed to me there's a need to write about not what Northern Ireland was supposed to be, but what it actually was like at that moment. And so I came back with the express purpose of letting *Fat Lad* write itself out of what was there.

'Between the Boundaries'
AN INTERVIEW WITH MARGARET ELPHINSTONE

Lisa Babinec

Margaret Elphinstone is a writer who has lived an itinerant life. In addition to being involved in the women's peace movement at Greenham Common, she lived in Shetland for eight years and spent time in the 'new-age' Findhorn community. Elphinstone now teaches literature at the University of Strathclyde, and her writing reveals versatile interests: three novels, a collection of short stories, a collection of poetry, two books on organic gardening, numerous short stories in a variety of different journals, critical essays on Scottish literature, as well as an edited collection of garden verse.

Elphinstone finds a place in the Scottish female literary tradition because her writing shares thematic preoccupations with several other Scottish women writers such as Emma Tennant, Janice Galloway, and Candia McWilliam. A central concern with female subjectivity and female community dominates her first two novels, *The Incomer* (Women's Press, 1987) and *A Sparrow's Flight* (Polygon, 1989); similarly, her most recent novel *Islanders* (Polygon, 1994) rewrites the history of women in Norse Shetland. Elphinstone's fiction also venerates and pays homage to the Scottish literary tradition by exploring the different realms of fantasy and reality. Both *The Incomer* and *A Sparrow's Flight*, the two novels discussed in this interview, are set in a fantastical fictional world which resembles the historical past and recognizable present. The characters in both novels make it very clear that some unspeakable harm has been done to the earth and, as a result, life is hard and based only on taking food from the land and making clothing and homes which accommodate survival. Time and place cannot be firmly established in either novel, and the culture that Elphinstone explores in these books is non-materialistic and steeped in folk tradition. Music, tales, and dance permeate the characters' lives.

Significantly, Elphinstone's alternative fictional world challenges the ways in which women are constructed and confined as passive subjects by overturning conventional gender hierarchies and expectations. In *The Incomer* and A *Sparrow's Flight*, women, rather

MARGARET ELPHINSTONE

than men, are in 'control' of the households and maintain a spiritual connection with the land. Elphinstone designs a fictional world where contemporary power structures are inverted. Women are allowed and encouraged to develop relationships and creative potential, and the novels reveal women to be powerful and independent subjects when they are not limited by social and cultural policies that favour men. Likewise, her writing illuminates threatening subversions of reality for the literary establishment because she interrogates the traditional roles and relationships women and men hold in society, offering readers new visions of egalitarian alliances between women and men. When Elphinstone subverts the fine line between fantasy and realism, she estranges readers from conventional interpretations of reality and invites us to think more poetically about how women are typically alienated from cultural codes and practices.

During the course of my doctoral research in June 1992, I met with Margaret Elphinstone to talk about the nature of Scottishness, Scottish literature, Scottish women's writing, and certain aspects of *The Incomer* and *A Sparrow's Flight*. The following interview sheds light on Elphinstone's role in the vibrant tradition of contemporary Scottish women's literature.

LSB: *What does being Scottish mean to you?*
ME: Well. I'm not sure that I am Scottish in so far as I grew up in England. My father's family is Scottish and as a child growing up I was always told I was partly Scottish. Of course, when I arrived here, I'm English. So it's being caught between two boundaries, I think, which has been very important. Belonging and not belonging. Being outside and inside at the same time. I think it's a very familiar position for a lot of people, on the edge of things and not knowing quite what they are. It can be quite uncomfortable and quite creative.
LSB: *Emma Tennant spent her childhood in Scotland and when she went down to England, she felt like an outsider. She says that very much affected her use of language and dialect and the way that she thinks. Can you relate to her feelings at all?*
ME: What I would relate to is the language aspect of it. Every time I open my mouth it's perfectly clear that I'm from the south of England. I'm quite happy to be from the south of England, but it leaves you in a very tenuous situation to be writing in terms of any particular culture when you know you come from several. I think coming from several is a strength and I'm glad that I'm all these things. But linguistically, teaching Scottish literature when I don't

really speak Scots is quite an intriguing situation and sometimes it's uncomfortable, but it's another outlook.

LSB: *How would you define a Scottish literary tradition?*

ME: I think it took me years to define it at all. I did English literature at Durham University for my first degree and the Scottish literature we did nobody described as 'Scottish'. We did Henryson and Dunbar and I'm sure it says in my lecture notes somewhere 'and by the way they were Scottish', but that was about it. We looked at the ballads. We didn't look at any of the Scottish novelists: no Scott, no Stevenson, no Hogg, nothing like that. It was years before I realized that you could try to define a Scottish tradition. Of course when I did, I realized I was very familiar with it, because I had been brought up on a lot of the books; I was given Stevenson and I read some Scott in my early teens. MacDonald's fairy tales were my favourite books aged about seven or eight, but I certainly didn't think 'this guy is Scots'. I think it was years later, partly through Douglas Gifford, that I did define it. He wrote that he saw *The Incomer* as part of the Scottish literary tradition. I thought, 'how do you see that?' Talking to him I began to think, 'goodness, maybe that's where I get it from'.

LSB: *How would you define a Scottish female literary tradition?*

ME: I think it's very hidden. I would include myself in a Scottish female literary tradition. I think it's very interesting how much of it has been about borderline situations, borderlines of madness, borderlines of reality. Look at Emma Tennant, it's this absolute on the edge feeling. I think it's because Scottish women have been so marginalized in their own reality that it comes out in weird, exciting, and very different and very dynamic ways. I think I'm beginning to feel, recently I suppose, there's definitely a struggle going on for women's writing to emerge in Scotland; it's up against very rigid patriarchal attitudes. I want to include myself in that group whose voice should be heard.

LSB: *In a review of* An Apple From the Tree, *Douglas Gifford wrote 'Elphinstone has a dark view of progress, akin to that of George Mackay Brown, but with an added feminism which is never strident, but insists on the prime role of women in renewal and resistance to the poisoning of the world'. How do you feel about this comment?*

ME: Well I liked that comment when I read it. I certainly like being told I'm akin to George Mackay Brown because I admire him greatly and to have somebody say that, it's quite affirming. But with the added feminism ... I think that's probably fair. What it makes me think of is the place where I really started writing, when I was staying down at Greenham Common. The first short story I did,

'Spinning the Green', certainly came out of a quite active involvement in issues about poisoning of the world and so on. But I didn't think 'we're going to get a point about the environment in here'. I don't mean that I'm totally or naively unconscious, but in fact what I think I'm saying is that I have a much stronger line than I often realize on the way I perceive things and the way that I do things and the life I've led. I often don't realize that perhaps for a lot of people, this isn't very mainstream and that when it comes out in my work, they see this as more borderline than I do.

LSB: *In an interview with Jennie Renton, you say that you 'don't like the idea that I'm writing only about women for women. I write about men and women, though I have often had a woman protagonist'. Would you say that you are aware of being a woman writer, or would you define yourself simply as a writer, a feminist writer, or anything else?*

ME: Yes, I'm aware of being a woman writer and it's been quite interesting to me that I've had the theory after the practice. This year I taught a course with Alison Thorne on feminist theory and women's writing. I hadn't done much theory at all before I came here, because I was out of academia for sixteen years when all the theory happened. The way we did the course was that she would teach a theory lecture and I'd teach a lecture on a text that I chose to illustrate the theory, to an extent. That course made me think a lot about how I am aware of being a woman writer. I'm quite intrigued, but I find some of the theory quite reductive, even though it's certainly made me think. What I don't want to do is ghettoize, and sometimes I would rather not be published by The Women's Press, because I think in practical terms there are a lot of men who don't pick up Women's Press books. I did a reading in Aberdeen last week and afterwards a man in the audience said to me, 'I thought you were going to be some feminist, but you're quite a normal person. How do you feel about being published by The Women's Press?' I said, 'would you buy a Women's Press book in the bookshop?' He said, 'well, I might now'. I guess it's because I didn't have three heads. I don't want that initial barrier. I don't want men to think that 'this is not for me' or that I'm in a sort of woman's world. I'd rather that what I write is available for anyone to read who likes it, or doesn't like it. There are so many factors and though gender is one of those important factors, it's not the issue. I think feminism must come through my writing just like compost heaps do, because it's part of what I think about.

LSB: *Would you say that contemporary Scottish women writers have evolved themes, imagination, and narrative forms that are their own?*

ME: Yes, I would. I hesitate to generalize but I've described in an essay how the fantasy element fascinates me because I do see that as a theme that recurs in very different writers.[1] Put Sian Hayton and Muriel Spark side by side and you've got these ghosts and strange beings in both and yet there's difference in treatment. Emma Tennant – never quite knowing what's real. Liz Lochhead does it too and she can be very surreal in her dramas. There's the exploring of psychological states through stories that are on the edge of reality in *Dracula* and there's quite a lot of it in *Mary Queen of Scots Got Her Head Chopped Off*. It's very intriguing to me how many Scottish women writers have gone back and very explicitly revised male texts; many of them have gone back to the nineteenth century, not all as explicitly as Tennant, for example, but they go back and revise it.

LSB: *It's interesting. I think that a lot of people would probably say that this revision is unoriginal, but I don't see it that way. I think it's just taking a tradition and showing it from another perspective that's been ignored.*

ME: It's a necessity, I think, in terms of history. It seems to be that women in Scotland have almost no acknowledged history and it has got to be discovered, because of course women have existed. The novel I've just written, *Islanders*, is about Norse Shetland and it's very much about women. There are a lot of men in it too. But I think certainly with the Vikings, you read the historical accounts and they occasionally give you an account of brooches that have been dug up and you think, 'oh, they were worn by a woman, they existed'. But you'd think from historians that the Vikings were a society that was 99% male and obviously it wasn't, so I thought about rewriting that history, going back and filling in the gaps between the very fragmented evidence we have.

LSB: *Like many of Emma Tennant's female characters, your protagonists often seem to be on a quest to define or to understand a female self. Do you find that the struggle to formulate an identity leads to a dissociation from self?*

ME: I think that's spot on. These defined images that women are surrounded by, like the wee granny and the young lassie, are so unquestioned. When I've been in the States or even in England, I've felt this sense of liberation – not because the US is such a liberated country – but because a lot of the defined selves that are imposed

---

[1] See Margaret Elphinstone, 'Contemporary Feminist Fantasy in the Scottish Literary Tradition', in *Tea and Leg-Irons: New Feminist Readings from Scotland*, ed. by Caroline Gonda (London: Open Letters, 1992), pp. 45-59.

upon me had vanished. Nobody wanted to know 'are you Scottish, are you English?' If I said I was Scottish, anyone would have believed me. People thought it very romantic if I lived in Scotland; but the constriction that every time you opened your mouth you defined yourself had fallen away. It may be very superficial stuff but there's this sense of a brick being lifted off your head when it's new to you. I've lived in a lot of different places and had many different roles in life. In the 60s I did my hippie number and in the early 80s I was living at Findhorn.

LSB: *Was Findhorn important to you?*

ME: Yes. Actually, it was my first encounter with American women who seemed to me to be so free to state how they felt. I was in Shetland for many years before I went to Findhorn and a lot of my friends at that time were so-called hippies and I grew from that to this. I suppose because I've moved from place to place and I've dropped out and I've dropped in and have also been a mother, I've had a lot of selves put onto me. Now some have gone again because my children are away from home, but I think I've this sense of all the parts you play, things you're supposed to do, roles you get into, and identity is somewhere. It's all there in Burns, personae and things, and I think that it is very typical of the Scottish literary tradition. I think I get my identity from talking to my friends and going for walks or being out alone in places. I work things out by talking to people, and those are the things that matter. All these roles are almost like a game.

LSB: *Would you describe yourself as a feminist?*

ME: Yes, but often I don't say so when it's not convenient. Yes, definitely in terms of what I think about, where I come from, what my life's been like. I would say that feminism means what I mean it to mean, which goes back to the 1960s charter of women's liberation. I remember when that happened and it was important to me, and the gradual realization of what oppression is and what it means not to be 'I', you're 'other', you're object not subject and all that. But I wouldn't walk into a room full of hostile men and say, 'here I am, I'm a feminist'.

LSB: *How would you feel if your fiction were to be defined as feminist fiction?*

ME: Well it often is and I feel fine. What annoys me of course is what other people think feminist means.

LSB: *Emma Tennant and Janice Galloway examine myths of femininity or what it means to be female in contemporary society. Would you include yourself in this type of analysis?*

ME: Yes, quite definitely. Although I think I see myself closer to Tennant in terms of method. I've used images of utopia and dystopias, creating other worlds of possibilities. I think I'm moving closer now to exploring this world. My recent short stories are contemporary and they're still fantastic, they're still weird and quite surreal, but not necessarily supernatural. Of course, they are about contemporary society or they wouldn't have any relevance to anything.

LSB: The Incomer *is set in a world distant from a dominant male order, without many images of dominant patriarchal ideology. In your opinion, does the novel represent how women can achieve and survive in an environment free from male oppression?*

ME: Yes, I think that was certainly what it was intended to do, what would it be like for women in an environment almost free from male oppression. But in Milton's paradise, there's no plot, it's a pretty boring place, nothing happens. You've got to have a plot which means you've got to have a devil, you've got to have some sort of serpent in the garden. What it represents is how women can achieve and survive in a world *almost* free from male oppression but it's also got to relate to what we do deal with, so in those terms it's a paradigm for contemporary reality. Here and now, rape is something that women have to deal with. There they know what it is, but it's almost unheard of. I think I was trying to get the distance of how it would be if rape was such an extraordinary thing; but it also happens in that world because if it didn't, it would be too far from where we are.

LSB: The Incomer *also focuses on relationships between women and a female community; in other words, it seems to me that women in the novel are defined in relationship to each other, rather than in relation to male power. Could you comment on this?*

ME: Yes. In fact it's interesting that some of the negative comments I've had in reviews – and I haven't actually had any horrid reviews of *The Incomer* – suggest the men aren't strong enough, or there's not enough about men, that the men are peripheral. I was trying to create a world in which women's networks predominate and the men are more peripheral. No doubt in that world, the men have their own community, but I didn't describe it. In terms of how the place is run, the sort of politics of Clachanpluck, I see a definite women's network of how they talk about things, arrange things, sort things out. You couldn't say there is a hierarchy and there's not meant to be; that's meant to be quite anarchic. It's through the women that I see things happening. It's quite a threatening paradigm that men have become peripheral in terms of the novel. There's no male hierarchy at all and the men, like women, certainly have their place in the society – they are in no way excluded – but they belong to a household that is centred around a woman. They're defined in relation to that household, but they have autonomy. They're not oppressed. They don't belong to anybody, so it's nothing like the situation in which most women have lived under patriarchy, and yet it's perceived as very threatening and disempowering to put a man in that situation.

LSB: *In my interpretation,* A Sparrow's Flight, *like* The Incomer, *is a quest for female knowledge and the recognition that in order to come to terms with a female or a male self, one must confront the past. Do you agree with this?*

ME: I would agree that a major theme in the book is dealing with the past. Yes, I think it's to do with past conflicts and this load of guilt that stops you being who you are. You can't run far enough from it and it's following you everywhere and the only thing to do is turn and face it, which is probably, I would imagine, what monsters are about. You can't go on carrying guilt. Well you can, but it will kill you. It won't go away by you trying to get further and further from it, and so they literally make this journey back to where the guilt was for Thomas and they meet Naomi's along the way. I think confronting the past is a lot to do with confronting guilt and confronting one's own limitations. They didn't get it right and they've both had to make choices that were wrong and they've both perhaps made terrible mistakes, even if Naomi's choice was correct. Even though nobody's judging her, there's always – you know that Frost poem, the road less travelled – there's always the way you didn't go, and that's something that also has to be lived with.

LSB: *Both novels also involve a commitment to music, dance, privacy, myth, and social ritual. Do you feel this is part of Scottish literature and the Scottish literary tradition and therefore permeates your writing? Or are there other reasons for these imaginative creations?*

ME: Let's take that in two parts. I think that music and dance are very explicitly part of the Scottish tradition, and music keeps turning up in my writing. In Shetland I got very interested in folk music, and it got me interested in ballads. I'm also intrigued because I'm quite ignorant about music. I can't make all the right noises in criticizing it. I'm interested in a pagan past. I'm not interested in being a pagan in the present – it's pretty irrelevant. I read books about folklore and myth like Marian McNeill's *Festivals*. I think we're terribly lacking in ceremonies and rituals. I grew up in a religious household and we always had grace before we ate. I wouldn't dream of doing that now, certainly not to a patriarchal God, but it was a ritual, a ceremony – you knew when you were eating and when you weren't. My children haven't had that. I think it's useful to mark things and passing seasons, and living in the city,

I really miss knowing where the moon is. I used to know all the time. I think this is important in the Scottish tradition. I think it's also from a lot of other sources as well.

LSB: I find Naomi and Thomas's friendship and interaction in *A Sparrow's Flight* compelling and compassionate. Would you say that their relationship is an attempt to show that men and women can share the same feelings, emotions, and support similar to the ones that communities of women can generate?

ME: It is. I didn't want these two in a sexual relationship and the simplest way was to make Thomas gay. It's not the only reason why he's gay, and once I'd started writing, the theme grew, but initially it was that simple. They weren't to fall in love because I wasn't going to write a love story. This novel is about love and friendship and of course Naomi is attracted to Thomas, but it's not reciprocal and she has to settle for friendship. After the earlier book, I did want to look closely at a man because it is true that *The Incomer* is largely about women in a community, and this is a book about a relationship between a man and a woman and knowing how Thomas feels by getting inside his head. When I was writing it, I felt I knew those two terribly well and everybody else is a sort of chorus to this relationship and meant to be. I got very involved between Naomi and Thomas. I felt the intensity as I was writing of that relationship.

Lisa S. Babinec is a freelance teacher of English and Scottish Literature. She is currently writing a book on Contemporary Scottish Women Writers based on her Ph.D thesis for the University of Glasgow, from which the above interview is taken.

Ciaran Carson

interview with Niall McGrath

Carson is a native of Belfast, where he works as Traditional Arts Officer for the Arts Council of Northern Ireland. An outstanding contemporary poet, he has published four collections: The New Estate *(1976);* The Irish For No *(1987);* Belfast Confetti *(1988), winner of the Irish Times prize for poetry, and* First Language *(1993), which won the T. S. Eliot prize.*

NMc: *Why did you begin to write poetry? Were you encouraged at school?*
CC: I think that the urge to write comes when you see something that you admire and think 'that's very nice, I wish I could do something like that'. I don't thing it comes from wanting to say something or from needing to **release your psyche**. It's about the urge to invent a story, at the end of the day. To me, poems emerge out of a story structure.
NMc: *Would you see yourself as a social writer, rather than a nature or urban poet, for instance?*
CC: I don't think I'm social at all! I wouldn't see myself as being someone who has 'something to say'. All I can do is observe things and invent stories about it all. What sort of ties my poems have with the world I don't know. At the end of the day it's a song or a tune or a story.
NMc: *Formally, how would you describe your poems?*
CC: I would describe them as being based on the structure of a reel, for instance the line is based on the length of four bars of a reel, or it's the long line of the Irish song, or it's the long line when somebody embarks on a story when you're at a bar – 'well, there was this man now I'll tell ye and there was this man now…' It's also

CIARRAN CARSON
Belfast, June 9th 1994

Photo: Niall McGrath

about the length of a Japanese haiku. It's got all those ideas in it. The line has to sing in some way. It's very important to get a flow in the line; it has to sing or speak and if you haven't got that it just won't work. At the back of my mind there would be the idea of a tune or something like that. Also, you want to go against the standard iambic line, to get that edge, so you don't get an absolutely stock line.

NMc: *What do you think is the role of humour in your poetry?*

CC: It's just … fun. If you can't laugh at things, you're dead. I would hope that what would seem to some people as obscure is really only a laugh, a wee joke.

NMc: *Do you consider* First Language *to be very different from previous collections and if so is this a deliberate change of style or subject matter?*

CC: Well it rhymes, for a start! That was accidental. Anything at all that occurs is largely an accident, or inspiration. I think it started when I was doing the version of Rimbaud's 'Le Bateau Ivre' and it actually had to rhyme. The rhymes are, as you can see, a bit upside down and askew. But I found that whole idea of rhyme an interesting thing. And I found in a way rhyme helps you to find a story. If you hunt around for an idea or a theme or whatever it might be it's not so much that there is a theme there, but you can root, that the rhymes start off something, go in a certain way or acquire ideas en route. Once I started on that I discovered it was an interesting thing to do and also it's fun. The hard work of going through all the rhymes – it's almost as if you walk across a landscape of asps: some sort of a sahara, and there's a rhyme there and away out there about a mile away another there, says 'I want to be in the poem', but this moving dune says 'Sorry boys, I'm not going to have you in the poem'! This idea that the rhyme invents a story almost of its own accord. And there's a sort of randomness involved in it as well, of course. An interesting edge between writing the story yourself and allowing the story to occur via rhymes.

NMc: *Do you think that's how some of the surreal aspects got prompted, by the different rhymes?*

CC: Yes, to a certain extent. Because the very idea of rhyme itself is accidental and surreal: it's not how you think, it's not how things really are. In the ordinary world there are no rhymes. Rhyme itself is an artifice; you have a set edifice inside which you have to operate, that you find some odd edge of the thing you're actually involved with.

NMc: *Which European writers have influenced you?*

CC: In *First Language* I guess there's a slight influence of Rimbaud and Baudelaire, whom I learnt at school; that stuff was lying around at the back of my mind. There is some relationship between sight and sound and smell and so on; and the access to whatever you have in your mind can be sparked off by either a sight or a sense or a smell or a sound or whatever.

NMc: *You mean the kind of thing Ezra Pound was getting at in 'A Station In The Metro'?*

CC: Yeah.

NMc: *Would you, in poems like 'Sonnet' see poems, as in Robert Duncan's 'Poem Beginning With A Line From Pindar', as mosaics, with images set together rather than needing to be coherent narratives?*

CC: In 'Sonnet' there's maybe four or five storylines in there, and they recur and go in some sort of a zigzag way and it's really like a jigsaw in a way, it's up to whoever reads it to handle it in his own way. So, the ostensible thing which is involved in it can be A, B, C... or B, B, A...

NMc: *As in life, there are several relationships, or roles we play, which overlap and progress at uneven intervals?*

CC: Yes.

NMc: *Has* First Language *been inspired by childhood experiences or parenthood, in the main?*

CC: That's part of it. I've got three young children and if you observe them beginning to talk, it's a very interesting thing how they arrive at speech. How they can form an abstract idea of the world. You would imagine that they would start off by having specific words for things, but instead it's the other way around: they start off with an abstract idea. So that 'dog' would mean a dog or a cat or a cow or any four-legged animal; they start off with abstract ideals. After a while they can see that a cat isn't a dog and so on. It's that interesting relationship between specifics and abstract ideas. And also, I was brought up with Irish at home, so at an early age I was aware that there was the English and the Irish language. And at the end of the day if something is said in Irish it's not the same as if it is said in the English language. So there's no final way of saying **here is how it is**. There isn't finally an answer to the objective structure of the world. So that what is going on here, in terms of how things are expressed and things are said with absolutes, that there's only one way, it has to be this way or that way; from a very early age I understood that it's not like that. It depends on the language.

NMc: *So do you write in English more because you feel you can reach a wider audience?*

CC: I write in English because the Irish that I spoke was the Irish of the home and I wouldn't be able to write in the same way in Irish as

I can in the English I have. If I were to write in Irish I'd have to go back and learn it all over again very well. And I feel at times that the idea that I should write in Irish because it's the language of the Irish soul or something like this is a bit off, anyway.
NMc: *The collection* First Language *contains many translations. What do you think is the value in this exercise?*
CC: It tended to spark things off. I was asked to do the passages from Ovid. It so occurred that the bits I did were in line with what I was already doing.
NMc: *Ships seem to be the prevalent images in this collection. What symbolic importance do they have for you?*
CC: I don't know, it just happened that way. I guess you could see the ship as being an ark, or Star Trek: the idea that there are strange new things out there and you don't know what they are. Or, you're on a ship and nobody knows where it's going and the ship is very structured and layered inside it, but nobody knows why they're on it. The ship is...
NMc: *Destiny?*
CC: It's an island, too. And a state.
NMc: *What stimulated 'The Ballad of HMS Belfast' and why write about this particular ship?*
CC: Because of the name, just. And also it's connected to 'Le Bateau Ivre'. I was stuck on it for a long time, at the end of verse five I think – what am I going to do next. I went back to Rimbaud's, and there's a bit where he says, 'I've been immersed since then... ' and instead of giving accounts of 'first I did this, and then I did that...' he gives a whole lot of stories.
NMc: *Like a sailor telling his dits in a random order?*
CC: Indeed.
NMc: *You've always used these long, sinuous lines, for example in* Belfast Confetti. *Why do you adopt this form of line in 'Grass' (in* First Language*), and is it influenced by Joyce?*
CC: All the words in that came from Eric Partridge's *A Dictionary of Slang and Unconventional English*. I just picked it up one day and there was this daft word and another... The idea that everyone has a language of their own – a language for being inside, for being outside, if you've got a job, involved in sport...
NMc: *Jargons?*
CC: Yes. You can say it this way or that way. And at the end of the day it's all just babble-babble, anyway. And what you're really saying is you don't know what the hell you're saying.
NMc: *And 'The Brain of Edward Carson' I suppose is because of the obvious link with your own name? Another satirical piece?*
CC: I remember as a child I'd be hitting the shop and you'd hear,

'Ach, here's Carson again, And that oul' Lord, wasn't he one of your people?' and all this sort of crack. And because of the ambiguity of the name, though it's usually connected with one side of the divide. And I remember as a child being taken for a walk around Stormont by my father; there's the statue of Edward Carson, this huge iron thing that represents the name Carson. And I'm a Carson too, so that disparity between iron rule and order and your own life... That there was this state that you didn't accept but it was still there. And what was exuding that idea, what was inside the statue? And other things going on, scales and shackles and so on.

NMc: *And he has this iron image yet was supposed to be a neurotic man, not sure what he was doing?*

CC: Indeed, as is the case, you often have to have those iron absolutes in a state of uncertainty. And the fact that Stormont existed as a grandiose structure amidst a state of immense uncertainty. It's almost a law that if a country is in a state of being uncertain it invents iron laws and rules and statues.

Niall McGrath is a graduate of Edinburgh University and is currently researching contemporary Anglo-Irish Literature at the University of Ulster. His poetry has been published in several magazines and journals, including *The New Statesman & Society* and *The Honest Ulsterman*.

POETRY FROM THE SIX COUNTIES

JOHN BROWN

MARTIN MOONEY

JAMES SIMMONS

PAT RAMSAY

MEDBH McGUCKIAN

GERALD DAWE

FRED JOHNSTON

FRANK ORMSBY

JOHN HEWITT

The Singer's House

John Brown

Cuchulain stalked round a rosebed.
Slunk behind a dank privet. A dull thud.
A crimson rivet hammered home in a forehead.
Darkcrushed dawn grass where he lay.
Charlie Chaplin feet splayed heavenward.

Out of the singing house would try at song.
The streets are all wrong
The lift and lilt leave the lips.

Funerals at funerals. Moonhelmet men
Stop, circle, hedgehogged in batons, rifles:
A perspex wagontrain. Apaches don't circle
But come over the top with a starting handle, milkbottle,
A flailing tomahawk from the coalhouse skuttle.

Out of the singing house would try at song.
The streets are all wrong
The lift and lilt leave the lips.

High over Divis a tin bee hovers,
Dips its white proboscis tip
Into the red brick flower of the city,
Sunshafts at midnight slant along the battlements.

Out of the singing house would try at song.
The streets are all wrong
The lift and lilt leave the lips.

A Misidentification of Birds

Martin Mooney

These are things I need to explain
before I read this last poem of the night.
Up here on the worried coast
the term for stranger is *blow-in*
and my lover, Jack our four-month-old
and I are blow-ins, like the weed
fermenting down there on the slipway
that only a north wind will clear.

Till then the swallows graze the midge-herds,
I risk remarks on tide-times, and
next door's bachelor corrects
my misidentification of birds.
His smile is a settled smile, through which
the history of our cottage is unfolded
like some patchwork heirloom
it's a privilege to be shown.

You'll need to know this too –
how, constantly outsmarted, the Excise
built this station on the smuggler's
own farm, a stone ear cocked
for Scotch and sheep. How Jack's
are the first baby's cries to rattle
the farmyard since the Second War
left the yellow lookout on the headland
and the phosphorous flares that still
wash up, sizzling, on the beach.

Stretching the point, an army
helicopter buzzes the island, cockily
goads the gulls into a white
frenzy of feathers and bitching.
This is a weekly manoeuvre, so low
you can see the crew's sarcastic grins.
Jack, woken, repeats his accidental
only word, *Inge*, his imaginary blonde.

I imagine her too – tolerant, witty,
beautiful, what would she make
of all this local colour?
I'd have to tell her, and you, how
five calves froze to death in May, and how
they say the helicopter exercises
are something a real native shrugs
and buckles down to, like work.

I want the poem I'm about to read
to ask if we have to put up with this
to live here. I hope it's more
than a grizzle of details, swallows
and anecdotes. This is for Inge.
Thank you for coming. Safe home.

Lake Event

James Simmons

Once, when water called my name
I discovered the sky as a liquid element,
swimming in a clarity so blue
the firmament floated under me.
I gazed into nothing
so clearly that
for a moment
I was unsure of up or down
backward or forward
time ahead or behind.
Just this,
that is all,
just *this*,
an orientation that could not be described
full of the sound of water rubbing past my ears.
So I came away from something people call swimming
washed clean of time
unable to remember
the name the water called me.

Water
   deeper than bone
   bluer than thought
   colder than stopped breath
   vaster than a meditator's eye
   more changeable than ways I have changed
since knowing this water.

One dip
and the cold stays with you
wringing out your capillaries
marbleizing your skin.
The great blue lake
inoculates with light.
The horizon stretches against your chest
drawing your body into its cobalt haze.
Though you may only wade or swim the edges
or travel its glittering surfaces,
this lake fuses inner spaces with its vistas,

a merger of landscapes
in which arises the permanent lake
the one you will never be able to leave
because it reminds you of you.

Water
> *deeper than bone*

Sestina of the Seaboard

James Simmons

The nylon rope slapping the metal mast,
a forest clapping coldly in the dark,
and I alone unsleeping, close to the roof.
No other vessel had a man on board.
The small yacht strained against the mooring rope.
'Rangoon by morning!' Captain Billy cried.

'The rising sea's too much for me,' I cried.
Fear and mistakes. There was the broken mast
and only Billy who could climb the rope
his competence a beacon in our dark.
Two assholes and a sailor were aboard.
He climbed into our swaying shattered roof.

Nerve was like metaphysics. We called roof
what was beyond us as we whinged and cried,
keen but incompetent to be aboard
so thin a vessel with so high a mast
that in full daylight left us in the dark,
two lubbers with a slack and useless rope,

in crisis lost, though smart enough with rope
in light winds. Now I feel the shallow roof
press on my head. I feel the lonely dark.
When she went off with someone else I cried
and felt no seaman's feeling for the mast
we all gazed up to as we came aboard.

Aboard, ashore, aboard, ashore, aboard.
You buy a boat and tie it with a rope.
You look up scared by far too high a mast,
but sleep well underneath the lowly roof.
And even Captain Bill might have cried
along in the small cabin in the dark.

A boat is for exploring. Moored in the dark.
with no companions, the one man aboard,
I cried alone, and many would have cried.
Don't hand us from the yard arm by a rope

who should have stuck beneath our family roof
now and before ... frightened to climb a mast,

to climb a cross in darkness, the high mast.
They hacked at the boarded windows, the thatched roof.
Crying, we felt them hack home's last straw rope.

Overlooking Belfast Lough

Pat Ramsay

Looking out, you dream of distant shores,
Of loves in foreign cities, to be free,
Shrug off the dull responsibility
Of house, job, wife and kids – domestic chores –

And start again with the ideals of youth,
Live on energy and raw nerve. Find you're
Alone once more, slightly soiled, insecure,
Yet on amicable terms with the truth –

Whatever *that* is. It's a useful dream
But that's all it is. The good life's here –
Both prospective and real. Your proper sphere
Lies in the rituals of hearth and home.

The secret's remaining flexible, skilled.
Like anywhere, *here* is a place to build.

Some Days

Pat Ramsay

There are some days which should weep with shame,
Days when you call at certain hotel counters
To collect your parcel of that day's sorrow,
Your re-heeled shoes of pain; the sharp taste
That inhabits your mouth is recondite, hard,
The ghost of unused things, a perfect lozenge
Of someone else's tears turned to sudden stone.
Strangely penitent, you let them wickedly demand
Their tax of hobbling, their incantations
Of swearing under your breath. These are the days
When even being loveless is an act of faith,
The half-hoped doubt of martyrdom. The heart's
Cancer of dead petals, smouldering wormwood.

In close rooms, bedsits, the hotel you have just left,
The nothingness that happens throbs like a wound,
Fired not by the memory of love or misfortune
But the knowledge that the approach of light
Will prove them senseless, without a moral
Of any kind. In these pastless, withered rooms
You know no lovers sail the treacherous seas
That is some other body and in every street
Each man reads the passing of his minute
As a poem not written but already fallen to ruin
With the weight of words, the free syllables
Suggesting merely the idea. They look and know
That your body is but a misanthrope's conception
Of a witticism, his disapproval of weakness.

The Scissors Collection
Medbh McGuckian

Red house, red week-red springtime:
card-carrying freshness hoarded from childhood.
Though we did not reach the empire of signs,
I overheard in your child-verb-city
all the earth's principal languages
spoken in hushed voices-spoken in torrential
but everyday voices, by the gracious,
distant, antiquated silhouette
of the fir trees, unreeling miles and miles
of voice powerful enough to kill moonlight.

Timbered porches, balconies hanging over
empty space stole our instincts. Our poetry
boutique was a sort of pastry palace on two levels
reined in by a double sweep of stairs.
Its rooms were not designed, with their pointed,
clover-leaf windows, to be lived in by day.
Like a living creature entered
in a coat of arms, old Europe
couldn't raise a cup to our lips, but held
our eyes on overturned chairs for a swallowed time.

I was appeased by the endless, oversized
sky, that felt like part of the morning,
or nature where there is no nature, wearing
a cavalry badge on her gold bracelet.
Ave Maria time altered the lighting
on your past; it wrapped our shoes in felt
like mountains walled into their own happiness.
Stone flames arose from pots, a granite piano
decorated a composer's grave, we suffered
through one Mozart, two Schuberts and four Liszts.

Though they have music built into their names,
their spirit of havoc, vital, reassuring disorder,
we were ill-assorted, semi-experiences,
my porcelain washbasin with slate blue flowers
wept all the tears in my body. I covered
the lamp on my night-table with a handkerchief,

like a small, irregular breast. Your father
buried in his red Garibaldian shirt
suddenly kissed my black-clad father's
worker's hands for ten minutes.

Palm's breadth of green water. So beautiful
when it is beautiful. The wild new life
of a blond-wood desk felling something sure
in a Bible paper word. Even if a brother died
the day a bird was brought home, embellishing
your signature with another sharp, we are
only responsible for our lives starting
on a particular day ... an unusually long-held
wavering first-hand shot, blurs the kind
of incandescent ... long hair that you love.

Turning the Sleep Spindle

Medbh McGuckian

Druidic wind, running without a sweatband,
your womblessness sows its white smile
near my face: I use your linen lord's antlers
as a book rest in my woman-hour
with you against a wall in June light,
waiting to be shot or lamed or nailed
up like a jackdaw on a barn door.

Rosette-formed T-cells in my blood
drink the threefold scent of live and dying roses:
when the bull-sleep of a man who has been 'out',
or a boytroop of three brothers, begetting
the same child, breaks like a nut
my shabby, wing-sleeved peace, the only stirrup-cup

bids from a birth-ladle so big
Setanta and Scathach
could have lain together in its praise.

Moving

Gerald Dawe

Some things are becoming clear
such as the seaweed baths at Enniscrone;
or the dogs barking as we came near
the waterside one Sunday morning early.

Gulls scavenging in the carpark at Seapoint;
couples window-shopping before their tea
and the girls upstairs getting ready.
Your ancient fur-coat, my blue two-piece suit ...

But there is someone else talking here and now;
the scene changes. Under this roof,
under these stars, the garden tips far below
and the house falls into an airy silence.

Rogues

Fred Johnston

A word implying good-natured rule-bending,
forgivable moral decrepitude,
shadowy string-pulling, favouring a few
what we'd all do, if we had the nerve

admirable, those who earn the name
how else to endure under gombeen and taxes –
they know by nature what to do
eviction, transportation, the best of teachers

they have learned the hows and wheres
the semaphore of wink-and-nod
they know that God's a chancer too,
you understand that early, and move on

they'll look you in the eye and tell you
My father worked his fingers to the bone
giving you to take from that
the same mistake won't be made again

mention words like *fair play* or *straight*
they'll talk about Black and Tans,
Victoria letting Ireland starve,
getting nowhere in this world being slow

the odd thing is they mean well –
they believe in themselves, are patriotic
to a man, won't hear the county bad-mouthed
are genuinely sorry for the neighbours out of work

they are Mass-goers and can hold a pint
there are certain things they won't discuss,
such as divorce, men loving other men,
mention *women's health*, and they're finished

but they've uncovered the slot
in every man's heart where the coin
should be dropped – you've had it
when they whisper We *know* you.

Sunday Afternoon

Fred Johnston

Downstairs, he plays Chopin on a Japanese piano
the wooden house is full of chords and arpeggios

Upstairs, we watch an episode of *Star Trek*
four of us, not a word, Chopin and Captain Picard

Years ago the British Fleet sat at anchor in the bay
we can see the empty water from the kitchen window

Whores gathered under the skittering Quay Street lamps
children were told the devil walked there by night

The town sent its men to Flanders or under the North Sea
so few understood that quiet Post Office revolution

Or wanted it. A piano playing Chopin on a Sunday
afternoon. A girl's dress played with by the sea wind.

History is a large dog dozing across the threshold.
Do not disturb. I make tea, consider Connolly in his chair.

Two Cradle Songs

Frank Ormsby

I

**for Matthew Rogers
b. 29 December 1989**

The world is six days old.
He lies white
in a white room
and January light
attends his cradle.
We watch his restful face
come into its own.

Will he open his eyes?
In his own sweet time he will,
on us, on the Cave Hill –
old head-in-the-mist
dreaming blues and greens
a mile from his window,
his first present of spring.

II

**for David Rogers
b. 5 April 1993**

The spirit of Lent is broken. On holiday
for the first time in years
he finds in us his happy hour.
The raising of his glass
is a lost art recovered.
His Easter self
sleeps in Maternity,

will wake to the name David,
treating his kin
(exhausted in all but loving,
schooled in love
by his tearaway elder)
to the best gift of this or any season:
a new place and reason for love to begin.

The Gap on my Shelf

Frank Ormsby

Smaller than life, episcopal in death
he lies, browns frowning
the length of his body.
the *Poems* of Mrs Hemans under his chin.

The lips sink in his face, his paunch settles
as the hump of a grave levels at last with the earth.
Empty of self, he fills us with the tug
and ebb of his absence.

Where has he gone? When I try to imagine his soul
in flight before dawn, or fluttering down at last
on the clouds of a catechism heaven,

what floods my head is dislocated light
and rain at the window,
some n-place, like the space where yesterdays go;

all I can see, the book-sized gap on my shelf,
wordless with loss, where poems used to be.

Ossian's Grave, Lubitavish, Country Antrim
John Hewitt

We stood and pondered on the stones
whose plan displays their pattern still;
the small blunt arc, and sill by sill,
the pockets stripped of shards and bones.

The legend has it, Ossian lies
beneath this landmark on the hill,
asleep till Fionn and Oscar rise
to summon his old bardic skill
in hosting their last enterprise.

This, stricter scholarship denies,
declares this megalithic form
millennia older than his time –
if such lived ever, out of rime –
was shaped beneath Sardinian skies,
was coasted round the capes of Spain,
brought here through black Biscayan storm,
to keep men's hearts in mind of home
and its tall Sun God, wise and warm,
across the walls of toppling foam,
against this twilight and the rain.

I cannot tell, would ask no proof;
let either story stand for true,
as heart or head shall rule. Enough
that, our long meditation done,
as we paced down the broken lane
by the dark hillside's holly trees,
a great white horse with lifted knees
came stepping past us, and we knew
his rider was no tinker's son.

Widely regarded as being the father figure of the current generation of Ulster poets, John Hewitt actively promoted the development of art and literature in Northern Ireland throughout his life. He was born in Belfast in 1907, and was educated at Methodist College Belfast and Queen's University Belfast. His poetry was first published in left-wing journals such as the *Irishman* and the *New Leader* in the 1920s. Between 1948 and 1972 he published two collections and six pamphlets of poetry. From 1930 to 1957 he worked in the Belfast

Museum and Art Gallery. During this period he was also active in socialist politics and – with John Luke, Colin Middleton and others – formed the Ulster Unit, a progressive art group. In 1957 he became the art director of the Herbert Art Gallery and Museum in Coventry. On his retirement in 1972, he returned to Belfast, where he died in 1987. His last years were remarkably productive, seeing the publication of seven collections and two pamphlets of poetry, one book and two monographs on art, and a study of the weaver poets of Antrim and Down, *Rhyming Weavers*. His lasting contribution to the arts in Ulster is celebrated at the John Hewitt International Summer School, held each year in Garron Tower on the Antrim coast.

From *The Collected Poems of John Hewitt* (1993), edited by Frank Ormsby and published by The Blackstaff Press, Belfast, by whose kind permission this is reprinted.

ALLUSION, THEFT
&
FREE TRANSLATION

AN OSSIANIC MISCELLANY

MURRAY PITTOCK

FRANK KUPPNER

EDWIN MORGAN

MACDONALD DALY

THOM NAIRN

JAMES MACPHERSON
From the Painting by Reynolds in National Gallery, London

Oisin Oisian Ossin
Suibne Subney Sweeney
Osuine Oswine Ossian Ocean
A (Mock?) Heroic Miscellany

> We, the Fenians, never used to tell untruth;
> a lie was never attributed to us.
> By truth and by the strength of our hands
> we used to come safe out of every danger.
>
> *Ossian, to St. Patrick, in the Dialogues of the Sages*

AS THE WORLD prepares for a Burns bicentennial bonanza in 1996, there is another Scotsman, the bicentennial of whose death on February 17th 1796 may pass comparatively unnoticed. Yet the writing of James Macpherson, the Badenoch Bard, was in its day the toast of Europe, and gave to the burgeoning Romantic movement a model Noble Savage in the form of the ancient warrior poet Ossian almost half a century before the Waverley pen first began to scratch a picture of the misty Highlands. It may be considered ironic that for Burns 'the world found no fitter business than quarrelling with smugglers and vintners, computing excise-dues upon tallow, and gauging ale-barrels', as Thomas Carlyle phrases it in his essay of 1828, while the infamous 'forger' Macpherson made his fortune, returned to the land of his birth in the role of magnanimous laird, and was buried in Westminster Abbey.

The connection between the two is interesting. A matter of a single generation – twenty-six years – separates the Edinburgh which hailed the Gaelic translator of the Northern Homer in 1760 from the Edinburgh which took the Ayrshire plooman to its fireside in the winter of 1786, a period short enough for there to be roles for the same players in each drama. George Laurie, minister of Loudon in Ayrshire, was present at the meeting in Moffat which first introduced Macpherson to the literary coterie headed by Dr. Hugh Blair, and it was Laurie who later sent a copy of the Kilmarnock Edition of *Poems, Chiefly in the Scottish Dialect* to the capital in

1786, so causing Rab to borrow a steed and ride to Edinburgh rather than emigrate. Henry Mackenzie, whose essay on the Kilmarnock edition published in *The Lounger* in December 1786 introduced him to Edinburgh society, was appointed head of the Commission established in 1804 by the Highland Society to investigate the Ossianic controversy.

Both Macpherson and Burns offered to the Enlightenment city a vision of the rural Scot. Macpherson's Gaelic image was as noble as the Classical model so beloved in the Athens of the North, but Burns, for all his sentimental moralising, belonged to the Scots 'Doric' world, rather than the Classical. He may have wept spontaneously at a fine painting hanging in a drawing room by day, but at night he caroused the taverns, singing baudy songs. Macpherson was University-educated, 'starched and reserved'; Burns, according to Mackenzie, was a 'heaven-taught ploughman' whose effusive emotions are now legend. Put bluntly, the young Macpherson fitted humbly in, and his idealised Highland past was exactly what a city bereft of its regal and parliamentary significance wanted. Burns, after the initial lionising was over, did not – let it not be forgotten that it was his sentimental poems in English that Mackenzie, author of *The Man of Feeling*, first praised, though what qualities Burns had to offer were at home in the coarn rigs and barley rigs of Ayrshire, not the drawing rooms of the capital city.

From a distance of almost two hundred years, the careers of James Macpherson and Robert Burns seem interconnected – it might even be that the embarrassment caused to Blair and the Edinburgh literati by Macpherson's 'forgery' was sufficient cause for the coining of the term 'true British poet', as used by Carlyle to praise Burns. As Angus Calder, paraphrasing Voltaire, puts it: ' ...if Burns hadn't surfaced, with the publication of a volume of poems in Kilmarnock in 1786, someone would have had to invent him. There was nothing inauthentic about Burns.'

Macpherson, though broadly accused of being a counterfeiter, was never punished in his lifetime; Burns, considered to be 'true' even to his own loss, was never rewarded. Perhaps, in the last two hundred years, posterity has taken it upon herself to settle these accounts. Now, as 1996 approaches, the shadow that hangs over James 'Ossian' Macpherson should be illuminated, by the light thrown from the concept of intertextuality on the dim-lit corners of 'authority', 'plagiarism' and 'forgery'.

If the provenance of Macpherson's *Ossian* is uncertain, his motivation is not, for it was in the shadow of Ruthven Redoubt, a substantial garrison established in 1719, that James Macpherson was born – it has even been suggested, though there is no proof extant, that his mother was the 'Mrs Macpherson of Ruthven' who appears in a letter written in 1745 by the commander, as 'barrack-wife' to the redcoats stationed there. Whatever the detail, his youthful Highland pride must have been sorely stung – imagine him around the age of ten, witnessing the arrival of the ragged but still considerable band of men who had escaped Culloden, crossed the Nairn and made their way to Ruthven under the leadership of Lord George Murray and Cluny Macpherson. This destination was not coincidental, for the barracks had fallen to the Jacobites early in 1746, and as Alan G. Macpherson tells us in the clan history *The Posterity of the Three Brethern* (1993), 'the Macphersons formed the rearguard of the retreat as the fugitive army fled through their lines.' At Ruthven they raised the standard once more and sent a message to the Prince, to the effect that he still had followers keen to continue to fight. Their three-day long wait for Charlie's disappointing reply – 'Let every man seek his safety in the best way he can' – and Murray's searing admonition in response to it, was a last defiant stand worthy of any Ossianic ballad.

What follows here is a cut-and-paste miscellany, in the spirit of Macpherson, of sense and nonsense relating to the 'Ossianic controversy' and its dark age origins. We begin with an account of a chance find in 1732, during the building of General Wade's road from Crieff to Dalnacardoch, part of a route over the Pass of Drumochter into Badenoch, which may have been the first unintentional act in the eighteenth century resurrection of the 'Northern Homer' – literally, a rolling away of the stone traditionally known as Clach Ossian.

RAJ.

A Glen for John Hewitt

Murdo Macdonald

A balance is threaded across my map
from that Ossian's grave which your heart marked
to Clach Ossian lying like a sky ship's anchor
lost on the floor of the glen of my memory.

High above that broukit and disshevelled place
in a wide territory where quartz shines from peat
the drifting irony of the pipes catches my breath
a sharp web traced on the wind's contour.

I listen for the shouts of the curious roadmakers –
Ossian was re-made in the echoes of their spades
waiting three hundred years to re-enter history
on the open moor with the hare and the buzzard.

There rocks lie like the bones of some beached creature
tugging me back into the vast museum of my childhood –
whale ribs trapped majestic among the pillars
of that constricting, dead, and yet inspiring place.

A museum, like a cairn, can be a true nekropolis
giving birth in due time to a city of soul and body –
in your fine city you endured each question and defeat
and held with understanding to your lack of faith.

Clach Ossian, the Sma' Glen; View from the South.

1. About fifty years ago, certain soldiers employed under General Wade, in making the military road from Stirling to Inverness, through the Highlands, raised the stone by large engines and discovered under it a coffin full of burnt bones. This coffin consisted of four grey stones, which still remain, such as are mentioned in Ossian's Poems.

Ossian's Stone, with the four grey stones in which his bones are said to have been deposited, is surrounded by a circular dyke, 200 feet in circumference, and 3 feet in height. The Military Road passes through its centre... ...The people of the country, for several miles around, to the number of four score of men, venerating the memory of the Bard, rose with one consent, and carried away the bones, with bagpipes playing, and other funeral rites, and deposited them with much solemnity within a circle of large stones, on the lofty summit of a rock, sequestered and of difficult access, where they might never more be disturbed by mortal feet or hands, in the wild recesses of western Glen Almond, and many other persons yet alive, attest the truth of this fact, and point out the second sepulchre of the son of Fingal.

There is on the summit of the steep slopes of the west of the Almond, at 1750 feet above sea, a great cairn. Perhaps it is this spot that now contains the bones revered as those of Ossian.

2. In July 1726 we come upon... ...a deplorable picture of the pollution with which Badenoch was impregnated by the establishment of the barracks at Ruthven, built by the Government of the day a few years after the Rising of 1715, on the site of the old castle of the Comyns... ...in the immediate neighbourhood of the barracks stood the village of Ruthven, which for many years previously was distinguished as possessing the only school of importance from 'Speymouth to Lorn.' Here in 1736 was born James Macpherson, the celebrated translator of Ossian's poems, where for some years, after finishing his studies at King's College, Aberdeen, he filled the honourable position of parochial schoolmaster. The site of the old village is now indicated by the farmhouse of the same name. The Kingussie session could not apparently see their way to extirpate the rowdy Lowland garrison bodily; but they did not hesitate, as the following extract shows, to adopt the most summary measures to have the abandoned and disreputable followers of the alien redcoats banished out of the district:-

> '*July 10th,* 1726. – The sessions, understanding yt yr are a great many stragglers and vagabonds come into this parish without testimonials, as also a great many dissolute and unmarried women from different parts of the Kingdom, commonly follow the soldiers at the barracks of Ruthven, and are sheltered in some houses in the parish, where they and the soldiers have frequent meetings, and very often upon the Lord's Day, to the great scandal of religion and prophanation of ye Sabbath: Therefore, the Session think it necessary to apply to the civil judge that all such shelter such women and vagabonds shall be condignly punished and fined in twenty pounds Scots *toties quoties,* and this to be intimated from the pulpit.'

3. The bowling green at Moffat about the middle of the [18th] century was a gay scene. There were present visitors from all parts of Scotland who were glad to while away the time between the intervals of drinking the sulphur waters which had gained fame for the village. Lairds and their wives from remote districts came to the wells, anxious to join rank and fashion which every season gathered there – 'nabobs' who returned from the Indies, possessed of lacs of rupees and bilious constitutions; 'Tobacco lords' from Glasgow with airs of consequence as pronounced as their accents; ministers in blue, professors in black, and lawyers in their brilliant scarlet coats, with ladies in their hoops and sacques of brilliant hues. On an October day in 1759, there met on the green Mr. Alexander Carlyle, the minister of Inveresk, and Mr. John Home, and Mr. George Laurie of London – a young minister, who afterwards was helpful

to Robert Burns. There, too, was a big stalwart youth of six foot three, standing substantially on thick set legs, encased in old-fashioned jack-boots. This was James Macpherson, tutor to young Graham of Balgowan, known afterwards to history as Lord Lynedoch, who was staying at the wells. ...

...This unknown youth had been born in 1738, in a little thatched cottage in Ruthven, where his father had a small farm. He had become a student at King's College, Aberdeen, with the intention of entering the Church, and had then gone to finish his studies at Edinburgh College. He returned to his native parish, and when barely twenty years old became the master of a charity school. An income of about £6 or £8 gave him enough money to live upon, and his scanty flock of scholars gave him leisure enough to study, for reading poetry, and writing verses beside his peat fire when the children had left for the day. Already, from the age of seventeen to twenty, he had written the portentous number of 4000 verses; and an ambitious poem called the 'Highlander', in six cantos, crept into light in 1758, and at once crept back into obscurity.

While teaching at Ruthven, he amused himself by listening to snatches of Gaelic ballads, which were recited by the people, from whose lips came verses transmitted from generation to generation. A few such relics of the past had been collected; and in 1756, in the *Scots Magazine*, a poem 'Alvin, or the Daughter of Mey,' with some others, had appeared, introducing English readers to unknown poetry from an unknown tongue. These translations from the Erse were by Jeremiah Stone, who had begun life when a boy as a pedlar, and ended it at the age of twenty-nine, as a learned schoolmaster at Dunkeld. Save from a few fragments, the world knew nothing of Celtic poetry till Macpherson gave his specimens...

...[At Moffat in 1759] a letter of introduction from Adam Ferguson had made the tutor known to John Home, who was always glad to make himself pleasant and useful to any one. They discussed that day many things, among them Gaelic poetry, customs, and superstitions, and the young Highlander mentioned that he had some pieces of Celtic poetry in his possession. When the author of *Douglas* begged to see some specimens, but owned he did not know Gaelic, 'How then can I show them to you?' he was asked. 'Very easily,' said Home, 'translate some of the poems which you think are good, and I imagine I shall be able to form an opinion of the genius and character of Gaelic poetry.' With reluctance he agreed, and in a few days produced a fragment called 'The Death of Oscar'. Some translations were also shown to Laurie. Both he and Hume agreed that an invaluable discovery had been made, and when they went to Edinburgh, each of them called on Dr. Hugh

Blair in Riddell's Close, to show the literary dictator these remarkable translations from an unknown Erse poet...

...Dr. Blair became eager to see James Macpherson in Edinburgh and, when he met him, urged him to translate still more for publication. The young man of twenty-two years was, however, a difficult youth to deal with, silent, reserved, and proud. He deprecated his power to find more originals, and after he had consented he tried to avoid the task, and several times wrote begging Laurie to get him released from his engagement, urging that his Highland pride was offended at only appearing to the world as a translator. His friend, however, was insistent, and Macpherson gave way; testily swearing that the blood of Ossian would be on the young minister's head...

...Coy publishing, while his friends were urgent, he at last, swearing he would never consent, consented...

...The year 1760 became eventful by the appearance in Edinburgh of an attenuated volume entitled *Fragments of Ancient Poetry collected in the Highlands of Scotland, and Translated from the Gaelic or Erse Language,* with a preface by Doctor Blair explaining that the work contained Gaelic verse of great antiquity, anterior to the clan system, and bearing no trace of Christian influence.

The success of these 'Fragments' was immediate. All Scotsmen were delighted at being able to boast that even the most barbarous parts of their despised country had been possessed of genius before England had risen out of savagedom. Hume and Home, Ferguson and Blair, Lord Elibank, Lord Kames, Lord Hailes – in fact every one – joined in the chorus of acclaim, and were fierce at any who dared to impugn their genuineness, or to slight their beauty. Had not these verses been handed down from remote ages? Did not chiefs keep their own hereditary family bards whose themes were the feats of their clan and the wars of Fingal? Had not Adam Smith heard a piper of Argyleshire repeat some of these very poems? Did not the distinguished chieftains – Mackays, Macleods, Macfarlanes – assert that they knew them well? Furthermore, were not the very names of the heroes, Fingal, Ossian, Oscar, Diarmid, still given in the Highlands to large mastiffs, as the English gave the name of Pompey and Hector, and the French the name of Marlborough to their dogs? So wrote, so argued David Hume full of his usual extravagant patriotism...

...This first success whetted literary appetite for more, especially as Macpherson stated that he had only given fragments of a great epic existing orally in the Highlands. We next find his admirers urging him to rescue the great poem from oblivion. They offered him funds to travel in search of the nebulous epic... ...He refused, he hesitated, but at last consented. Before many months were over, in September 1760, he mounted his horse, fixed his saddle bags and his wallet, and set forth on his voyage of discovery. How he had learned that such an epic existed he alone could, but did not, tell: the difficulty of proving his assertion may explain his reluctance to undertake the expedition. However, he departed, a young man of twenty three, with an imperfect knowledge of Gaelic and a perfect confidence in himself. Letters of introduction ensured him help and hospitality in distant glens and islands with lairds and ministers from Perthshire to far-off Benbecula, where unadulterated tradition and undefiled Gaelic were likeliest to be found... ...Onwards he travelled with Macpherson, the Laird of Strathmashie, his faithful friend and kinsman, over island and mainland. Schoolhouse, croft and manse welcomed him, and chieftains gave him the loan of treasured manuscripts containing household receipts, genealogical notes and old verse in chaotic confusion and distressed cacography – some were lent and never seen again.

After four months spent on tours of discovery, the literary explorer got back to Edinburgh in 1761. His patrons were naturally anxious as to the results. Soon the precise steps of Dr. Hugh Blair with Mr. Adam Ferguson ascended the dirty turnpike stairs of his lodgings in Blackfriars Wynd, and entered the dingy flat. There was James Macpherson, 'a plain looking lad dressed like a preacher,' with a manner starched and reserved. His little garret room was crowded with books, copies of verses, manuscript books in Gaelic, some of them 'stained with smoke and daubed with Scots snuff.' The visitors, after their interview, quitted the room highly satisfied with the assurances of Mr. James Macpherson that the great promised Ossianic epic had been found. Quickly news ran along, and society hummed with excitement. A Celtic Homer had been brought to light after he had been dead thirteen hundred years.

In a few months Macpherson took horse with his manuscripts in his valise to seek subscribers and publishers and a patron in London. David Hume meanwhile had written to his friend William Strahan, the printer, recommending him as 'a sensible, modest, young fellow,' a very good scholar, and of unexceptionable morals.' Lord Bute was then the court favourite, and his favour was secured, and with a humble dedication to his lordship, who was the most patronising of patrons, there appeared in December 1761, *Fingal, an ancient epic Poem, in six books, together with several other poems composed by Ossian, the son of Fingal, translated from the Gaelic language by James Macpherson.*

4. It is clear that there was some close collaboration between Macpherson and Blair (Macpherson lodged for a time below Blair's rooms), especially regarding epic theory; the Introduction and footnotes to Macpherson's poems show his influence strongly; the Fragments and, later, the full-scale epics were presented as ancient (third century) works translated from Gaelic; the historical roles of Scotland and Ireland were largely reversed in the plot and the Viking wars were pushed back into the period selected. This framework was supported by a mass of detailed and pseudo-scholarly argument in notes, etc., using sources such as Mallet's *Introduction a l'histoire de Dannemarc* (Copenhagen 1755–56) and O'Flaherty's *Ogygia*. The intention of this deliberate distortion was to show that an ancient Gaelic epic had been recovered and that Scotland was its locale, though there had been attempts to appropriate it to Ireland.

5. Now there was a stir in every literary circle; the poetry met, as Dr. Beattie, who was no believer, expresses it, with 'a universal deluge of approbation,' and it rivalled the Cock Lane ghost in the interest it excited in London. True, there were some notes of discord, the truculent Churchill had his sarcastic flings, and Wilkes had his jeers; for Scotsmen, and all who clung to Lord Bute, were the butts of every wit and witling. In Scotland, however, hardly one dissentient voice was heard. Here was an epic that cast Homer into the shade; here was a poem that shed a lustre on Scotland which England well might envy. At every Edinburgh breakfast table it was discussed and lauded, the dinner-table resumed the talk, and every supper-party got more enthusiastic as the wine passed round. The class-room at College was crowded by the rank and fashion of the town, as Dr. Hugh Blair, with the pride of a discoverer and the pomposity of a critic, descanted in his familiar burr on the age, the style, and marvellous beauties of the blind son of Fingal. When the lectures were published in 1763 his *Critical Dissertation* was hailed as a masterly and convincing performance. It was, indeed, as learned a disquisition as could be written by a man who knew nothing of his subject.

6. ...Homer is a more cheerful and sprightly poet than Ossian. You discern in him all the Greek vivacity; whereas Ossian uniformly maintains the gravity and solemnity of a Celtic hero... ...cheerfulness is one of the many blessings which we owe to formed society. The solitary wild state is always a serious one...

...The description of Fingal's airy hall, in the poem called *Berrathon*, and of the ascent of Malvina into it deserves particular notice, as remarkably noble and magnificent. But above all, the engagement of Fingal with the Spirit of Loda in *Carric-thura* cannot be mentioned without admiration. I forbear transcribing the passage, as it must have drawn the attention of everyone who has read the works of Ossian... ...*I know no passage more sublime in the writings of an inspired author...*

7. More debate, more talk arose when, shortly after these laudatory lectures appeared, the final part of the immortal work was issued – *Temora, an ancient Epic in eight books, composed by Ossian, the son of Fingal.* Here was, indeed, a surprising result of the Celt's travels for four months in the Highlands – not one, but two great epics which had survived the lapse of ages which lingered in the tenacious memories and flowed from the fluent lips of Highland crofters. By this time the translator had lost all diffidence. He went about London with a swagger; he was vain-glorious and aggressive. Fame had spoiled his character – not that there was much to spoil – and even his old supporters winced under his manner. Good David Hume retracted alike his faith in Ossian and the good things he had said so guilelessly of the 'sensible, modest fellow,' and now wrote to Strahan of his 'absurd pride and caprice – a mortal than whom I have never known more perverse and unamiable.' Three years before, he had been pleasingly diffident, and deferential to his superiors, being conscious of his poverty, his humble birth, his ignorance of the world. Now, however, that he was celebrated, patrons he owned no longer; he was impatient of the advice of friends, contemptuous of the cavils of opponents. See him with his big, brawny person, dressed in ill-fitting clothes, jostling his way along the Strand; his voice strident and blustering in the coffee-houses, looking down from his height of six feet three at his acquaintances, talking English phrases in Highland tones, and assuming the grand airs of a man of the world. He was aware that society was not so loud in its praises of the great Ossian as before; that it was more sceptical of its genuineness; and this made him all the more defiant in tone. In truth, the world was weary of the melancholy monotony of the verse, of the moaning winds and 'sounding shores', misty hills and 'halls of shells'. It found certainly more bombast in this last doubtful relic of antiquity. 'Why, sir,' said Dr. Johnson, 'a man might write such stuff forever if he would abandon his mind to it,' and in spite of Boswell's patriotic protests the Literary Club would treat Ossian contemptuously...

...To silence sceptics Macpherson placed in the hands of Beckett, his bookseller, certain Gaelic manuscripts; and the newspapers advertised that the 'Originals of Fingal and other poems were to be seen at the shop by all who desired to examine them.' 'Ossian' Macpherson was not highly gifted with a sense of humour; but surely there was excellent humour of a sardonic sort in this proposal that Englishmen should satisfy themselves of the genuineness of a Gaelic epic by looking at documents without a history, manuscripts without a date, in a language of which they knew as little as a Hottentot. For months the manuscripts lay uninspected in Beckett's back room, and then they were withdrawn in sulky triumph. Most of these documents were copies of recitals from Highland lips, with a few old papers, which sceptics like George Dempster declared were Gaelic leases from Macleod of Skye's charter chest ...

...The great questions regarding Ossian were for a while silent if not settled, but they suddenly started once more into life. Dr. Johnson made his famous journey to the Highlands in 1773, and he took with him his contemptuous incredulity to the land of the Gael. There he bullied chiefs and hectored ministers, snorted forth his contradictions and his flouts, till be reduced them to silence, and he mistook the courtesy of his hosts for the abjectness of the convicted. When the famous *Journey to the Hebrides* was about to appear, Strahan, the publisher, Macpherson's good friend and countryman, let out that some unpleasant passages and offensive charges were to appear in its pages. A civil note was written begging that any injurious statements might be omitted. No notice was taken of this appeal, and the temper of the Celt boiled over when the *Journey* was published, and a letter despatched by him to Johnson's Court, informing his assailant that 'his age and his infirmities alone protected him from the treatment due to an infamous liar and traducer.'

8. Notwithstanding his material good fortune and his literary renown, an element of bitterness had entered his life in the wake of his first triumph... ...due to the... ...acrimonious attacks to which he was personally subjected by his refusal to meet the just demands of public criticism. It was to be expected that if he had brought to light a national legacy so important he would also furnish the proofs that it was genuine.

Macpherson's most formidable opponent, it is well known, was Dr. Johnson, whose opinion may be given in the very words in which he afterwards in the Highlands expressed it to Boswell. 'That is just what I always maintained. He has found names and stories, and phrases, nay passages, in old songs, and with them has blended his own compositions, and so made he what he gives to the world as the translation of an ancient poem.'

This was really the verdict also of Malcolm Laing, native of Orkney, the searching legal critic who, next to Johnson, delivered the most telling attack, and it expressed the conviction of thousands of Sassenachs who regarded Macpherson as the original author and not the translator of *Ossian*. Johnson, of course, was mistaken in supposing that the Gaelic never had anything written but where were the Scottish Gaelic documents then to be found that were not in Macpherson's own possession? It was years after the death of the two original combatants in the controversy that the rich legacy of Celtic MSS. now preserved in Edinburgh came to light...

...In 1773 Macpherson published a new edition of his *Ossian*, and this gave occasion to Dr. Johnson to renew the attack, which he did in 1775, with all the more increased vigour, because he had visited the Highlands in the year that the new issue appeared, and he had returned more convinced than ever that Macpherson was an impostor.

In a letter to Mr. W. Strachan, publisher, Fleet Street, the bard wrote:- I find I cannot pass over the expressions contained in Dr. Johnson's pamphlet. I desire therefore that you use your endeavours with *that impertinent fellow* to induce him to soften the expressions concerning me, though it should occasion the delay of a few days in the publication.'

Not content with indirect pressure of this kind, it would seem that he hurled a challenge to fight, or threat of some sort against the Doctor, which drew forth the following animated reply:-

'MR JAMES MACPHERSON – I received your foolish and impudent letter. Any violence offered to me I shall do my best to repel, and what I cannot do for myself the law shall do for me. I hope I shall never be deterred from detecting what I think a cheat by the menaces of a ruffian. What would you have me retract? I thought your book an imposture. I think so still. For this opinion I have given my reasons to the public, which I here dare you to refute. Your rage I defy. Your abilities, since your Homer, are not formidable; and what I hear of your morals induces me to pay regard not to what you shall say, but to what you shall prove. You may print this if you will. (Signed) Sam. Johnson.'

9. History has up to a point vindicated Johnson's insistence that Ossian was a 'forgery': it now seems abundantly clear, from the work of scholars sympathetic in general towards Gaelic literature, that Macpherson constructed his 'epic' out of bits and pieces of folk tradition and that it had never existed as a whole in anything like the form which he gave it. On the other hand, if Johnson's own 'imitation' of Juvenal's satire was valid, if Pope's translation of Homer into eighteenth century couplets imposed an English form remote from the original metre, was it ever fair to castigate Macpherson for treating his oral and manuscript sources as others used the classics?

10. The future career of this indomitable Scot was one of active success. He was ready with his pen to back up any ministerial policy. Did the Ministry really want a writer to attack the mysterious Junius? He could write letters signed 'Scævola' which supplied in venom what was lacking in strength. Did a badgered Prime Minister require a pamphlet to defend his American policy? He was ready with a pamphlet which outdid his enemy Johnson's 'Taxation no Tyranny' in popularity. Did the ill-used Nabob of Arcot need an advocate to plead his claims against the East India Company? He became that potentate's advocate at a good price; and through his friend and brother Celt, Sir John Macpherson, he also became the Nabob's well-paid, highly pensioned agent... When in 1780 he became M.P. for Camelford, his vote was worth something, though he never made a speech...

...It was in 1785 that some enthusiastic Highland gentlemen subscribed £1000 to have the original Gaelic manuscripts of Ossian published, and they provokingly, but respectfully, begged the great man to undertake the task. More than twenty years had elapsed since the epic translation had appeared, and he said there were trunks in the attics, which he had not opened for years, full of manuscripts, both old and new, antique books to read, and fragments to arrange – he did not add that he had all the verse he had composed in English to turn into the supposed original Gaelic.

11. ...he had to sit down in cold blood and make his ancient Gaelic poetry. He had begun with a piece of literary artifice, a practical joke; he ended with deliberate forgery, which the more it succeeded, would leave him less of what was really his due for the merits of the English Ossian.

12. ...As he grew elderly, rich, and prosperous, Macpherson's heart yearned for his old Highland district, and he turned his eyes to Badenoch; there he resolved to buy land and build a home within sight of his native mountains. Two or three small farms were bought on the banks of the Spey, and soon a villa, bearing the Cockney title of 'Belleville', which had been designed by his friend Adam, the architect, rose from the wilds, two miles from Kingussie. People long remembered the great man from London, who came every year, bedizened with rings and gold seals, and clad in fur-edged coat. They told stories of the grand state he kept up as a Highland chief, his splendid table, his home filled with guests; of his sallying forth in the morning and bringing up bibulous lairds from houses far and near, who in the dining room, from whose walls portraits by Sir Joshua Reynolds looked down, kept high revelry till they and the

nights were far spent. But good things, too, were told of Macpherson, pleasant to remember; of his refusing from a grateful Government the forfeited estate of Cluny Macpherson, which was thereupon restored to its rightful owner; his generosity to the poor, whom he employed at high wages, which no Badenoch man had every dreamed of; his kindly remembrance of all about his native Badenoch. Now that his ambition was satisfied, now that his struggle with poverty and obscurity was over he could be the pleasant, affable man, the kindly landlord, and the genial host.

13. ...Tradition in Badenoch is unanimous in remembering his loyalty, kindness and generosity to the land of his birth. Familiarly, he was known as *Seamas Ban*, 'Fair James' and a countryman of his, recalling his day a century later, wrote of 'poor kind James, of unhappy connections' warning his tenants and dependants on the Balavil estate with uncanny foreboding of the changes attendant on a new race of proprietors: *Mo thruaighe sibh dar thig an Sassunach* ('woe unto you for when the stranger comes'). A Gaelic elegy composed at the time of his death described how Macpherson brought prosperity and wellbeing to his people, and amongst his many virtues praised him as *ciobar a chinne*, 'shepherd of the clan'.

14. It was on 17th February 1796 that Macpherson died at his Highland home... ...An obscure burial in a Highland kirkyard not satisfying his ambition, he left £500 to erect a monument on his land, and ordered that his important remains should be interred in Westminster Abbey. After travelling for eighteen days, the hearse finally arrived in London, was met at Highgate by many acquaintances, and a long range of carriages followed it to the Abbey, where the body was laid within a few feet of that of his enemy, Johnson, in the sanctuary where foes can war no more. Thus in pomp and circumstance ended the career of the poor schoolmaster of Ruthven.

15. So lived, so died, so acted and thought, the 'CLOUD POET', and after the storm and the shine of life he now sleeps with the heroes. Future times shall hear of him. They shall hear of the fame of the Badenoch bard and the voices he awakened from the past...

16. With him did not die the Ossianic controversy. Englishmen forgot it, but Scots were too eager for the credit of their country not to vindicate the credit of Ossian... ...A few years later the Highland Society formed a committee, under Henry Mackenzie, to investigate the sources of the famous work, and information was sought from those who best knew Gaelic poetry. The result was not satisfactory...

17. The Highland Society instituted an inquiry into the whole question but their conclusions were somewhat negative. They succeeded in establishing the characters introduced by Macpherson were familiar in the Highlands and that Ossianic ballads really existed, which Macpherson had utilized.

18. ... the Highlanders of India sent him a cheque for £1000 to enable him to vindicate the antiquity of their native literature. Macpherson at different times, and particularly towards the end of his life, seems to have had some intention of publishing the Gaelic of his Ossian, but he was naturally deterred by the feeling that his knowledge of Gaelic was becoming shakier with his continued absence from the Highlands. At any rate he left behind a quantity of Gaelic matter in MS. which was ultimately published by the Highland Society of London in 1807. This MS., however, was revised and transcribed by Ross and afterwards destroyed so that we are ignorant of its nature...

19. ...The *Red Book of the Clanranald*... ...was obtained by Macpherson in 1760 from Neil Macvurich, nephew of the last great bard, and it figured largely in the Ossianic controversy. In addition to poems in Irish by Neil Macvurich, who died at a great age sometime after the 1715, and other bardic matter, the MSS. now contain only three Ossianic poems, and these are in Irish. During the Ossianic controversy the *Red Book of Clanranald* was supposed to contain the originals of much of Macpherson's famous work; but, on the book coming into the hands of the enthusiastic Gaels of the closing years of the 18th century, and on its contents being examined and found wanting, the MS. was tampered with...

20. The Gaelic poems which were published in 1807, from a manuscript in the handwriting of James Macpherson, differ very widely indeed from those handed down by tradition; very widely indeed from all known traditions about the Fenian heroes in the Highlands. The kingdom of Morven is unknown either in traditional poems or stories... ...The language of the printed *Ossian* of 1807 differs entirely from that of the traditional ballads now ascribed to Ossian; it differs entirely from that of other published Scoto-Gaelic poetry... it differs entirely from Gaelic as spoken at present in the Highlands; and it differs entirely from that of the Ossianic poems which have been published by the Irish Ossianic Society.

21. I have frequently questioned old men concerning the Fingalians

in almost all parts of the Highlands, from Cape Wrath to the Mull of Cantyre. If they have heard of them – what they have have heard of them – and if they believed in them? I have never in one single instance met with a negative... ... Some, I believe, imagine, in the simplicity of their heart, that Macpherson, the translator, was the author of Ossian's poems. Perhaps it was Macpherson who also composed the thousand and one Fingalian tales that are floating through the Highlands? and all the anecdotes of the Fingalians? Well, if so, I can only say that Macpherson must have been very busy in his day.

22. I do not assert that the poet's name was Ossian. I deny on good grounds that it was James Macpherson. I maintain that a poet, and a Scotch Highlander, composed all those lines separately, if not together; and judging from my own knowledge of the people, and their ways, it is possible that these may be fragments of sentimental poetry different from the popular ballads, more modern, but certainly older than 1730.

23. In point of time, as reckoned by the Irish annalists and historians, the men of the Fenian cycle lived something about 200 years later than those of the Cuchulain era, and in none of the romances do we see even the faintest confusion or sign of intermingling the characters belong to the different cycles. One of the surest proofs – if proof were needed – that Macpherson's brilliant 'Ossian' had no Gaelic original, is the way in which the men and events of the two separate cycles are jumbled together.

24. The Scots seem to have oozed out of the north of Ireland upon the western coast of Scotland and its archipelago. The countries are nearer to each other than we are accustomed to think; from one great seaport to another, as from Greenock to Belfast or Drogheda, is a considerable voyage, but the Mull of Cantyre is only twelve miles distant from the county of Antrim...

25. ...Stories and placenames relating to Fionn and his men are abundant in Argyll and, like the Sons of Uisneach of an earlier age, the heroes evidently moved between western Scotland and north east Ireland as if it was one country... ...Place names in north Lorn include Dun Fionn at Benderloch, Tom Oisein, or 'Ossian's Mound' near Barcaldine and Carn Oisein or 'Ossian's Cairn' at Achnacree... ...There is also Rudha na h'Oisinne, presumably 'Ossian's point', on Loch Etive... ...On Lismore... is Sliabh nam Ban-fionn, or the 'Hill of the Fianna Women', the site of a great hunt by three thousand nobles with their dogs of the warrior band led by Fionn MacCumhaill and commemorated in a poem preserved locally and written down early in the 16th century by James MacGregor, Dean of Lismore... ...The hill is that on which the wives of the Fianna warriors sat and watched the proceedings. The Lismore site seems a little small for such a spectacular affair (even though there were forests and large deer there once) and the name may have been given by homesick Irish colonists in remembrance of the greater hill in Ireland... ...Nevertheless it is interesting that just offshore is Eilean Loch Oscair, an island named after Osgar... ...in addition there is Cnoc Fionn, 'Fionn's hill' nearby.

Of course some of the names could have been applied in later times when the reputation of the heroes had grown to supernatural proportions; there is more than one stone circle for example called 'Fingal's cauldron seat'. However, Larach Tigh nam Fionn on Lismore does suggest the memory of something more specific; it means 'the site of the house of the Fianna'.

26. ...The Book of the Dean of Lismore contains 11,000 lines of poetry, some of which are attributed to Oisein and his comrades, some to bards of the period. Probably a collection written from dictation, it gives according to the writer's ability a faithful representation of the current language and traditional poems of the district of Lorne in the sixteenth century. Even a few sheets of this publication prove beyond question that the groundwork of the first book of *Temora* had been made the subject of a Gaelic poem written down more than three centuries ago, but the poem of 1807 is not there. This MS., then, disposes of a great deal of the Ossianic controversy and clears the ground. Lorne is close to Morven, but there is no mention of Fingal or his kingdom. It is thus proved that Fionn and his heroes are not simply creatures of Macpherson's brain, or worthies who belong exclusively to Irish romance.

27. ...Zimmer developed a theory that Finn was really a Norseman, and that the Fenian cycle is in fact posterior to the Norse invasion, but this paradoxical theory has broken down, or at least has carried with it none of the other great Celtic savants. Mr. Alfred Nutt, on the other hand, has come to the conclusion, in his learned and interesting essay on the development of the Fenian Saga, appended to the Gaelic Folk and Hero Tales by MacInnes, that the whole groundwork of the Ossianic tales is mythical... ...According to this theory of Mr. Nutt's, both the Cuchulain and the Ossianic sagas were originally nothing but tribal myths, and probably myths belonging to different Gaelic tribes... ...There is yet another hypothesis of which Dr. Skene and Mr MacRitchie, and perhaps the great folklorist, Iain Campbell of Islay, were champions – that the Fenians were a non-Celtic race of men, allied to or identical with the Picts of history.

28. If Fionn is not a historical character, then how can we account for his existence as the national hero of the Gael? To answer this is to have the 'key of all mythologies'. How do the heroes and demigods of mythology arise? Fionn is, like Hecales, Theseus, Perseus, and other such persons of Greek myth, a culture hero – probably originally a local deity raised to a national place. He is an incarnation of the chief deity of the race – the Mercury, whom Caesar tells us the Gauls worshipped – a god of a literary and mercantile character. His grandson Oscar is a war god, and the other characters of the Fenian band no doubt the other personages of the Gaelic Olympus. Reverting to the question with which we started – 'Did Fingal live or Ossian sing' – we have to give the answer, that Fingal lived and Ossian sang only in the imagination of the Gaelic race, to embody their idea of all that is noble or heroic.

29. The actual data that we have to go upon in estimating the genesis and development of the Fenian tales have been lucidly collected by Mr. Nutt. They are, as far as is known at present, as follows:- Gilla Caemhain the poet, who died in 1072, says that it was fifty seven-years after the battle of Moy Muchruime that Finn was treacherously killed 'by the spearpoints of Uirgriu's three sons'. This would make Finn's death take place in 252, for Moy Muchruime was fought, according to the Four Masters, in A.D. 195. Tigearneach, the annalist, who died in 1088, writes that Finn was killed in A.D. 283 'by Aichleach, son of Duibhdrean, and the sons of Uirgriu, of the Luaighni of Tara, at Ath-Brea upon the Boyne'. The poet Cinaeth O'Hartagain, who died in A.D. 985, wrote – 'By the Fiann of Luagne was the death of Finn at Ath-Brea upon the Boyne'. All these men in the tenth and eleventh centuries certainly believed Finn to have been a real man...

...But, there is another proof of antiquity of the Finn stories which Mr. Nutt does not note, and in some respects it is the most important and conclusive of all. For if, as D'Arbois de Jubanville has I think proved, the list of one hundred and seventy eight historic tales contained in the *Book of Leinster*, was really drawn up at the end of the seventh or the beginning of the eighth century, we find that even then Finn or his contemporaries were the subjects of or figure in several of them...

...thus, Finn is sandwiched in as a real person along with his other contemporaries, not only in tenth and eleventh century annalists and poets, but is also made the hero of historic romances as early as the seventh or eighth century. Side by side in our seventh-eighth century list with the battle of Moy Muchruime, we find the battle of Moy Rath. The last, the battle of Moy Rath, we *know* to be historical; it can be proved; why should the first not be so also? It is true that the one took place four hundred and thirty-eight years before the other, but the treatment of both is absolutely identical...

30. This version [Sweeney Astray] of *Buile Suibne* is based on J. G. O'Keefe's bilingual edition, which was published by the Irish Texts Society in 1913... ...The basis of the 1913 edition is a manuscript written in County Sligo between 1671 and 1674. This manuscript is part of the Stowe collection in the Royal Irish Academy and O'Keefe believed that, on linguistic grounds, 'the text might have been composed at anytime between the years 1200 and 1500'. Nevertheless the thing was already taking shape in the ninth century. O'Keefe cites a reference in the *Book of Aicill*, a text dating from the tenth century at the latest, to stories and poems relating to Sweeney's madness; and other evidence from literary and historical sources leads him to conclude that the *Buile Suibne* which we now possess is a development of traditions dating back to the time of the Battle of Moira (A.D. 637), the battle where Sweeney went mad and was transformed, in the fulfilment of St. Ronan's curse, into a bird of the air.

What we have then, is a literary creation; unlike Finn McCool or Cuchulain, Sweeney is not a given figure of myth or legend but an historically situated character, although the question of whether he is based upon an historical king called Sweeney has to remain an open one. But the literary imagination which fastened upon him as an image was clearly in the grip of a tension between the newly dominant Christian ethos and the older, recalcitrant Celtic temperament.

31. Side by side with the numerous prose stories which fall under the head of 'Fenian', exists an enormous mass of poems, chiefly narrative, of a minor epic type, intermingled with others whose basis is a semi-dramatic dialogue between St. Patrick and Ossian. This poet was fabled to have lived in Tir-na-n-og or the 'land of the ever young' for three hundred years, thus surviving all the Fenians and living to hold colloquy with St. Patrick... Some of the Ossianic poems relate the exploits of the Fenians... ...many more consist largely of semi-humourous dialogues between the Saint and the old warrior; another is called Ossian's madness; another is Ossian's account of the Battle of Gowra which made an end of the Fenians, and so on... ...The Lochlannachs or Norsemen figure very largely in these poems, and it is quite evident that most of them – at least in the modern form in which we now have them – are post-Norse production... ...The spirit of banter with which St. Patrick and the Church is treated stops just short of irreverence...

...The conception of bringing the spirit of Paganism and Christianity together in the persons of the last great poet and warrior of the one, and the first great saint of the other, was truly dramatic, and the spirit and humour with which it had been carried out in the pieces which have come down to us, are a strong presumption that under happier circumstances something very great would have developed.

32. ...They [the Scots] had not been long settled in Scotland before... ...they were joined by the great spiritual potentate of their original country, Columba. The reigning monarch of Dalriada at the time of his arrival was Conall... ...The influence of the mission became conspicuous in the increased power and rank of his successor Aidan [N.B. – not St. Aidan, below]... ...Aidan was inaugurated to the throne with sacred sanctions of the most solemn character. He was anointed by the hand of the great missionary... ...the solemn ceremony was accompanied by a prophecy. The ambition and talents of Aidan seem to have given the saint some uneasy suspicions that he might aspire to the throne of his relations in Ireland. By his descent from Riadha he belonged to race of the Hy Nial or principal rulers of Ireland. To these Columba himself had a still closer relationship... ...so he uttered a prophecy:- 'Aidan, you and your posterity will be invincible in your throne until they do injustice to me and my race. Recommend, therefore, to your sons, that they also may retain their throne by observing the conditions of its settlement; for whenever they lift a hand against me or my relations in Ireland... ...the heart of man shall be taken out of them, and their enemies shall triumph over them'. A prophecy believed to have been fulfilled at the battle of Moyra...

...A certain Congal Claon, representing one of the houses struggling for authority, had killed Subney Mean, the King, or the most powerful among the Kings, of the north of Ireland. His successor, Domnal, attacked Congal and defeated him at the battle of Dun-Reherm. Congal took refuge in Dalriada, and offered his services to his uncle, Donald Brec, king of the Scots, should he pursue the project of trying for empire in Ireland. Donald is said to have collected a large mixed army of Scots, Picts, Strathclyde Britons, even Saxons, which he landed in Ireland in the year 637. Here he was met by King Domnal at Mach Rath, now known as Moyra, in the county of Down, and there was fought a decisive battle. It is described as lasting for seven days. Any accounts of it that can be depended upon are as bare as possible. They say nothing but that the battle was fought and the invading army utterly defeated. The victory of Moyra was more than the decision of a mere contest between dynasties. The presence of combatants of a foreign race and tongue made it a victory in a struggle for national independence; and its memory became more significant and important when, after a lapse of centuries, the Saxon return to enslave the Celt. Its immediate effect was limited to a district in the north, but it... ...became the Marathon of all Ireland... ...about the time of the English invasion, the various traditions of the battle had been drawn into a great epic story, the work of several distinguished bards – the banquet of Dun na N-Gedh, and the Battle of Magh Rath, an ancient historical tale... ...first published from a manuscript in the library of Trinity College, Dublin, with a translation and notes by John O'Donovan. This work, like Ossian's poems and the romances of Arthur's Round Table, at once declares itself the work of a period centuries after the story it records, by abundantly introducing the practices of chivalry and the armour and weapons of the Crusaders.

33. ...the basis of Professor Zimmer's argument... ...is that Finn was really a Norseman, and that the Fenian cycle is posterior to the Norse invasion. Professor Zimmer lays great stress on the fact of Finn being the Irish translation for 'white', and of the Irish therefore calling the Norse vikings Finians (Fian, Fianna, The Fenian militia) – ie. 'White Strangers' – as later they called the Danes black or dark strangers. According to Professor Zimmer, also, Lochlann – the Lochlin of Macpherson – which was hitherto considered to be Norway, is explicable as Lake-land: and Lochlann to be an Irish rendering of Laland, the island from whence came the Danish vikings, and first designated the Danes's country alone...

34. Oscarach, orscarra, bold, fierce, Ir. *oscar*, champion; from the heroic name Oscar, son of Oisian (Ir. *Oisin*, little deer or *os*, qv.) Possibly Oscar stands for *ud-scaro-, 'out-cutter', root *scar* or *sgar*, qv. Zimmer derives it from the Norse 'Asgein, spear of the Anses or Gods', and *Oisian* from the Saxon 'Oswine, friend of the Anses'...

35. Osuine belonged to the house of Deira where he ruled for some years in great prosperity, while Osuiu reigned in Bernicia. Later the two disagreed and went to war. Their armies assembled near

Catterick and Osuine, perceiving the enemy to be in much greater strength, dismissed his own army. One faithful companion, Tonderi, remained with him, and the two concealed themselves in the house of one whom Osuine regarded as the most trustworthy of his followers, but he betrayed the trust and Osuine was killed. Even Bede was moved to stern language by the heinousness of this crime brought about by the treachery of a trusted warrior. Bede is full of praise for the murdered Osuine and it is of interest to note the qualities for which he praises him – his tall stature and graceful appearance, his friendly courtesy and his generosity, qualities which inspired men of the highest rank to come from neighbouring provinces to seek service with him.

36. Aidan, or Ædan, first bishop of Lindisfarne, a monk of Hii (Iona), was sent by the abbot Senegi to Northumbria, at the request of King Oswald, A.D. 634-635. He restored Christianity, and in accordance with the traditions of the Irish episcopacy chose the island of Lindisfarne, close to the royal city of Bamborough, as his see... ...He survived Oswald, and died shortly after the murder of his friend Oswine of Deira...

37. Oswald, (c.605-642) King of Northumbria, was one of the sons of Æthelfrith, and was expelled from Northumbria on the accession of Edwin. He appears to have spent some of his exile in Iona, where he was instructed in the principles of Christianity...

38. Oswio, (c.612-670), King of Northumbria, son of Æthelfrith and brother of Oswald, whom he succeeded in Bernicia in 642 after the battle of Maserfield... ...He succeeded in making the majority of the Britons, Picts and Scots tributary to him. At Gilling in 651 he caused the murder of Oswine, a relative of Edwin, who had become king of Deira, and a few years later took possession of that kingdom.

39. With the 16th century we reach the later treatment of the legend [Ossianic cycle] in the *Battle of Ventry*. In this tedious story Daire, the king of the whole world, comes to invade Ireland with all his forces, but is repulsed by Finn and his heroes. The *Battle of Ventry*, like all later stories, is a regular medley of incidents taken from writers of antiquity and European medieval romance.

40. Macpherson was neither as honest as he claimed nor as inventive as his opponents implied. In *Fingal*, his most elaborate work, we can identify twelve passages, some of them fairly lengthy, in which he used genuine Gaelic ballad sources, sometimes specific versions... ...he used many names from the ballads, often distorting them violently, and he juggled historical data to suit his own ends...

41. If anyone is still found to repeat Macaulay's hackneyed taunt about our race never having produced a great poem, let him ask himself if it is likely that a country where, for a hundred years after Aughrim and the Boyne, teachers, who for long before that had been in great danger, were systematically knocked on the head or sent to jail for teaching; where children were seen learning their letters with chalk on their fathers' tombstones, other means being denied them; where the possession of a manuscript might lead to the owner's death or imprisonment, so that many valuable books were buried in the ground or hidden to rot in walls – whether such a country were a soil on which an epic or anything else could flourish. How in the face of all this, the men of the eighteenth century preserved in manuscript form so much of the Ossianic poetry as they did, and even rewrote or redacted portions of it, as Michael Comyn is said to have done to 'Ossian in the Land of the Young', is to me nothing short of amazing.

42. The day is gone when the stupid outcry against Macpherson's 'Ossian', as no more than a gigantic fraud, finds a response among the lovers of literature. We all know, now, that Macpherson's 'Ossian' is not a genuine translation of authentic *Dana Oisin mhic Fhion*, but for all its great and enduring beauty, a clumsily-constructed, self-contradictory and sometimes grotesquely impossible rendering of disconnected, fugitive and for the most part, oral lore. Of the genuineness of this legendary lore there is no longer any doubt in the minds of those native and alien students, who alone are qualified to pronounce a definitive verdict on this long disputed point...

43. What is advanced, in this short Dissertation, it must be confessed, is mere conjecture. Beyond the reach of records is settled a gloom which no ingenuity can penetrate.

44. From the beginning in the 1760's, because of Macpherson's association with the powerful Scottish Earl of Bute, and the administration of George III, *Ossian* became caught up in the complexities of Anglo-Scottish political relations. What this meant was that almost from the moment of initial publication, Anglo-Scottish interest centred on one question only: were the works of Macpherson genuine or fraudulent?... ...As a result of this preoccupation with

the authenticity question, *Ossian's* impact in England, despite the enthusiasm of writers such as Thomas Gray and Horace Walpole, was relatively muted. Such was not the case elsewhere...

45. The appearance of Ossian fitted in with the era of sentiment which had sprung up – sentiment which was domestic in *Clarissa Harlowe*, romantic in Walpole's *Castle of Otranto*, poetic in Percy's *Reliques*... ...Ossian may be no more read, yet it cannot be ignored, for it was a great force in literature... ...One remembers how Burns, whose favourite authors were deplorably sentimental, enumerates 'Ossian' as one 'of the glorious models after which I endeavour to form my conduct' – how, or why, or when, he does not explain.

46. The appearance of Macpherson's Ossianic 'translations' in 1762-3 seems to have prompted Thomas Percy, later Bishop of Dromore, to publish the contents of a seventeenth century manuscript of English ballads he had acquired, together with similar poems, as the well-known *Reliques of Ancient English Poetry* in 1765. He had been in correspondence with the Reverend Evan Evans, who as early as 1758 had been collecting Welsh poetry, urging him to produce 'an elegant translation of some curious pieces of ancient British Poetry', which appeared as *Specimens of the Poetry of the Ancient Welsh Bards* the year before Percy's own *Reliques*... ...In Ireland, Charlotte Brooke's *Reliques of Irish Poetry* (1789) acknowledges its debt to Percy in its title.

47. The published work of James Macpherson of Balavil was a revelation to Europe. When his writings appeared in the 1760's, they appealed strongly to contemporary taste in literature, the mood of which was shifting from the rational to the romantic, to a search of the past for the Noble Savage, mystical Druidry and the values of a primitive society.

48. In every period human manners are a curious spectacle; and the most natural pictures of ancient manners are exhibited in the ancient poems of nations. These present to us, what is much more valuable than the history of such transactions as a rude age can afford – the history of human imagination and passion. They make us acquainted with the notions and feelings of our fellow-creatures in the most artless ages; discovering what objects they admired and what pleasures they pursued, before those refinements of society had taken place, which enlarge indeed and diversify the transactions, but disguise the manners of mankind.

49. Macpherson's work in turn was one of the most important inspirations for the 'Romantic' movement in Britain and on the Continent, shaping literary and artistic styles well into the nineteenth century. A comment on the historical influence of James Macpherson, which deserves to be better known and is difficult to contest, came in 1919 from the pen of Peter Hume Brown, the first Professor of Scottish History in Edinburgh University:

> It struck the most resounding note in European literature of the eighteenth century, and laid its spell on the greatest man of action and the greatest man of thought, Napoleon and Goethe.

50. The plangent, elegaic tone connected specifically with widespread sense of loss among Macpherson's fellow Gaels, but more generally with fears in intellectual circles, not only in Scotland but in Rousseau's France and throughout Europe, that luxury and over-improvement were destroying essential human virtues:

> Often have I fought and often won in battles of the spear. But blind, and tearful, and forlorn, I now walk with little men. O Fingal, with thy race of battle I now behold thee not. The wild roes feed upon the green tomb of the mighty King of Morvern.

Jefferson loved this. Goethe loved this. Napoleon loved it. The major British 'Romantic' poets, from Burns and Blake onwards, were all deeply affected by Ossian. However, Macpherson did not bring adequate reinforcement to the egos of quasi-nationalist Scottish professors because spoilsports, mostly English, objected that Macpherson wasn't *really* 'translating'.

51. ...the Ossianic vogue was everywhere expressed in a wide range of artistic forms: Ossianic plays and melodramas in Scotland, France, Germany and Italy: settings of songs from *Ossian* by Schubert, Brahms, Weber, and a variety of other less famous composers; at least two operas; a great range of paintings on Ossianic subjects in France, Germany, Scotland and other countries. In the early nineteenth century the Ossianic world had become part of the permanent romantic landscape of Europe and America.

52. ...The translation of Cæsarotti initiated a new poetic school in Italy. In Germany, then going through its romantic stage, it was hailed with rapture. Klopstock wrote turgid odes after its worst style; Herder gloried in it; Burger versified it; Schiller found rare beauty and grandeur in the life of Celtic past with its background of mist; and Goethe tried his skill in translating it; and his *Werther*, to express his agonised emotions turns to the melancholy bard of the North, and in his strains pours forth his abject woes. Voltaire laughed his dry laughter like the crackling of thorns over it, and for a while France was unthrilled. At last even it gave way to the spell, especially when Napoleon, who knew it through the Italian translation, and loved the grandiose, was moved to admiration for 'Ocean', as he spelt it... French parents found baptismal names for their children in its pages, and either to please his master or his own taste, Bernadotte took a name from Ossian for his son, who became Oscar I of Sweden, and transmitted his name to his successors.

53. It was I – I made them the fashion. I have even been accused of having my head filled with Ossian's clouds.

54. The author or translator of Ossian won his great success fairly, by unfair means. To call him an impostor is true, but insufficient. When Ossian dethroned Homer in the soul of Werther, the historical and antiquarian fraud of Macpherson had very little to do with it. Werther and Charlotte mingle tears over the 'Songs of Selme'; it would be an insult to Goethe to suppose that he translated and printed these 'songs' merely as interesting and philological specimens of the ancient life of Scotland.

55. ...He [Macpherson] brought to bear his knowledge of the Classics, of Milton, and of the Authorised Version of the Bible to produce his measured style. John J. Dunn thought that his achievement had been overshadowed by the fact that greater writers (eg. Blake, Coleridge) 'developed the artistic direction that he was among the first to take' and E. H. W. Meyerstein regarded him as one of the main originators of free verse. He had a pernicious effect on later Gaelic writing but also indirectly stimulated much Gaelic collection and research.

56. Make the part of what is forged, modern, tawdry, spurious in the book as large as you please, there will still be left a residue with the very soul of the Celtic genius in it, and which has the proud distinction of having brought this soul of the Celtic genius into contact with the genius of the nations of modern Europe and enriched all our poetry by it. Windy Morvern and echoing Sora, and Selma with its silent halls! we owe them a debt of gratitude, and when we are unjust enough to forget it, may the muse forget us.

57. But lead me, O Malvina! to the sound of my woods; to the roar of my mountain streams. Let the chase be heard on Cona; let me think on the days of other years. And bring me the harp, O maid! that I may touch it, when the light of my soul shall arise. Be thou near, to learn the song; future times shall hear of me! The song of the feeble hereafter will lift the voice on Cona; and looking up to the rocks, say, 'Here Ossian dwelt!' They shall admire the Chiefs of old, the race that are no more! while we ride on our clouds, Malvina! on the wings of the roaring winds. Our voices shall be heard at times in the desert; we shall sing on the breeze of the rock.

NOTES AND SOURCES:

1. Thomas Newte, quoted in the *Proceedings of the Society of Antiquaries*, 'Report on Stone Circles in Perthshire, (1910). p. 95-7. The story is first recorded, though not so descriptively, in *Letters from a Gentleman in the North of Scotland*, (1732), by Edward Burt, who was Wade's agent and surveyor.
2. Alexander Macpherson, *Glimpses of Church and Social Life in the Highlands*, (1893), p. 31, currently being reprinted in 3 vols by the Clan Macpherson History Society, Newtonmore.
3. Henry Grey Graham (HGG), *Scottish Men of Letters in the Eighteenth Century*, (1901), pp. 226-8.
4. *Companion to Gaelic Scotland*, ed. Derick S. Thompson (DST), p. 189 Thomson is also the author of a seminal work on the subject, *The Gaelic Sources of Macpherson's 'Ossian'*, (1952).
5. HGG, ibid. 3, pp. 230-2.
6. Dr. Hugh Blair (HB), *Critical Dissertation on the Poems of Ossian*, published in *The Poems of Ossian* (1860), pp. 70, 90.
7. HGG, ibid. 3, pp. 233-5.
8. Magnus MacLean (MMac), *The Literature of the Highlands*, (1903), pp. 230.
9. Angus Calder (AC), 'Varieties of Enlightenment', in *The Enlightenment*, (Open University: 1992), p. 172.
10. HGG, ibid. 3, p. 236-7.
11. W. P. Ker (WPK), *The Cambridge History of English Literature*, vol. H, p. 230.
12. HGG, ibid. 3, p. 240
13. Hugh Cheape (HC), 'Were But the White Billow Silver: Ossian and Macpherson' in *Scottish Book Collector*, vol. 3 No. 3
14. HGG, ibid. 3, p. 246.
15. MMac, p. 232.
16. HGG, ibid. 3, p. 240.
17. Encyclopædia Britannica, 11th edn, vol 5, p. 635.
18. Ibid., p. 637.
19. Ibid.
20. H. Maclean, quoted by WS, ibid. 26, p. xxi.

21. Alexander Carmichael, compiler of *Carmina Gaedelica*, quoted by WS, ibid. 26, p. xxii.
22. J. F. Campbell (1822-85), author of *Popular Tales of the West Highlands*, quoted by WS, ibid. 26, p. xxi.
23. Douglas Hyde (DH), *The Story of Early Gaelic Literature* (1895), p. 121.
24. John Hill Burton (JHB), *History of Scotland*, (1853-70), vol. 1, p. 212.
25. Euan W. Mackie, *Lismore and Appin; an Archeological and Historical Guide* (1993), pp. 20-2. For a more detailed examination of the geography of the Scottish Ossian, see *Lismore in Alba*, Ian Carmichael (1948).
26. William Sharp (WS), Introduction to *The Poems of Ossian*, Centenary Edition (1896), p. ix. Under the name 'Fiona MacLeod', Sharp published many poems and a number of visionary novels set in the ancient Celtic world. Along with Patrick Geddes, he was a central figure in the Celtic Renascence of the late 19th century in Scotland and was a friend of W. B. Yeats.
27. DH, ibid. 23. Alfred Nutt was author of *The Waifs and Strays of the Celtic Tradition*, quoted by WS, ibid. 26, p. xii.
28. Alexander MacBain, 'Who were the Feinn', published in *Transactions of the Gaelic Society of Glasgow*, Vol II (c. 1895), quoted by WS, ibid. 26., pp. xiv-xv, as 'an excellent synthesis of the chief views on the subject, comprising as it does criticisms of Professor Zimmer, Mr. Nutt, and other eminent specialists'.
29. DH, ibid. 23.
30. Seamus Heaney, introduction to *Sweeney Astray* (1983). Heaney's translation is a fascinating contemporary comparator to Macpherson's Ossian.
31. DH, ibid 23.
32. JHB, ibid. 24, pp. 320-1, 323-4.
33. DH, ibid 23.
34. Alexander MacBain, *Etymological Dictionary of the Gaelic Language*, (1917).
35. Peter Hunter Blair, *Anglo Saxon Britain*, (1959), p. 209.
36. Ibid. 17, vol. 1, p. 435.
37. Ibid., vol. 20, p. 364.
38. Ibid., p. 365.
39. Ibid., vol 5, p. 24.
40. DST, ibid. 4., pp. 189-90.
41. DH, ibid. 23, p. 135.
42. WS, ibid. 18, pp. xiii-xxiv.
43. James Macpherson, *Dissertation on the Æra of Ossian*, (1773).
44. Andrew Hook (AH), *History of Scottish Literature*, vol. II, pp. 313-16.
45. HGG, ibid. 3, p. 241.
47. HC, ibid. 13.
48. HB, ibid. 6, p. 90.
49. HC, ibid. 13.

50. AC, in 'Scotland in the Eighteenth century', ibid. 9, p. 443.
51. AH, ibid. 44, p. 316.
52. HGG, ibid. 3, p. 242.
53. Napoleon Buonaparte, in conversation with Lady Malcolm, wife of the naval commander of St Helena, quoted by AH, ibid. 44.
54. WPK, ibid. 10, p. 231.
55. DST, ibid 4., p. 190.
56. Matthew Arnold, *Celtic Literature*, (1865), p. 153.
57. ???

John Trumbull (1756-1843)
'Lamberg and Gelchossa'
a scene from Ossian's Fingal, 1792

Toledo Museum of Art

Otto Rünge (1777-1810)
'Comhall's Death and Fingal's Birth'
from a series of illustrations to Ossian

Hamburg Kunsthalle

Ruthven Barracks, 1994

'Ossian receiving the warriors of the Revolution into Paradise' (1801)
Anne-Louis Girodet de Roucy-Troison (1767-1824)

Chateau de Malmaison

Forging North Britain in the Age of Macpherson

Murray Pittock

> If countries have had their ages with respect to improvement, North Britain may be considered as in a state of early youth guided and supported by the more mature strength of her kindred country.
> *The Edinburgh Review* 1755-56 (Preface)[1]

I

It was a divided, uneasy Scotland that James Macpherson was born into in 1738 and although it has been suggested recently that he was 'a sophisticated and latitudinarian Scottish Whig', Macpherson was in fact deeply rooted in two kinds of Jacobite society: the clan country of his background and the Scoto-Latin inheritance of King's College, Aberdeen. Born and brought up at Ruthven in Badenoch, Macpherson as a boy witnessed both General Cope's advance against Prince Charles Edward Stuart's army and Major-General Gordon's attack on Ruthven Barracks. At the Rising's end, Macpherson may have joined his cousin in 'hurling stones at the troops who were setting fire to the Chief's house'. In his early poetry, such as 'The Hunter' or 'On the Death of Marshal Keith', Macpherson uses Jacobite metaphors and topoi in subject matter charged with wish-fulfilment and regret. The latter was to predominate in an Ossian cycle which acted as a:

> dirge for the ancient civilisation which in his own day and in his own strath he saw dominated and depressed by the course, dull emissaries of the raw materialistic civilisation of the south.[2]

Despite John Pinkerton's denunciation of Ossianic patriotism as 'the last effort of Celticism to injure the history of Britain', Macpherson's 'dirge' can be read as a distancing of sentiment from history, rather than recreating its presence there. Macphersonian landscape is vacant and ruined into sublimity as surely as the heroism of his characters is extinguished in pathos. The loss continues, the victories of the past pass away: what the poet provides is a spectacular elegy which sublimates Jacobite history under the historyless zone of primary epic. The songs are over, the times are finished: heroic Celticism is iconized, and in so doing the iconographer detaches it from the narrative of human history and its continuing agendas.[3]

II

In *What is History?* E. H. Carr argues that not every fact about the past is a historical fact, but that only those occurrences selected by historians for interpretation count as such: a privileged minority whose admission to history is, in a revelatory metaphor, likened by Carr to election to a club. Implicit in this is that the club is a London one and the list of 'historical facts' about eighteenth century Scotland are largely those which have not been blackballed by this kind of British history.[4]

So the traditional British history of eighteenth century Scotland reads like this: debates preceding the Union 'had alerted the Scots to the problem of a small country with a defective constitution and an underdeveloped economy'; the Scottish Enlightenment was a phenomenon made possible in a post-Union era where 'constitutional and economic problems' having been tackled by the Union, 'cultural problems' could be dealt with. Politeness drives out factionalism and the dark night of Scottish religious fanaticism. A contemporary account of the relation of Scots to their own past suggests that they 'were only too well aware that it was the new dawn of Union and Anglicisation which had dispelled the nightmare of Scottish feudal oppression and backwardness'. The 'burying of national pretensions' was the result of the realization that 'the bankrupt Scots had only a set of discredited institutions and a debunked ancient constitution in their historical treasury'. This 'lacerating self-criticism' was the sign of a new 'maturity', part of the belief that 'refinement was a product of modernity': a process seen in the way in which 'primitivist instincts' were 'reined in' by writers like Scott.[5]

Admission to clubland is part of maturity's rite of passage and it is remarkable how often the paradigm of Scottish immaturity/British adulthood rises up like a dragon's tooth in the furrows ploughed across eighteenth century studies north of the border. From the 'early youth' confessed to by the *Edinburgh Review* above, through the adolescence of Scott's romantic nationalists who finally succumb to adulthood and commonsense or else perish in irreconcilable folly, Scotland's emergence from the 'long brawl' of its divided independence is marked with approval. Even in later cultural typology, the overt Scot – betartaned, chippy, drunk, moody and probably left-wing – is a figure to be contrasted with his canny countryman of engineering, financial, legal or medical fame – a douce adult, cautious and decked in probity, often identifiable only by a mild accent. Such a Scot has really grown up.[6]

In the argument that follows, two ends are planned – first, an examination of the dominant historical narrative to reveal the complexity it so often ignores; and second, the placing of the concept of forging in play in both its senses: construction and counterfeiting. For the foundation of the 'North British' club is not merely titular, but involves a process of selection for membership which has long outlived this faded label. Scotland's 'historical facts' in the age of Macpherson are still often those sponsored by conformity with a British paradigm. Since this paradigm has in the past stressed stability, continuity and religious/social convergence close to homogeneity, Scotland must undergo a process of radical discontinuity from its own past. Following centuries of hostility, Scotland drifts into conformity within a couple of generations. This process has important consequences for the paradigm. Besides those outlined here, these include the downplaying of anti-Union feeling and the treatment of Scottish Nationalism as a modern phenomenon. North Britain is portrayed as a new birth from a long-labour of 'nightmare', 'oppression', and political 'faction', and it grows rapidly from childhood to forge a place in the British Empire. Meanwhile the term 'Scotland' counterfeits its past with a nationality recognized only in conformity with the state of which it is now a part. All other assertions are treated with suspicion. By 1792, even the radical Alexander Aitchison's claims of liberty depended on 'the English constitution so long ago as the days of King Alfred' when 'every man had a vote in choosing his representative, and that in these days parliaments were annual'. It is a potential embarrassment for the concept of the Scottish Democratic Intellect that 'English rights acquired by incorporation provided a more convincing platform for Scottish radicalism' than did their home-grown equivalents, though some radicals such as Thomas Muir were nationalists. But essentially, across the political spectrum Scottish history was being steered into a localised iconography of gallant losers and one winner (Bruce), coupled with spasmodic bouts of patriotic antiquarianism, such as Patrick Walker's attempt to have George IV fly the Scottish quartering north of the border. As I have argued elsewhere, the only partial exception to this was the continuing power of a radical critique which had taken over certain features of the Jacobite analysis.[7]

This, apparently, is where Scotland stands in the eighteenth century. Focussing on Edinburgh, we see the strong outlines of increasing social stability, a 'refinement' produced by the 'modernity' into which the city is emerging, which gives rise to an Enlightenment seeded by the stability of the Union and the end of religious fanaticism in an age of more moderate Protestant divines. Scots everywhere are busy growing up double quick, adopting politeness, ridding themselves of 'the halitosis of a Scots tongue', as they prepare for their part in the civic dimension of a new world of Anglo-British Protestant patriotism, imperial opportunity and growth of trade. The deep interest of the Enlightenment in social progress is a distinctive Scottish statement of the increasing homogeneity of a Britain in which leading Scots begin to describe themselves as 'English'. While Edinburgh is transformed and Glasgow grows on the back of colonial trade, Scotland north of the Forth/Clyde line is left behind. But Highland and Lowland are not always carefully separated. The description of the Jacobite risings as 'Highland' is an example of the strategic gains of factual selectivity, for as we will see, in reality a large proportion of troops and support came from outwith the Highlands. This description treats the risings as not national but dynastic: 'the last battle of the Highlanders against the Strangers'; and marginalises them socially, linguistically and geographically, (not to mention religiously, as 'Catholic'). To acknowledge Jacobitism as existing in what was simultaneously a modernising Lowland urban society would have been to acknowledge its vitality in areas which belonged to the 'future' rather than the 'past'. It is much easier to regard Jacobitism as an anachronistic spasm when its supporters are visualised as shoeless Gaels armed with poles, forced out by political opportunists or irreconcilable reactionaries, than it is when we know how many canny lawyers, established east coast artisans and tradesmen *volunteered* to risk their lives among the blades which proclaimed 'Prosperity to Scotland and no Union'. Such a broadly-based Jacobitism is potentially national and nationalist. In entering space already occupied by the 'historical facts' dedicated to asserting Scotland's easy assimilation into Britain, it becomes a dangerous intruder. In contrast, the myth of the 'Highland Army' defending a vanishing way of life assures Jacobitism of the status of heritage rather than history; that is, it is part of an irrevocably supervened order which can be revisited in comfort, while the Lowland burghs are kept in the quarantine of stability, progress, Enlightenment and Britishness.[8]

Of course there are much more alert and sensitive readings of eighteenth century Scotland available than this, as well as sophisticated defences of the above position and revisionist attacks on it. But attitudes move in the wake of scholarship: Keynes' acerbic observation that those who praise common sense are in reality the slave of some long dead economist holds good for history too. Nor is this vision of 'North Britain' quite defunct. In the context of Macpherson's achievement, long despised as it has been, truly remarkable comments are still available from distinguished historians. In 1983, Hugh Trevor Roper writes that Macpherson was a forger who transplanted Irish myth into Scotland; in 1992, Linda Colley, in her acclaimed *Britons*, made the quite extraordinary suggestion that Macpherson 'invented the romantic Celtic hero Ossian'. The forger is thus seen as a fantasist, and his part in the Highland 'invention of tradition' is distanced yet further from the happy productions of the rational Enlightenment. In a broader frame, the Forty-five has recently been called 'the preservation of England against a Highland rabble', in the New Oxford History. It has also been suggested that the reforms of 1747-48 in the aftermath of the Rising enabled Scots to recognise 'that political union had allowed Scotland to leap centuries of national historical development'. Trevelyan's view that 'Scotland, where the age of barbarism was at last coming to an end' by the close of the seventeenth century, could after 1745 not tolerate 'an Afganistan...within fifty miles of the "modern Athens"' is complemented by A. J. P. Taylor's crushing admission of *his* historical club's location:

> The Scotch, though in very recent times not the Irish, know that the important political institution is Parliament, which can be called English or British according to choice. The difference is a triviality interesting only to nationalist cranks.

These examples are not particularly untypical – and I have left out comparisons of the Jacobites to savages. Such structures in historical narrative are not altogether eradicated even in the apparently more neutral framework of 'four nations' British history.

> Between 1689 and 1747 a dwindling number of Scotsmen struggled to maintain a separate, independent state. Hopelessly riven by religious antagonism, deep seated political factionism and particularist institutional interest groups, this proto-nationalist tendency was divided and bought off to maintain England's imperialist dominance.

Despite a more balanced approach to the location of historical facts, we are still the audience of a narrative which evaluates specifically Scottish history as 'hopelessly riven', a 'dwindling remnant of the 'long-brawlers' being weaned off their 'deep seated factionalism' and fanaticism by the lactation of imperial opportunity – a narrative in which the admittedly deeply divided seventeenth century is taken as a synechdocal paradigm for all the pre-British history of Scotland, rather than as an exception partly brought about by Scotland's anomalous political status after 1603.[9]

The progressive model of British history, towards stability and Union with a broadening path of liberty at home and a widening sphere abroad, smoothly discards the failures of the past: and Scotland itself is considered one of those failures. This model renders the violence and division of England's past an aberration overtaken by developments, while Scottish violence confirms the flaws of the former Scottish state. Britain was destined to succeed, Scotland to fail: the flaws in the one are redundant, in the other diagnostic.

III

Edinburgh was both the cockpit of the Union debates and the centre of 'the remarkable experiment in rebuilding' which was to become the Scottish Enlightenment. It was a big city, not only in Scottish terms. With a population approaching 40,000 at Union and 57,000 by 1755, it was bigger than any British city outside London, larger than Norwich and almost twice the size of Bristol. True, London had more than half a million inhabitants, but Scotland's urban centres were not grossly underdeveloped in British terms: Aberdeen and Dundee were larger than many English provincial cities such as Bath, Ipswich, Leeds, Nottingham or Portsmouth, while even Inverness was bigger than Leicester or Derby in mid-century.[10]

It is important to be aware of these dimensions when gauging Edinburgh's social and political climate. Without doubt, many of the changes which have been classified as 'rebuilding' were taking place in a city reorienting its cultural direction in the aftermath of Union, but enlightened culture had a long history in Scotland, both in the context of the Scottish humanist tradition and in Episcopalian Royalist circles; and many Jacobites such as the Duke of Perth, the Earl of Mar, Brigadier Mackintosh of Borlum and Cameron of Locheil, were improvers. James VII sought to make Edinburgh 'an intellectual centre of Stuart Royalism' when he came to Scotland as Duke of Albany. The 'institution of the Advocates Library and the Royal College of Physicians, as well as the Order of the Thistle' bore witness to his efforts, and may have helped to plant the Enlightenment. Unlike the subsequent Presbyterian regime, James' Episcopalian administration did not seek to meddle with the curriculum of the University.[11]

Although many of the changes in eighteenth century Scottish society were reflected in fresh intellectual preoccupations with social progress and a new civic rationale, the origins of Enlightenment Edinburgh were not miraculous endowments of the United Kingdom. Far from being 'a sort of enchantment', effective 'soon after... 1745', it was part of a process of adjusting to a new environment. As the number of Jacobite and nationalist improvers makes clear, there was no distinct march between 'forward' and 'backward' looking Scots. Many Enlightenment figures had friends or relations on the Jacobite side – David Hume for example had links with Chevalier Ramsay, the Jacobite apologist – while in the world of the French Enlightenment, Voltaire and Montesquieu had connections with Charles Edward Stuart. Edinburgh, the 'widowed metropolis' of North Britain, was not so politically stable in mid-century as might appear. The defence of the vernacular and the era of patriotic publishing in the capital has been well-documented, but events such as the Porteous riots of 1736 and the entrance and occupation of the Jacobite army in 1745 are more than aberrations of a new-found 'maturity', despite Winston Churchill's assurance that 'the cities had long accepted Hanoverian rule'.[12]

In 1745 the governor of Edinburgh Castle had so little trust of the town that he was prepared to turn the guns on its inhabitants rather than submit to Jacobite blockade. The Lord Provost stood trial because it was thought he had conspired to let the Prince's forces in, and the records of the guard even after the town was recaptured show Jacobite disaffection. The earlier Porteous Riots were only one example of the distrustful peace which could obtain between the British authorities and Edinburgh's inhabitants. On 10 June 1721, King James VIII's birthday, 'a parcell of boys... gott together, having whyte roses in their hats, near the Netherbow', and the Canongate guard opened fire, killing a man and a woman who were bystanders: 'Tho this was... contrary to all law, we are not to expect any redress'. On December 20, 1748, Charles Edward's birthday in the year that Hume's *Enquiry Concerning Human Understanding* was published, 'the Lion, the Crest of the Scots arms placed above the outer entry of the parliament House... was found dressed in a white wig and a blue bonet *(sic)*, with a large white cockade on one of the sides of the bonet... the mob (a very numerous one) cried several times "Huzza! huzza! the blue bonnet has won the day! the blue bonnet has won the day forever!"'. 'One of the eyes' of Cumberland's picture on the Crown Tavern signpost 'had been scraped out', and the mob cried 'that Cumberland had gratten out both his een to see the lion better busked than himsell'. A bonfire was lit on Salisbury Crags, and some fifty people marched down 'the Canongate to the Abbay gate' in 'blue bonnets, with white cockades'. This was behaviour in keeping with the 'riotous' entry of Charles Edward in 1745, when the '"common" people and the women' flocked to him. Disaffected meetings continued in Leith until at least the early 1750's, while in the 1770's the Jacobite Episcopalian congregations were still counted in hundreds.[13]

In the Rising of 1745 itself, by 9 September the British authorities had raised only 124 men prepared to defend the city, and although six days later they had scraped together a notional 700, it was an ineffective force which dwindled to forty-two at the prospect of combat. Subsequently, an Edinburgh Regiment was raised for the Prince's forces. Although many in its ranks were not from the city, some 150 volunteered to fight: a not unreasonable recruitment given the risks involved, the fact that urban recruits could not easily be pressed, and that a single hostile witness, easily found in a large town, could play a disproportionate part in sending many to the gallows. Edinburgh produced a total of 49 Jacobite officers, more than anywhere else. In the Press Act of the 1750s, the city's contribution was 140, a figure comparable with the Jacobite's army's tally a decade earlier. Moreover

> From Edinburgh, Haddington, Dunfermline and Stirling a large proportion of those joining were either tradesmen, craftsmen or workmen. These men came from classes on whom no economic pressure, of the kind found in the Highlands, could be exerted, and joined presumably for personal or private financial reasons. Their adherence was apparently voluntary – few complained of being forced out and none of being hired out.

Jacobite support was not insignificant. Among the most obvious non-combatant supporters were women, and it is revealing that a Whig memorandum survives, the aim of which was to prove that not all ladies were Jacobites, indicating there was a widespread suspicion that this was the case. 'An Impartial and Genuine List of the Ladys on the Whig...or...Jacobite Partie' counts 194 Whig and 134 Jacobite ladies in Edinburgh and environs, also assuring us that the 'Whigs are...not inferior in Rank, Beauty or Sollidity'.[14]

We would thus do well to view the politics of the capital as mixed and tense in the mid-eighteenth century. But there are arguments for looking at the events in society from other perspectives. It is easy for example to forget that at the time of James Macpherson's birth more than half the population of Scotland lived benorth the Tay. On the east coast and in its hinterland, support for Jacobitism and Scottish independence was rife. Of some 112 field and general officers who held significant command in the Jacobite army of 1745, only just over two in five were Highlanders, with the northeast, east coast and Perthshire supplying the bulk of the rest.

Small towns such as Arbroath and Banff supplied several companies of men, with perhaps a battalion coming from the Montrose area, while a small town like Brechin supplied some 70. The Stonehaven fishing fleet kept a British warship out of the harbour so that arms could be landed for the Jacobite forces, and 118 carts were provided to transport these supplies to Laurencekirk, while Franco-Irish troops landed in the eastern ports. In Aberdeen there was support for the government, but a strong minority favoured the Stuarts and one pro-Hanoverian commentator of time, far from citing the Highlands as the epicentre of disaffection, commented that 'the seat of the rebellion in Scotland is likely to be in Perth, Angus, Merns *(sic)*, Aberdeen and Banff shires'. Government intelligence spoke of the small number of the well-affected in the Brechin area, and later the Hanoverian high command were not fooled (as some historians may have been) by 'loyal' celebrations of the victory of Culloden:

> what is still more extraordinary, every one thought themselves obliged to put on the appearance of being pleased, altho' their neighbours well knew they were otherways affected. In the little town of Keith in Strathbogie, all was galyly & good humour, expressed by the Ringing of Bells, Bonefires, & drinking of Healths, so much were they convinced of the Total Defeat of their Friends.

Pro-Stuart sentiment in the 'conservative North' of the Lowlands had a long history. In 1640, even the feudal claims of the Earl Marischal were unable to squeeze more than two companies of men from Aberdeen to fight for the Covenant, a figure apparently more than matched by Jacobite recruitment, which had far greater obstacles to overcome in 1745. In 1644, Aberdeen men were pressed to fight in a national and supposedly nationalist force defending a Presbyterian country. In 1745 they volunteered for a Catholic prince. In the hinterland, Jacobites were 'thickest about Carnoustie, Achmedden, Pitsligo, Fraserburgh Altri in Old Deer Parish, Inverugy, Fyvie, Monwheiter'. Of the many factors involved in sustaining such levels of support, one of the most central was the role of the culture of Episcopalianism, possibly the church commanding majority support north of the Tay only half a century before the Forty-five and still a powerful force in defence of 'Learning, social order, the aristocratic graces' against a Whig state. Both Episcopalians in Scotland and their 'British Catholic' counterparts in the Nonjuring church in England regarded themselves as politically and religiously distinct from an Anglican establishment which had compromised itself by accepting a Lutheran king. The dying speeches of such theological Jacobites, hanged after Culloden, show the strength of their commitment. One speaks of the 'once glorious' 'part of the Church Catholick… Her oratories have been profan'd and burned, her holy altars desecrated, her priests outragiously plundered and driven from their flocks'; another professes to 'die a member, not of the Church of Rome, nor yet that of England, but of a pure Episcopal Church'. The Nonjurors had attempted an early ecumenical rapprochement with the Orthodox in the early eighteenth century, and in the north-east of Scotland some saw Fenelon, the Archbishop of Cambrai, as more of an authoritative religious leader than the conforming Anglican hierarchy. There were also a considerable number of Roman Catholics in the area: 200 may have been confirmed in a single day on Deeside, and the early eighteenth century saw a seminary opened in Loch Morar, then in Glenlivet.[15]

The government forces understood the religious dimension of dissent in the north, one linked in cultural terms to the Scoto-Latin ethos, culture and learning, which finally disappeared only with the death of James Melvin in 1853. Around the time of the 1715 Rising, dragoons had been used against Episcopal congregations: in the aftermath of the 'Forty-five, Episcopalian meeting-houses were burnt, their priests dispossessed, and penal legislation passed against them. By the end of 1746 *'no Scottish* (Episcopal) *Priest, whether he took the oaths* (to Hanover) *or not was to be allowed to officiate'*, and Scottish orders were deemed void: only Anglican or Church of Ireland priests might officiate. It remained true that an Episcopal priest could not officiate in the Church of England until 1840, and the Episcopalians did not join the Anglican Communion until 1867.[16]

Such penalties, together with the banning of the tartan, fed a culture of oppression for thousands of people. The stability, prosperity, commerce and commonsense aspects of mid-eighteenth century Scotland are only one dimension of the experience of the people who lived there, and one not present in every locale. Groups remained in arms after Culloden, and as late as 1770, agents reported 'stirrings' among the clans. Recruitment of French troops continued in Scotland at some level until 1789, and included men drawn from the disaffected east as well as the Highlands. At the same time as some Scots were pushing into the openings made in the cause of British imperial expansion, others were serving in the French forces which were their country's greatest rival and competitor. Although the numbers were smaller than those of the Irish myriads under French arms in the eighteenth century, among the thousands of these Scots were leaders lost to their communities, for 'the Jacobite movement was not simply a clique of fossilised ultramontane reactionaries, but... contained within its ranks some of the finest talents of the age'. In military terms, these included men such as Field Marshal James Keith (on whose death the young James Macpherson composed the elegy mentioned earlier), Macdonald Duke of Taranto and Marshal of France, Admiral Thomas Gordon who developed the Russian Navy, and lieutenant-generals Ogilvy and Drummond, both commanders in the Forty-Five. Senior Jacobite diplomats included the Earl Marischal, Ambassador Extraordinary of Prussia, and 'governor of the Prussian canton of Neuchatel when Rousseau was in temporary residence there' and Ricardo Wall, the Spanish Foreign Secretary. In the context of improvement and enlightenment were men like James Stuart the economist and Bernard Ward, whose 'economic thought deeply influenced the *philosophes*'. In government and commerce was a range of achievement from John Law, 'comptroller-general of French finances in 1720' through the Swedish and Danish East India Companies to numerous business communities in France, Brittany and Spain. Closer to home, Lord Forbes of Pitsligo was the most prominent military Jacobite among those who contributed to the political and theological dimensions of Nonjuring thought in a group which contained many talents, while after 1745 English Jacobites contributed much as 'manufacturers and industrialists'. An array of gifts had passed into exile and internal exile.[17]

IV

In the sense that James Macpherson sublimates his own Jacobitism in the lost regions of primary epic, detached from history, his work could be argued as leading to the excluding historical narrative characterised earlier. Yet such a critique of his role ignores the interesting fact that he has proved no comfortable figure to canonical British criticism. The dismissiveness towards Macpherson shown by the historians quoted is only an extreme echo of the negative literary judgement which views Macpherson as a forger of the most uncomplicated kind – an assessment not shared by Gaelic scholars. Far from being a Scottish Chatterton who succeeded,

Macpherson is more like Burns: the difference being that instead of dressing oral material as his own, he passed it off as a dressy version of itself. Macpherson's adaptions are far clumsier than Burns's, admittedly, and he has more the air of the opportunist: but his categorization as culture-villain shows that there is something destabilising about his work and its claims.

Perhaps this leads us back to the question of forging with which we began. Macpherson's non-admission to the club, called canon in its literary manifestation, may now seem reasonable on aesthetic grounds, since it seems that few now read him with pleasure. But his difficulties are of an earlier date. Maybe Pinkerton was not so far from the truth: in suppressing the Jacobite elements he sets out to celebrate, Macpherson not only gives them a shadowy energy useful to the primitivist aspect of Romanticism, the sublimity of Wordsworth's 'old, unhappy far-off things, and battles of long ago'; he also gives an ennobled status to the Gaeltacht at a time when it was still controversial: 'At the height of the Scottish Enlightenment, Scotland was presented as an anti-Enlightenment culture, to the delight of all Europe'. Macpherson's 'patriotic view "that the Irish Ossianic ballads were ultimately derived from Scotland" served only to underline the cultural nationalism' of an enterprise which, while it detached Celtic Scotland from history, confirmed in it qualities that its detractors never found. So Macpherson became a forger, but his counterfeiting was a metomyny of transcendence: the Fianna were Jacobite, and the Fianna were victorious, as Fergus's Scots had been in 'The Hunter'. As in that early poem, the knowledge of what really happened is present as a foreboding of loss.[18]

Such foreboding is the price of romance, and the price paid by all metonymic icons: whether that of Mary Queen of Scots, Montrose of Bonnie Prince Charlie himself. The lustre of depoliticized sentiment casts a glow over political defeat symbolized by images torn out of history to grace the niches of romantic veneration and its commercial pastiche. They are thrust out from the contextualising world of fact, the struggle to be Scotland rather than remember it. So between Holyrood and Edinburgh castle, Charles Edward smiles from a thousand whisky bottles and shortbread tins, trailing like a cloud the glorious myth of his selfless and romantic Highland clans in the heart of the Lowland commerce which supposedly rejected them, while the times in which he lived, the political and ideological context of those who supported his cause, are facts not always dignified by the adjective 'historical', not always present in the club where sits the comfortable old armchair of British history.

NOTES

1. Cited in Nicholas Phillipson, *Hume, Historians on Historians*, (London: Weidenfeld & Nicolson, 1989).
2. Colin Kidd, *Subverting Scotland's Past*, (Cambridge: Cambridge University Press, 1993), 223; Pratt Insh, *The Scottish Jacobite Movement*, (London, 1952), 168, 174; Fiona Stafford, *The Sublime Savage* (Edinburgh: Edinburgh University Press, 1988), 18, 20, 48, 58.
3. Kidd, 253; Claire O'Halloran, 'Irish Recreations of the Gaelic Past: The Challenge of Macpherson's Ossian', *Past and Present* 124 (1989), 69-95; Murray G. H. Pittock, *The Invention of Scotland*, (London and New York: Routledge, 1991), 73-79.
4. E. H. Carr, *What is History?*, 2nd ed., (London: Penguin, 1990 (1987)), 12, 23.
5. Phillipson, 6-7; Allan Armstrong, 'Jacobite or Covenanter, Which Tradition?', in *Jacobite or Covenanter*, (Scottish Republican Socialist Forum, n.d.), 15-36 (31); Colin Kidd, *Subverting Scotland's Past: Scottish whig historians and the creation of an Anglo-British identity, 1689-c.1830*, (Cambridge: Cambridge University Press,1993), 259, 267, 279, 280.
6. For an examination of this phenomenon in Scott, see Murray G. H. Pittock, 'Scott as Historiographer: the Case of *Waverley*', in Hewitt and Alexander (eds.), *Scott in Carnival*, (Aberdeen: Association for Scottish Literary Studies, 1993), 145-53.
7. Phillipson, 32; Kidd, *Subverting Scotland's Past*, 248; Murray G. H. Pittock, *The Invention of Scotland* 90 and passim.; cf. Rosalind Mitchison, 'Patriotism and national identity in eighteenth-century Scotland', in T. W. Moody (ed.), *Historical Studies XI: Nationality and the Pursuit of National Independence*, (Belfast: The Appletree Press, for the Irish Committee of Historical Studies, 1978), 95
8. Colin Kidd, 'The ideological significance of Scottish Jacobite Latinity', in Jeremy Black and J. Gregory (eds.), *Culture, Politics and Society in Britain 1660-1800*, (Manchester: Manchester University Press, 1991), 110-30 (112); Kidd, *Subverting Scotland's Past*, 279; National Trust for Scotland video, Culloden Battlefield (1984). For differing accounts of Lowland mercantile support in the 'Fifteen and 'Forty-five, see 'Memoirs of the Rebellion in 1745 and 1746 far as it concerned the counties of Aberdeen and Banff' in Walter Biggar Blaikie (ed.), *Origins of 'Forty-Five: And Other Papers Relating to that Rising*, (Edinburgh: T. & A. Constable, 1916), 111-64, and Jean McCann, 'The Organisation if the Jacobite Army in 1745-1746', unpublished Ph.D. thesis, (University of Edinburgh, 1963).
9. Hugh Trevor-Roper, 'The Invention of Tradition: The Highland Tradition of Scotland', in Eric Hobsbawm and Terence Ranger (eds.), *The Invention of Tradition*, (Cambridge: Cambridge University Press, 1983), 15-41 (15); Linda Colley, *Britons: Forging the Nation 1707-1837*, (New Haven: Yale University Press, 1992), 86; Paul Langford, *A Polite and Commercial People: England 1727-1783*, The New Oxford

History of England, gen. ed. J. M. Roberts, (Oxford: Clarendon Press, 1989), 197; Kidd, *Subverting Scotland's Past*, 208; G. M. Trevelyan, *England under the Stuarts*, 19th edn., (London: Methuen, 1947 (1904), 379; *History of England*, 3rd ed., (London, New York and Toronto: Longman Green and Co., 1952 (1945)), 538; A. J. P. Taylor, reply to J. G. A. Pocock, 'British History: A Plea for a New Subject', *Journal of Modern History* 47 (1975), 622-23 (622); Daniel Szechi and David Hayton, 'John Bull's Other Kingdoms: the English Government of Scotland and Ireland', in Clyve Jones (ed.), *Britain in the First Age of Party 1680 1750: Essays Presented to Geoffrey Holmes*, (London and Ronceverte: Hambledon Press, 1987), 241ff. (259).
10. Phillipson, 6; Geoffrey Holmes and Daniel Szechi, *The Age of Oligarchy:Pre-industrial Britain 1722-1783*, (London and New York: Longman, 1993), 345 ff.
11. Bruce Lenman, *The Jacobite Risings in Britain 1689-1746*, (London: Eyre Methuen, 1980), 149 and passim; David Allan, *Virtue, Learning and the Scottish Enlightenment*, (Edinburgh: Edinburgh University Press, 1993); Pittock, *Invention of Scotland*, 17-18; Hugh Ouston, 'York in Edinburgh: James VII and the patronage of learning in Scotland, 1679-1688', in John Dwyer, Roger Mason and Alexander Murdoch (eds.), *New Perspectives on the Politics and Culture of Early Modern Scotland* (Edinburgh: John Donald, n.d. [1983?]), 133-55.
12. Frank T. Galter, 'On the literary value of some Scottish Presbyterian writings in the context of the Scottish Enlightenment', in Dietrich Strauss and Horst W. Drescher (eds.), *Scottish Language and Literature, Medieval and Renaissance*, (Frankfurt, 1986), 175-92 (175), cited in Pittock, *Invention Scotland*, 17; Frank McLynn, *The Jacobites*, (London: Routledge and Kegan Paul, 1985), 139; *Charles Edward Stuart*, (London: Routledge, 1988), 344-45; R. Mudie, cited in Phillipson, 6; Sir Winston Churchill in *A History of the English-Speaking Peoples Volume III: The Age of Revolution*, 7 vols., (London: Cassell and Company Ltd., 1957), 110.
13. National Library of Scotland MS. 17525 ff. 139, 140; *Letters of George Lockhart of Carnwath*, ed Daniel Szechi, Scottish History Society 5:2, (Edinburgh: Scottish History Society, 1989), 165 (letter to James VIII of 15 June 1721); Bishop Robert Forbes, *The Lyon in Mourning*, ed. Henry Paton, Scottish Text Society 3 vols., (Edinburgh: Edinburgh University Press, 1895), II, 221-22; III, 119, 305-07; McLynn, *Charles Edward Stuart*, 148,159.
14. National Library of Scotland MSS. 290, 293, 3142 f.49; MS. 17505 f.98; McCann, 96-9
15. *Scottish Population Statistics*, ed. James Gray Kyd, Scottish History Society Third Series Volume XLIV, (Edinburgh: T & A. Constable, 1952), xviii; Alastair Livingstone of Bachuil, Christian W. H. Aikman and Betty Stuart Hart, *Muster Roll of Prince Charles Edward Stuart's Army 1745-46*, (Aberdeen: Aberdeen University Press, 1984); McCann, 96-99.; National Library of Scotland Adv. MS. 23.3.28, ff. 96, 277 (Eaglescarnie Papers); MS. 17522 ff.35ff.; *Jacobite Corre-*

spondence of the Atholl Family, During the Rebellion, 1745-1746, ed. by Messrs. Burton and Laing, (Edinburgh: Abbotsford Club, 1840), 95ff; cf. also 116; *The Miscellany of the Spalding Club Volume I* (Aberdeen 1841), 356; Cf *'The Aberdeen Doctors'*, in *Aberdeen Notes and Queries* IV (1911), 286-87; 290-9; 297-99; Edward M. Furgol, *A Regimental History of the Covenanting Armies, 1639-1651*, (Edinburgh: John Donald, 1990), 61, 165; *The Miscellany of the Spalding Club* Volume IV, (Aberdeen, 1849), 322; Bruce Lenman, *The Jacobite Risings in Britain 1689-1746* (London: Eyre Methuen, 1980), 223; cf Henry Broxap, *The Later Non-Jurors*, (Cambridge: Cambridge University Press, 1924), 39; Forbes, *Lyon in Mourning*, I, 13, 15, 23; 'State of Religion, etc., in Upper Deeside Two Centuries Ago', in *Aberdeen Notes and Queries* IV (1911), 145-46; Peter F. Anson, *Underground Catholicism in Scotland 1622-1878*, (Montrose: Standard Press, 1970), 111, 113; G. D. Henderson (ed.), *Mystics of the North East*, (Aberdeen: Third Spalding Club, 1934).

16. Lenman, 225; McCann, 138; Rev. Canon George Farquhar, *The Episcopal History of Perth*, (Perth: James Jackson, 1894), 171; The Very Revd. W. Perry D.D., *The Oxford Movement in Scotland*, (Cambridge: Cambridge University Press, 1933), 37.

17. Fitzroy Maclean, *A Concise History of Scotland*, (London: Thames & Hudson, 1988 (1970)), 184; Linda Colley, *Britons*, 128; Stephen Wood, *The Auld Alliance: Scotland and France, the Military Connection*, (Edinburgh: Mainstream, 1989), 77, 86, 90-92, 102-06; McLynn, *The Jacobites*, 130-31 135ff., 141.

18. *The Oxford Authors: William Wordsworth*, ed. Stephen Gill, (Oxford: Oxford University Press, 1990 (1984), 319; Pittock, *Invention of Scotland*,73, 78; Derick S. Thomson, 'Macpherson's *Ossian*: ballads to epics', in Bo Alanquist, Seamus Ó Cathan and Padraig Ó Healain (eds.), *The Heroic Process: Form, Function and Fantasy in Folk Epic*, (Dublin, 1987), 243-64 (261-62).

Dr Murray G. H. Pittock is Reader in English Literature at the University of Edinburgh, and has published extensively on the Jacobite period.

extracts from
TARTAN WISDOM

Frank Kuppner

9. IF A LION *could talk we would all wish to learn the name of his trainer.*

*

12. We have a colour system as we have a number system. Do the systems reside in our nature or in the nature of things? How are we to put it? *Not* in the nature of numbers or colours. (WITTGENSTEIN)
This is not right. A rainbow clearly shows a system of colours, whereas nowhere in nature (except where human beings are concerned of course) do we see a system of numbers. That is, we see colours directly; colours are an actual part of what we see – whereas numbers are not. There are no numbers in nature until it produces arithmeticians – and not even a Pythagoras ever directly saw, heard, smelled, touched or tasted a number.

True, there may be four ships in one harbour or seventeen sailors on three boats, and so on; but there is no brute, bare 4, 11, 7 or 3. That is: there is no abstract autonomous numerical component visible, only collections of objective physical things. There's a difference.

The fact that a system invented by humans may allow the development and proliferation of further vastly complex systems or sub-systems as a result, does not in the least argue that these elaborations, or the totality, carry on a separate existence wholly independent of human thought. Those who invented the moving film did not mean to invent slow-motion or reverse films – but that does not show that these were somehow not human inventions too.

*

16. Someone who doesn't know English hears me say on certain occasions: 'What marvellous light!' He guesses the sense and now uses the exclamation himself, as I use it, but without understanding the three individual words. Does he understand the exclamation? (W)
Well yes – if he really MEANS 'What marvellous light!' by it. (Which he seems to. What else can 'as I use it' mean?)

It is, however, more than a little surprising, not to say unrealistic, that someone with such an obvious flair for language should habitually use an expression the general sense of which he seems to have picked up at once, without ever bothering to enquire more closely into the structure of the exclamation – is it not?

✹

34. At the beginning of a piece of music it says crochet = 88, written there by the composer. But in order to play it right nowadays it must be played crochet = 94: which is the tempo intended by the composer? (W)
Well, crochet = 88, obviously.
Evidently someone else thinks it sounds better when played slightly faster. (For if, say, the composer's 88 = modern 94, there is no choice of tempo involved.)
(This is mere sleight of hand. What is the – evidently infallible – authority for the quicker speed?)

✹

35. *The road to heaven is paved with bad intentions.*

✹

66. I know that this world exists.
That I am placed in it like my eye in its visual field.
That something about it is problematic, which we call its meaning. (W)
(One derives the meaning of something by settling its place in the scheme of things; by setting it against other considerations.

What meaning could the All POSSIBLY have? What is it being compared to or set against? (How important is it? Compared to WHAT?)

I refer to All that exists here, in whatever form.

Split off part of it and call it 'the world', if you like. And let the rest (the other part) be called 'God'. Now the meaning of part one is somehow derived from a – baffling and unfathomable – part two.

Yet the basic question remains: what is the meaning of it ALL? Of part one and part two considered as a unity? Or, to repeat: what possible meaning CAN the totality have?

None.

What, one might ask, would be the POINT in being God?

God would have better grounds for thinking 'Oh, how pointless all this is!' than we do. We are details, internal to the universe; our meaning and significances are to be established by contrast and comparison with other things, with other parts, other details. But what would God be supposed to calibrate himself against? Nothing.

If God had a meaning, it could only be in the context of a greater God. And what meaning would this greater God etc.

Only real parts of the real universe can have meaning, in the context of the remainder which is inert, amoral and so forth. Meaning is a phenomenon of the details, and necessarily so.

To ask, with an air of triumph, 'But what is the point of it all if there is no God?' may be satisfying, but it is ill-advised. Quite apart from the fact that this would not be an ARGUMENT for God's existence anyway, it invites the precisely equivalent response, 'But what would be the point of it all, even if there were a God?' (An answer like, 'The point would be to love and serve God' does nothing here. This is still only relating one part to another, along the lines of 'The point is to make life better for my fellow men'. The question remains: what would be the point of the WHOLE THING; including the loving and serving God?)

*

90. *There may very well be innumerable unuttered truths, but there is no such thing as an unutterable one. Truth is a linguistic quality – a saying of something that is in fact so. A truth is, whatever else it is, something which may be uttered.*

Well: what ARE these 'mystic, unutterable truths'? Obviously, 'they' cannot be uttered. But if so, what are they? What do they say?

Presumably, they must be FEELINGS of some sort.

But, quite apart from the fact that all feelings must be expressible to SOME degree or other – though it be no more than a circumstantialization of its elusiveness – truth is not a property of feelings. Of course, one may genuinely, deeply, passionately, with utter certainty (and so forth) feel that such and such IS the case. In other words, 'truth' in feelings is not a guarantee of truth. And who has never felt utter certainty about something that turned out not to be true? Not many, I dare say.

Besides which, if this 'truth' cannot be uttered, what can it actually be? What but some extremely vague sensation about something or other? If it is something more than this, then what is it? Which is to say, make it more explicit. Utter it.

To have recourse to 'unutterable truths' (an extremely subtle verbal phantom) is merely to throw yourself into a soothing verbal resonance, corresponding to nothing real – beyond perhaps a ludicrous self-flattery which at the same time avoids the tedious criticism which so many of one's truths, if uttered, tend so deplorably often to attract from the base vulgar.

∗

93. There are, indeed, things that cannot be put into words. They make themselves manifest. They are what is mystical. (W)
   This is weighty froth; obscurantism; the higher mumbo-jumbo.

   If they make themselves manifest in words, then obviously they can be put into words. (They just HAVE been, after all.)

   If they make themselves otherwise manifest, then they, like any other manifestation, can be described.

   That they cannot be described entirely, cannot be caught wholly, in words, is hardly significant. After all, what can be caught wholly in words? Anything that is not merely verbal cannot be rendered in its entirety in words. (The reason for this is obvious enough: no description is itself the thing it describes. What would be the good of such facsimiles, for communication? What is required are manipulable abstractions, which may be tried this way and that.)

   But so what? You try to get into words an amount adequate for some particular, real purpose. (Of course, you can make a career out of unreality, if you prefer.)

∗

99. *Nothing changeless can be a living thing.*
   Indeed, nothing changeless can be a thing at all – unless it

were an entire, homogeneous omniverse. This is all a 'changeless' or 'unchanging' God could ever really amount to – so why use such a misleading term?

(Unless, of course, you intend to mislead.

I may as well repeat here how fatuous it is to complain that life is transient. As if it could be available on any other terms! As if you could have life (i.e. real life, in this universe – life like this) much the same as it is, only NOT TRANSIENT. *Were it not a transient universe, there would be no life at all – which, whatever else it requires, requires differentiation within the universe. Transience takes us away, true; but it was the process of transience that brought us here in the first place. Without it, we would never have got to be here at all. To lament that life is transient is to lament that life is life.)*

✷

101. *Only the physical – and that which is being expressed through the physical – actually exists.*

To be wholly divorced from the physical is to be non-existent.

(Of course, neither of these are real states of being.)

✷

123. *Perhaps only God can pretend to be alive.*

✷

127. One can own a mirror; does one own the reflection that can be seen in it? (W)

Yes; but don't try to sell them separately. That will mean sure disappointment for someone.

✷

135. Why do you demand explanations? If they are given you, you will once more be facing a terminus. They cannot get you any further than you are at present. (W)

This is not quite right, for at least two reasons.

Firstly, one might not understand what x means; but understand what y (its explanation: as in 'what is x/' – 'It is y') means. Secondly, one can be brought nearer to the level of 'it just is so' – that is, nearer the ultimate terminus.

(To know where a place is not the same as being able to get there. After all, we know where the Andromeda Galaxy is.)

Incidentally, is the ultimate available wisdom about the universe that 'it just is as it is?' Certainly this is where wisdom STOPS. What else could a final explanation be, if not an articulation of the point where explanation at last rolls to a halt? It is either this (which may not be much), or nothing at all.

By the way, this is pretty well the 'unutterable truth' that Zen Buddhists can go through years of struggle attempting to reach, before realizing that it was there all the time, too obvious to be appreciated. I should think that the ultimate available WISDOM about the universe would involve knowing the entire universe, being aware of everything that was the case – which is impossible for PART of the universe itself to do (and indeed would also be impossible for the entire universe itself.)

However, if 'it just is as it is' is not the ultimate wisdom (and perhaps it is), it does at least have surely unbeatable claims to be the single profoundest truth about the universe, and it can be framed in a leisurely ten words, nine of them monosyllables. In the end, the universe just is as it is. (One could make it a straight ten, by calling the universe the 'world'.)

If there are better claimants, one would of course be delighted to hear them. For me, the runner-up is: PANTA RHEI. All things flow. All things are in flux. This pair of truisms gets deeper than all the sacred books of the world – which, typically, are magisterial refusals to face reality.

For some reason, Zen Buddhism has to pretend that remarks like this cannot be said, or do not get it well enough. But, after all, the acolytes had to make a living somehow – or cadge one, at least. Mystique, I suppose, can be a great help towards attracting the financial support of others. Or perhaps I am missing something.

✸

140. *All this talk about truth 'lying beyond the stars' and so forth. Beyond the stars there are only more stars.*

✸

146. *Can anyone seriously believe that the universe is frightened of us?*
That the universe is envious of us?

That the universe loves viruses?
What a bizarre, self-regarding view, that the universe loves US!
One might as well believe that the universe wants to sell us a worn suit.

*

147. *The universe does not need to be given an alibi.*
It is perfectly POSSIBLE to be normally happy in it while knowing it for what it is.

*

165. The genius does not have more light than any other, decent man – but he gathers this light into a burning-point through a certain sort of lens. (W)
This tells us more about lenses than it does about genius.

*

184. *Unless one is willing to make the bizarre and barely coherent suggestion that new matter (or energy) is being added to the universe at times (from where?), one has to assume that all change and novelty comes as a result of rearrangements of already existing material.*

To suppose that, because it is all 'only rearrangement', it therefore cannot REALLY be novelty to get oneself caught up in a perhaps not very fruitful verbal debate. If by 'novelty' you mean something like matter or energy or whatever, newly created out of nothing – and how might that POSSIBLY happen? (I only ask) – then I suppose there can indeed be no novelty in the universe. But so what? You cannot therefore deduce that everything must always be the same, since no novelty exists – for the question remains unanswered, whether, WITHIN the hermetic universe, things that were not there before can appear. If they can, and one does not wish to call this novelty, then well and good. But one is going to have to call it something, and it would be highly misleading to call it SAMENESS. (Minor terminological query: what is the opposite of 'a novelty'?

For instance, you have five lettered titles which spell out ENSES. Since the plural of ENS is ENTIA, ENSES does not quite (I assume) give us a word. How may one develop a meaningful word from this still somewhat inchoate sequence? Well, one could add to it completely new material: to give TENSES and LENSES and so on. Or one could rearrange the existing material. Thus, if one swaps around the first pair of letters with the second pair, one gets SEENS. Has something new appeared or not? I suggest that it has, even though it is still not quite unproblematically a word. But now a fairly simple relocation gives us SENSE. Does it seem to you that SENSE is more like ENSES (and therefore 'less novel') than LENSES is?

Which is to say, new things can emerge from the rearrangement of the old material. How else, for example, did life arise in the universe? (How else, for that matter, does death arise?) Nothing was physically added to the universe between, say, four thousand million years ago and four years ago, but life has somehow in the interim EMERGED. There was such a thing in the later state, and no such thing in the earlier. From a continual process of interaction emerges everything, including things that are qualitatively different from what went before. Life emerged; language emerged; self-consciousness emerged; polyphony emerged; unreal numbers emerged. All from a re-ordering of the previous material, and presumably in the direction of greater organisational complexity.

As to what further potentials may yet be realized, if any – that we do not know. Since the salient feature of the emergent phenomenon is absent from the individual ingredients which produce it, emergence is unpredictable in principle. We do not, as it were, notice its absence. Only by emerging is it here. That which has not yet emerged is not actually anywhere – which is to say, it does not exist.

※

186. *With regard to what ordering can do: if the twenty stepping-stones that let people across the river are taken out and piled up neatly and completely on the bank – well, where is the difference in material terms? We still have the river and we still have the stepping-stones. But where is the crossing now?*

※

188. *Only individuals can feel that they have transcended individuality. (Which is to say, it is a delusion. They are still individuals who are feeling this. It is all only one more state of an*

individual mind – as would surely be fairly obvious to an onlooker.)

※

234. *Even the hands of a backwards-moving clock are going forwards in time. (or the numbers if it is digital, etc. When the clocks 'go back an hour', it does not mean that the same real hour actually repeats itself.)*

But time is not a sort of thing, a sort of container, inside which events run forward. (With regard to 'the four dimensions' – the mere fact that the first three are effectively interchangeable, whereas the fourth is always and only time, is enough to suggest that, at the very least, there lurks a gross anomaly within this equably labelled group.)

It is not that events might have run backwards or sideways, but that, as a matter of fact, they just happen to run forwards. No: this 'running forward of events' actually IS time. This is what time is. Regulatory measuring devices may be superimposed, of course, but without this basic change, this x becoming y, this forward motion (of, for instance, the states of the measuring device itself), there would be no time there to be measured. (And no-one wishing to measure it too, of course.)

If certain current equations in physics leave it an open question whether time is positive or negative – whether, that is to say, it runs forwards or backwards – this tells us nothing additional about time, which can only run forwards. (Which IS the running forwards.) It tells us that the equations, to at least the degree that they cannot get the only actual direction of time unequivocally right, are at best incomplete, insufficiently precise – and, at worst, wrong.

To 'travel backwards in time' is of course rank impossible. As any one event or moment succeeds another you are going forwards in time. (And however you might care to alter watches or turn back calendars, it is still only now.)

※

239. *Insofar as it is a problem at all death is a problem that solves itself.*

(Millions of bluebottles killed in irritation; and not a single one – I trust – ever knew why.)

※ ※

Recycling, Mosaic, and Collage

Edwin Morgan

It is an irony which makes the subject so interesting: that our twentieth century, which has seen the laws of copyright become more and more complex, nippy, and extensive, has also produced, from early modernism, right through postmodernism and beyond, an almost programmatic defiance of the very concept of copyright with the spread of (to be polite) intertextuality or (to be impolite) plagiarism among a wide range of authors from the irreproachably innovative to, shall we say, the careless (and that is being *very* polite in some cases). Since intertextuality can only grow more voracious in the age of E-mail, hypertext, interactive creativity, and the looming Internet, so voracious indeed that copyright will be hard put to it to survive at all, in any sense related to meaningful control or reward, it seems a good moment to float a few observations on the matter, tentative though they must be.

Whether the recycling of others' texts is or is not a sin, it certainly is or may be a crime under today's laws, and it can be a crime even if the recycled material is added to or altered, so long as the original remains recognizable. There have been some notable cases in recent decades. In the United States, a case was brought against Alex Haley for his book *Roots* (1976), a much discussed and highly praised account of Black history in America, also made into a successful TV series. It was argued that he had plagiarized an earlier novel, *The African* (1967), by Harold Courlander, which had so many passages similar to passages in *Roots* that it must seem impossible to deny a connection. Haley at first did deny this, but later was forced to admit that at least three passages in his book had their origin in *The African*. He alleged inadvertency rather than theft, but settled the case out of court, paying Courlander a large sum of money, reportedly half a million dollars, which would suggest that recycling is not something to be undertaken lightly, or by the poor. In another much-discussed case in France, in 1981, Françoise Sagan was taken to court for her novel *Le Chien couchant,* which was said to be plagiarized from a short story, *La Vieille femme,* by Jean Hougron, published in 1965. Like Haley, she too was found guilty, and the novel was ordered to be destroyed and Hougron to be paid half the royalties on what was already the six-figure sales of the book. In a foreword to her novel, Sagan had acknowledged a debt to Hougron, thanking him for his 'involuntary' assistance, but the Paris court decided this was no defence, since she had not asked his permission.

If this severe judgement was to be taken as typical, it might well make all novelists jumpy, and that is true even if money is not the prime consideration. When a claim was made against the Australian novelist Thomas Keneally for his novel *Season in Purgatory* (1976), alleging plagiarism from Bill Strutton's *The Island of Terrible Friends* (1961), and making, it has to be said, a strong case, Strutton commented: 'There is no possible doubt that his book derives from mine and I want him to admit it. I'm not in this for the money. But what Keneally has done doesn't strike me as the sort of thing one writer should do to another.' This form of indignation does not command universal support (as we shall see), but it is a very natural reaction, and many would consider D. M. Thomas lucky in getting away with *The White Hotel* (1981), a novel which made extensive verbatim use of Anatoli Kuznetsov's *Babi Yar* (1970). A brisk correspondence about the appropriations enlivened the pages of the *Times Literary Supplement,* with the plagiarism being equally strongly attacked and defended. Thomas had taken the precaution of briefly acknowledging Kuznetsov's book on his copyright page, but the Sagan case shows that that might not have saved him if he had been taken to court. Controversy might well have been avoided if he had been willing to use a mosaic rather than a recycling method, putting the Kuznetsov passages in quotation marks and giving the reader a binaural perspective. However, Thomas remained unfazed by the charges laid against him, and compounded his malfeasance, if malfeasance it was, by doing much the same thing in his later novel *Ararat* (1983). With what must seem like hubris, as if he was courting his fate, he had an Author's Note giving a list of sources, including, as 'principal source for factual detail relating to the Armenian massacres', Christopher J. Walker's *Armenia* (1980). Christopher J. Walker duly wrote a pained, though more angry than pained, letter to the *London Review of Books,* quoting extensive parallel passages and pointing out that 'principal source for factual details' was a rather mealy-mouthed way of describing substantial verbatim recycling. Whether Thomas's confident self-defence would have survived the legal probing given to Haley and Sagan, is of course another matter. What is clear from all these examples is that a dislike of plagiarism is far from dead, whatever critics and literary historians may say about the ancientness and respectability of recycling. (Romans recycled Greeks; the authors of *Genesis* recycled earlier Flood stories; ballads and folk-songs are recycled over both time and space, as are football chants and playgroup games.) If an urge to expose plagiarism exists, it must also of course be remembered that the exposer too is at risk, and had better play a full hand of hard facts. Pam Ayres sued the *Sunday Express* and a Mr Daniel McNabb in 1978 for claiming in print that she had plagiarized McNabb's Oxfordshire dialect poems. She won her case, and McNabb and Beaverbrook Newspapers had to pay her what was described as 'substantial damages'.

Legal questions, then, will always shadow plagiarism, where copyright is present. How far there are moral questions too, would be a matter of dispute. The American poet Charles Olson, himself no mean plagiarist, praised Herman Melville for his brilliant and extensive plagiarism. In *Call me Ishmael* he says of Melville: 'He was a skald, and knew how to appropriate the work of others.' Yet in practice it is not difficult to find examples where you are bound to feel some uneasiness. Hart Crane plagiarized the unpublished poems of a young New York Jewish poet called Samuel Greenberg who died about 1918 around the age of twenty, of tuberculosis. He was almost illiterate, but the poems are very striking in a bizarre sort of way and have marked potential, even if one has to say they are not achieved poems. Crane was shown these MSS by a friend, took them away, and used them in his own poetry; one of his poems, 'Emblems of Conduct', is simply a mosaic of lines and phrases from different Greenberg poems. It might be argued that Greenberg is given a kind of hidden immortality by this method, whereas otherwise he would very probably have been forgotten altogether. But there is still something ruthless and underhand about Crane's use of him which reminds us that there is a moral problem involved.

Plagiarism affects, of course, not only literature but all the arts, and particularly music, where in the nature of things, and even as recognized by convention, similarities will often be found. There is a whole range of effects from inadvertent echoes to openly announced 'Variations on a Theme by X'. Where there is deliberate recycling, does it suggest any ideas that might be useful in thinking about literary plagiarism? Shostakovich's last symphony, the 15th, uses passages, motifs, melodies, taken clearly and unmistakably from Rossini and Wagner – the *William Tell* overture in the first movement, parts of *Die Walküre* and *Tristan und Isolde* in the last movement. Shostakovich's obituary in *The Times* in 1975 referred to these as 'enigmatic quotations', and later analyses of the symphony are not very much more confident in saying what precisely these quotations are doing. The Rossini is placed in a jaunty, satirical context, as if Shostakovich felt that as a greater composer he could use Rossini, could both mock Rossini and at the same time mock whatever it is he sees through and behind Rossini. But when he comes to the Wagner, he is dealing with an equal, and the main impression is of a reinforcing of the sense of death and fate and disaster which the symphony is working out. Yet this interpretation does not satisfy. The symphony ends with an extraordinary series of percussive clicks, scarcely music at all, as if the orchestra was being conducted by a praying mantis. The end is so bleak, so desperate, that you then look back at the plagiarized passages in the light of a great artist's questioning of his mediums: neither Rossini nor Wagner nor Shostakovich can express what Shostakovich feels, living in Russia, and the world, in 1970.

And that questioning of the medium is something we find in literature too, increasingly throughout the twentieth century. Just as Berg felt he had to incorporate Bach, or Stockhausen Beethoven, or Schnittke Mozart, so also Eliot ingests Shelley, MacDiarmid, John Cowper Powys, Lowell, and Thoreau, in ways so totally unexpected that we are forced to reconsider the mechanisms and strategies of creativity. Nor are matters any simpler in the field of painting. In 1987 the authorities at the Edvard Munch museum in Oslo had to consult their lawyers when Andy Warhol proposed to sell, at a high price, lithographs of Munch's most famous painting, *The Scream*, which he had reproduced in new colours and with his own signature appended. 'Pure plagiarism', said the director. But was it? Was it not now a Warhol picture? And were the considerations as much commercial as ethical? The original painting brought lucrative reproduction fees to the museum, which would now be compromised. On the other hand, the opposition could argue that feverish interest in Warhol might well augment rather than diminish demand for reproductions of the original Munch. Perhaps Warhol was performing a public service? And think of the irony: here is the man famed for his laid-back passivity and taciturnity purloining a piece of expressionist agony – what a scream!

But do such provocative interlockings of past and present point to anything as glib as 'the death of the author', or the exhaustion of the Romantic premium on individuality and originality? It might seem so if anyone wanted to argue that Hugh MacDiarmid incorporated (without acknowledgement) in an autobiographical passage of *In Memoriam James Joyce,* a substantial passage from J.C. Powys's *Autobiography,* simply because he could find no better way of putting it. Yet even if this is true, there are counter-arguments lurking in the background. Any single borrowing by such a committed borrower as MacDiarmid ought to be placed in the broader context of his lengthy poems, where he is able to impose, on what is a cento of quotations, the unmistakable sense of his own style, his own originality. Others might claim that he is taking a pick to the idol of property, and democratising the material of art on an all-is-grist-to-the-mill basis. And if the plagiarized start to telephone their lawyers, this only shows what skinflints and dinosaurs they are, unaware of the way literature is moving back to Shelley's future of 'that great poem which all poets, like the co-operating thoughts of one great mind, have built up since the beginning of the world' (*A Defence of Poetry*)? The whole matter, in fact, like a spill of mercury, begins to escape in all directions as soon as we try to fence it in. Marianne Moore, whose work is almost a mosaic of references and quotations, went so far as to say (in 'A Note to the Notes in her *Collected Poems*) that 'in anything I have written, there have been lines in which the chief interest is borrowed' – but is this only a more extreme, or more honest, expression of something that has been widely exemplified?

It may still be surprising to consider the number and range of writers, in both prose and poetry, who have taken the risk of using non-original material, either overtly or covertly. To take a few examples from many. Sean O'Casey in *The Plough and the Stars* transcribed actual political speeches by Padraic Pearse which were published in 1922. Arnold Wesker in his *Trilogy* made use of his own father's (unpublished) autobiography. Tom Stoppard (apart from the obvious and rather special case of *Rosencrantz and Guildenstern are Dead*) recycled in *Every Good Boy Deserves Favour* a Russian dissident's account of his incarceration in a mental hospital (Viktor Fainberg, in *Index on Censorship* Vol. 4 No.2 – his words are spoken in the play by character called Alexander). W. H. Auden plagiarized from Anthony Collett's *The Changing Face of England* not only in his play *The Dog Beneath the Skin* but also in one of his best-known poems, 'O Love, the interest itself in thoughtless heaven', even in one of its best-known lines, 'Some possible dream, long coiled in the ammonite's slumber'. Samuel Beckett included in his trilogy of novels whole paragraphs copied from his own private letters to his friend Thomas McGreevy – presumably he had thriftily kept copies and decided they could be recycled! Norman Mailer in *The Executioner's Song,* a piece of 'faction' which reads like a novel and is meant to be so read, presented an almost seamless web of collage, since the book is made up of interviews, news items, reports, letters, poems, any kind of documentary material connected with the life, trial, and death of the murderer Gary Gilmore. William Burroughs, in his 'cut-up' compositions, produced collage effects exactly the opposite of Mailer's – splintered, impressionistic, repetitive, hypnotic. Hans Magnus Enzensberger in his poetic sequence *Mausoleum* (English translation by Joachim Neugroschel, 1976) presented a collage of famous Europeans (Newton, Machiavelli, Gutenberg, Darwin, Lenin, etc.), with his own poetry in roman type intercut by documented writings and sayings in italic, so that you have a clear collocation of social and scientific comment. Frank Kuppner in his long poem *In a Persian Garden* created what he called a 'collaborative' text, which is 'a radically altered version of that *Rubaiyat of Omar Khayyam* which Richard le Gallienne paraphrased "from several literal translations" before the Great War'. Although roughly estimating that 'some 60 per cent of the present volume comes from the original; some 40 per cent from me', he described the whole operation as 'a pretty independent-minded affinity' – as indeed it is. After all that, is the rebirth of Shakespeare's *The Tempest* as a science-fiction film, set on Altair-4 in the twenty-third century, *Forbidden Planet*, in the least exceptional? Or, to enter another field, is the approved and indeed highly admired technique of *honkadori*, 'allusive variation', in Japanese poetry not to be regarded as feebly traditionalistic but rather as ingeniously reinventive, brilliantly juxtapositional, hunky-dory in fact?

And the limits are – what? Towards the end of his life Robert Lowell was much criticized for using, in the poems in his book *The Dolphin* (1973), letters, postcards, telegrams, and even telephone conversations from the wife he had just divorced. In one of the poems he says:

> I have sat and listened to too many
> words of the collaborating muse,
> and plotted perhaps too freely with my life,
> not avoiding injury to others,
> not avoiding injury to myself –
>
> ('Dolphin')

– which one angry reviewer, Adrienne Rich, described as 'bullshit eloquence, a poor excuse for a cruel and shallow book'. Plagiarism such as that, moving across from art into real life and intimate relationships, is perhaps the most troubling and problematic of all. Even when actual documentation, such as Lowell's, is not used, any recycling of an identifiable living person by an artist is an extremely papery hornet's nest from which moral, legal, and financial stings may fly out at any moment. An excellent example – I almost wrote 'an instructive example', but I do not think anyone is quite sure what instruction the outcome produced – is the case which was brought by Professor Jane Anderson against Ted Hughes and others, in a Boston court in 1987, claiming defamation of character and invasion of privacy, in that the 1979 film version of Sylvia Plath's novel *The Bell Jar* contained a character, Joan Gilling, who was based on her and who it was suggested was a lesbian. The case was hotly contested on both sides, and at the centre was the issue of whether, and if so how far, Plath's novel was autobiographical. This was important because Anderson had known Plath – it was not as if someone had come in off the street crying defamation. They had dated the same man and had been patients in the same mental hospital (yes, the psychiatric patient later became a professor of psychiatry, another curious piece of recycling). The case had therefore to be taken seriously, and Hughes in an affidavit claimed that 'I can state without reservation that *The Bell Jar* is fiction ... Joan Gilling is not a real person; she is a created character in a novel.' However, this claim comes up against the fact that the book is generally 'regarded as being autobiographical' (Inga-Stina Ewbank), 'an autobiographical document' (Eileen Aird), 'this autobiographical work' (Elizabeth Hardwick). Eventually the court ruled that Dr Anderson was willing to settle for a payment of $150,000 and a public admission that the makers of the film had 'unintentionally defamed' her. This might give the impression that Hughes and the film-makers had lost, but in fact it was a compromise solution, since Professor Anderson had originally demanded $6 million and an apology. The verdict showed that plagiarism of a living person in a work of art may attract penalties, even where no intention can be proved. It was therefore a very modest, and even ambiguous victory for freedom of expression. *Romans à clef* will remain popular but high-risk ventures, whether the author tied the *clef* to the book or not.

In any case, how do you prove unintentionality? Bernard MacLaverty's novel *Cal*, whose central character is called Cal McCrystal, was published in 1983. At the time when it was coming out, MacLaverty received a telephone call from the deputy foreign editor of the *Sunday Times*, whose name was Cal McCrystal, who had just read the book and who said he was troubled by similarities between himself and the book's hero. Both had the same Christian name with Cal shortened from Cahal. Both had a brother called Brendan and an aunt called Mollie. Both their mothers died when they were eight years old. Both were born in Belfast on a street in which their families were the only Catholics. The journalist 'thought the author was being cheeky' and was preparing to take the matter further, but MacLaverty assured him that the similarities were entirely coincidental, and he accepted the assurance. As for MacLaverty: 'It was a very strange experience getting a telephone call from Cal McCrystal, a person I thought only existed as the character in my book. The hairs on the back of my neck stood up when he told me his name.' In this instance, both MacLaverty and McCrystal were decent and honest men, and nothing further came of the incident, as neither had any axe to grind. But if it had come to a court case, the novelist would have found his defence extremely tricky, depending as it did on such impalpables as where he got his characters' names from, assuming that he could even remember. A true defence, though a court would hardly be persuaded by it, could simply be that even more remarkable coincidences are happening all the time, as a backward glance through the pages of *Fortean Times*, a magazine devoted to such documentation, would clearly show.

Coincidence implies chance, and we tend to accept that there are operations of chance, with the mental proviso that if everything in the universe is interconnected (as reason suggests) it is only our present state of ignorance that prevents us from tracing links involving what we call 'countless' myriads of variables, though 'countless' is only 'so far uncounted'. In the world of chaos theory, it would be almost impossible to avoid the supposition that Cal McCrystal did somewhere, somehow, sometime impinge on 'Cal McCrystal', unlikely though it seems. Fortunately for authors, the idea of responsibility does not survive in the near-vacuum of such refinements of influence. But let us take up the case of authors to whom the conception of chance makes a direct appeal, encouraging kinds of recycling and mosaic composition different from those so far considered. How, if at all, are *they* to be held to account?

Hugh MacDiarmid, in one or two poems like 'On a Raised Beach' and 'In the Caledonian Forest', does something extremely unusual. He goes to the dictionary and picks out a batch of words which are linked only by the 'chance' that they interest him. They are uncommon words, but they are uncommon in different ways, both as regards derivation and as regards meaning, even though they tend to be drawn from one part of the alphabet. Some are dialect words, some are highly technical; and the fact that they have such incompatible backgrounds of denotation and connotation is what MacDiarmid, with a wild glint in his eye, determines to make use of: he will devise a context for them – a challenge of considerable difficulty – and insert them in a new mosaic where what is recycled is the dictionary itself. A good test of the process is the first part of 'In the Caledonian Forest', an innocently formal framework of three rhyming eight-line stanzas containing an extraordinary verbal explosion and self-purgation, where this least confessional of poets uses the distancing, the displacement, the *ostranenie* of his dictionary-Jack-Hornery to say things he could not otherwise say.

> The geo-selenic gimbal that moving makes
> A gerbe now of this tree now of that
> Or glomerates the whole earth in a galanty-show
>   Against the full moon caught
> Suddenly threw a fuscous halation round a druxy dryad
>   Lying amongst the fumet in this dwale wood
> As brooding on Scotland's indecrassifiable race
>   I wandered again in a hemicranic mood.
>
> She did not change her epirhizous posture
> But looked at me steadily with Hammochrysos eyes
> While I wondered what dulia might be her due
> And from what her curious enanthesis might arise,
> And then I knew against that frampold background
> This freaked and forlorn creature was indeed
> With her great shadowed gastrocnemius and desipient face
> The symbol of the flawed genius of our exheredated breed.
>
> As in Antichthon there among the apoproegmena
> A quatr'occhi for a long time we stood
> While like a kind of springhalt or chorea
> The moonshine flickered in the silent wood,
> Or like my own aporia externalised,
> For her too slight kenosis made it impossible for me to woo
> This outcast Muse, or urge the long-lost cause we might advance
>   even yet,
> Conjunctis viribus, or seek to serve her, save thus ek parergou.

(The earth-moon pivot which as it swivels makes a wheatsheaf of one tree after another, or twists the whole world into a shadow-show lit by the full moon, suddenly threw a dusky fog-halo round a tree-nymph, outwardly sound but inwardly decayed, lying among the deer-dung in this deadly wood, where I wandered again, with my migraine, brooding on Scotland's ineradicably thick race of folk.

She did not move from where she lay as if she was growing on a root, but she looked at me steadily with golden-brown eyes, while I wondered what sort of reverence might be due to her and what had caused her strange ingrown bloom, and then I realized that this forlorn moon-dappled creature, against that cross-hatched background, was indeed, with her great shadowed calves and empty face, the symbol of the flawed genius of our disinherited people.

As if we were on that second earth that is rumoured to be beyond the sun, in the midst of all the cut-off causes of things, we stood for a long time face to face, while the moonshine flickered in the silent wood like the muscular jerk of a horse's leg or the spasms of St Vitus dance, or indeed like the externalization of my own sense of doubt and perplexity, for her incarnation was too slight for me to woo this outcast Muse, or urge the long-lost cause we might advance yet, with combined strength, or seek to serve her in any better way than through this by-work.)

Some by-work! This wonderful poem, published in *Stony Limits* (1934), is a mosaic of words lifted from their normal contexts in medicine, law, navigation, biology, heraldry, theatre, woodcraft, photography, theology, and mythology and re-set as tesserae in a new context, a new pattern, the presentation of a writer's mid-life crisis. MacDiarmid uses the ancient topos of a poet going out into a landscape to encounter a Muse figure. In this instance, the flickering shadowy moonlit forest scene echoes the frustration and uncertainty the speaker feels both about his own art and about the fate of his country. The Muse, like similar figures in Burns and Yeats, is national as well as aesthetic. Although her eyes and the eyes of the speaker meet and hold, the two cannot speak, cannot communicate, they are a part of the 'silent wood'. The fact that they seem unable to gather their forces together, in order to cause meaningful desired changes in art and politics, is all the more movingly expressed through the difficulty of the language employed.

The introduction of chance to literary composition was of course recommended by the surrealist movement, but it is something different that is being discussed here. MacDiarmid uses a chance selection of words, mostly from the D-G section of the dictionary, to stimulate and initiate what eventually becomes a traditionally structured poem. Others have used chance in ways that refuse the swerve back towards recognizable structure, but without the deliberate courting of bizarre juxtapositions favoured by the surrealists. William Burroughs is an interesting case in point.

He tells us in one of his autobiographical essays ('Les Voleurs', in *The Adding Machine: Collected Essays,* 1985) how when he was at school a boy was caught copying an essay from a magazine and the young Burroughs was horrified by this first example of plagiarism, having been 'conditioned to the idea of words as *property*'; but later, when he began writing himself, he became, as he says, 'more adjustable' to the possibilities of literary recycling, and he describes how in *The Naked Lunch* (1959) the interview between Carl Peterson and Doctor Benvay was 'modelled on the interview between Razumov and Councillor Mikulin in Conrad's *Under Western Eyes*' – not that there was any resemblance between Benvay and Mikulin, but 'Mikulin's trick of unfinished sentences, his elliptical approach, and the conclusion of the interview are quite definitely and consciously used.' Later still, he moved further in this direction, taking the view that in our democratic age published works ought to be regarded as common property, and not the property of 'the sterile and assertive ego that imprisons as it creates'. That quotation is from a sort of plagiarist's manifesto he drew with his friend Brion Gysin and included in the essay already referred to. 'Out of the closet,' it begins, 'and into the museums, libraries, architectural monuments, concert halls, bookstores, recording studios and film studios of the world …' It ends with a lawbreaker's flourish: '*Vive* le vol – pure, shameless, total. We are not responsible. Steal everything in sight.' This, it might be thought, is very like what MacDiarmid had already done in his long philosophical poems, but in fact Burroughs's aims were different: instead of embedding, verbatim or near-verbatim, substantial passages from other writers in his own new contexts, he wanted above all else to reflect the quick-moving multiplicity of the modern world, its disjunctive self-shaping kaleidoscopic quality, and so his recyclings are usually of fragments, as in *The Ticket that Exploded* (1962), where the paranoiac wars are hypnotically studded with phrases from Shakespeare's *The Tempest* and Eliot's 'The Waste Land', 'Preludes', 'Prufrock', and 'Gerontion', to remarkable effect. Towards the end of that book, as the heroic Rewrite Department prepares to close down its broadcasts, Prospero's farewell begins to dominate:

> 'Indications enough written in symbols as the machine shut of July 26, 1962, Present Time – Just Time – Just Time–'
> 'The Board is relying on fading voices – Shut the whole machine off – Rub out the board – Is near right now to hear it – Mr Bradly Mr Martin five times guided poisonous cloud of parasites – These our actors bid you peaceful opaqueness in this monument to tiredness' – 'Thing Police all Board Room Reports now are ended – I foretold you were all spirits watching TV program – Terminal electric voices end – These our actors cut in – A few seconds later you are melted into air – Rub out promised by our ever living poet – Mr Bradly Mr Martin, five times our summons – No shelter in setting forth' –

'These our actors cut in' – or cut out, or cut up. Burroughs's 'cut-up' technique, which became almost his trademark, was used with varying degrees of deliberation, from a high cunning of montage to the idea of giving chance a chance. His experiments with reading *across* newspaper columns as well as down, or intercutting half a column from one context with half a column from another (often separated widely in time) produced results which could be startlingly far from nonsense, or at least results on which the reading mind (always searching for meaning) would impose a far-brought wide-eyed significance. And others have burrowed further than William S. into aleatorics and collage.

Jackson Mac Low is an American poet who is also a painter, composer, and playwright, and a man who has been active in politics, in civil rights and peace movements. His main work in poetry has been to experiment with chance, sometimes using dice, sometimes the I Ching, sometimes the Rand Corporation's book of mathematical tables, *A Million Random Digits*, sometimes methods devised by himself. Together with John Cage in music, he pioneered a series of aleatory effects and possibilities, and in his writings about his own work he has tended to link this with the particular brand of political anarchism he believed in. In poetry his use of chance is the equivalent of anarchy, but it is anarchy with a purpose, since his poems are very much reader-directed or audience-directed. The poem may be based on chance combinations of words, but there is some overall rule or principle of construction, and usually some overall subject or theme, which gives interest to the reader or listener, and it is the subtle combining of chance and constructional effects that Mac Low has brought to a considerable degree of sophistication – sophisticated that is to someone sitting down to analyze the poem, yet the poem may be accessible and attractive in a more immediate way to someone reading it aloud or hearing it. And indeed there is a Mac Low 'voice', just as there is a MacDiarmid voice through *his* collage, or as the John Ashbery collage poem 'To a Waterfowl', made up entirely of quotations from other poets, comes out uncannily like an original Ashbery poem. Here is what Mac Low says about his aims in a biographical statement he wrote for the anthology *A Controversy of Poets* (ed. Leary and Kelly, 1965):

> An 'anarchist' does not believe, as some wrongly have put it, in social chaos. He believes in a state of society wherein there is no frozen power structure, where all persons may make significant initiatory choices in regard to matters affecting their own lives... How better to embody such ideas in microcosm than to create works wherein both other human beings and their environments & the world 'in general' (as represented by such

objectively hazardous means as random digits) are all able to act within the general framework & set of 'rules' given by the poet 'the maker of plots or fables' as Aristotle insists – the poet is preeminently the maker of the plot, the framework – not necessarily of everything that takes place within that framework! The poet creates a *situation* wherein he invites other persons & the world in general to be co-creators with him! He does not wish to be a dictator but a loyal co-initiator of action within the free society of equals which he hopes the work will help to bring about.

In his sequence called *The Presidents of the United States of America* there is a particularly interesting mixture of chance and choice. In each of the poems he has given himself some freedom of artistic creation, but within limits which are quite severe and which depend on chance. The poems emerge as to a considerable degree meaningful, but surprising and often ironic. He describes his method as follows:

> *The Presidents of the United States of America* was composed in January and May 1963. Each section is headed by the first inaugural year of a president (from Washington thru Fillmore), and its structure of images is that of the Phoenician meanings of the successive letters of the president's name. The meanings are those given in *The Roman Inscriptional Letter,* a book designed, written, and printed by Sandra Lawrence in the Graphic Arts Workshop at Reed College, Portland, Oregon, in May 1955. They are: A (aleph) 'ox', (beth) 'house', C(G) (gimel) 'camel', D (daleth) 'door', E (he) 'window' or 'look!', F(V) (vau) 'hook', etc.... These letter-meaning words were used as 'nuclei' which were freely connected by other material. (*Open Poetry*, ed. Gross and Quasha, 1973)

A look at two of the poems, the ones on George Washington and Martin Van Buren, will show the strange meaningfulness that can emerge from the arbitrary ground-rules of this creative method. For example, in some well-known portraits Washington *does* have a camel-like look, and Van Buren's later admirer, Ezra Pound, has mysteriously begun to materialize in the Van Buren poem. (I have added the relevant letters for clarity's sake.)

1789

George Washington never owned a camel	G
but he looked thru the eyes in his head	E O R
with a camel's calm and wary look.	G E
Hooks that wd irritate an ox	W A
held his teeth together	S
and he cd build a fence with his own hands	H I

tho he preferred to go fishing   N
as anyone else wd
while others did the work *for* him
for tho he had no camels he had slaves enough   G
and probably made them toe the mark by keeping an eye   T O
                                                                      on them   N
for *he* wd never have stood for anything fishy.

1837
If Martin Van Buren ever swam in water   M
(if Martin Van Buren ever swam)
what kind of swimmer was he if he held onto an ox's head   A R
    (did he?)
to keep his own above the surface?
        (he knew about banks
            but
            what did he know about swimming?)
                      but
            what is Martin Van Buren now
                    but
            a series of marks I make   T
        with
                  my
      hand?   I
              (maybe
              Martin
        Van
            Buren cd swim like a fish!)   N
              do
                I
            make
                      these
            marks
                  with
        'my'
                    hand
                    can
                'I'
        catch
          this fish
                (i.
    e.,
            'I')?
A hook big enough to hang an ox from's   V A
a hook too big to catch a fish with.   N
Martin Van Buren lived in a fine big house in New York State   B
    before he was president
        but how did he get his hooks into   U

                          Ezra Pound's head: R
      look!   E
   I want to know how a poet became a
   rich old dead old politician's fish.   N

In his volume *Stanzas for Iris Lezak* (1971) Mac Low made another kind of approach, what he called the 'acrostic-stanzaic chance poem'. Here, the 'chance' component comes from the fact that the words are drawn from some book or newspaper, but not consecutively. The structuring is allied to the fact that the words of the title of the poem are echoed acrostically in the first letter of the words in each line, and also stanzaically in that if the title has six words the stanza has six lines, and this pattern will be repeated throughout the poem. So the overall effect of the poem on the page is like that of a fairly regular stanzaic poem, and the semantic side of it will usually be hovering on the verge of meaning, but only hovering, and tempting the reader or performer to think of it in a spatial rather than a linear way, that is, he imagines (wrongly) that if only he could rearrange the words they would all fall into place and present a clear rational meaning. Impressionistic, evocative, or humorous satirical effects are the most likely. In its outgoing suggestiveness the result is very far from Dryden's contemptuous 'Some peaceful Province in Acrostick Land'. Here are the last two stanzas from 'Mark Twain Life on the Mississippi Illustrated Harpers', to give a flavour:

> Miles. Also river kept
> The world – also is navigable
> Little is from engineers,
> One navigable
> The hundred engineers,
> Miles. Is since since is since since is proper, proper, is
> Is little little uniform since the river also the engineers, Delaware
> Hundred also river proper, engineers, river since
>
> Miles and river keeping
> The world, and in narrower;
> Lower in from empties
> Over narrower;
> The hundreds empties
> Miles in same same in same same in point point in
> In lower lower used same the river and the empties degrees
> Hundreds and river point empties river same

Comedy is clear in 'There are many ways to use Strayer's Vegetable Soybeans'. I give the poem complete:

> To hours, enough. Remove enough
> And. Remove enough

Minutes. And not Iowa
Water and Iowa simmer.
To or
Until simmer. Enough
Simmer. To. Remove and Iowa enough. Remove simmer.
Vegetable. Enough good enough to and buttered loaf, enough
Simmer. Or Iowa buttered enough and not simmer.

Tomatoes, hot egg. Roll egg.
Added. Roll egg.
Minutes. Added, nutty in.
Wash added, in soak
Tomatoes, overnight,
Until soak egg,
Soak tomatoes. Roll added, in egg. Roll soak
Vitamins – egg, giving egg, tomatoes, added, beans, largest egg,
Soak overnight, in beans, egg, added, nutty soak

In a note at the end of *Stanzas for Iris Lezak* Mac Low has a comment on these poems in relation to himself. He has been describing his methods of composition, which are obviously impersonal in that they allow so much sway to the operations of chance, and then he asks the question, as if it had just struck him, how far there could be said to be some personal element present:

> Probably the most 'personal' aspect of the *Stanzas* ... is the variety of source texts, which included practically everything I happened to be reading from May thru October of 1960. The titles of many of the sources appear as titles of poems – book titles, chapter titles, titles of articles, etc. Among them were books on Zen & Tibetan Buddhism, politics, poetry, & botany; *The New York Times,* especially the *Sunday Times Magazine*; the current issues of the *Scientific American* & the *Catholic Worker*; bulletins of other pacifist groups such as the Committee for Nonviolent Action & the War Resister's League; Spencer Holst's mimeographed edition of his *Twenty-Five Stories*; *Drugs and the Mind,* by De Ropp; Dorothy Day's autobiography, *The Long Loneliness*; an Olympia Press translation of de Sade's dialogue *Les Philosophes dans le boudoir* [sic]; the Wilhelm-Baynes translation of the *I Ching* ('Book of Changes'); 'La Jeune Parque', by Paul Valéry; a copy of *The National Enquirer;* & various leaflets & pamphlets, such as ones on using soy beans & on the Catholic Church of the North-American Rite ... One long poem incorporates, in one place or another, almost all of Robert Louis Stevenson's *A Child's Garden of Verses.*

This is very like what you find in MacDiarmid or Eliot or Pound or Lowell or Moore – they all make use of what they happen to be reading – and the result is both in a sense personal and yet highly impersonal. What Jackson Mac Low does is to bring in a greater element of chance, greater even than in Burroughs, and he does this in order to make the reader more active: the reader is to be tantalized into 'finding' more of the poem, or perhaps (as would please some recent criticism) making his or her own poem out of the material supplied by the poet. In all this, there is something old and something new. Ballads and folk poetry are collage texts; there is no finished or ideal text that can escape from the continual state of flux and growth and transformation, and more than one author is involved. In some of the ballads and songs collected by Burns and Scott, it is now impossible to disentangle the elements of the collage. But the idea of found poetry, or of a treated or recycled text, is particularly and consciously a twentieth century thing. Yeats opened his *Oxford Book of Modern Verse* in 1936 with a found poem, a description of Leonardo's Mona Lisa taken from a prose essay by Walter Pater, with the lines rearranged as verse and with one word added for the sake of rhythm and symmetry. Found and recycled texts certainly have links with developments in the other arts: the collage pictures of Kurt Schwitters, Mark Boyle's moulds of the earth's surface, Joan Eardley's landscape paintings which incorporate grass and seeds blown onto her canvas while she was painting, Ian Hamilton Finlay's transposition of Poussin and Claude and Dürer into the three-dimensional world of natural and sculptural objects in a garden, musique concrète using random noise which has been recorded and treated, cinéma-vérité, Tom Phillips's carving of new texts out of Victorian books, and many other examples one could list. Sometimes recycling seems to foreshadow virtual reality. If, as technology advances, actors can be recycled to digits, and the digits recycled to credible images of actors on a screen, 'all that is solid melts into air'.

Is status-uncertainty worrying, or pleasurable, or a bit of both? Who really are those scores of figures waving and signalling to us from the pages of the Index of Plagiarisms in Alasdair Gray's *Lanark*, an index which is not an index but an integral part of the book, printed Burroughs-style in columns contiguous with the story, and commented on occasionally in footnotes which add yet another dimension? Even non-plagiarisms are recorded: 'EMERSON, RALPH WALDO Ralph Waldo Emerson has not been plagiarized.' Only a naive reader would believe this without checking, such is the layering of claim and counter-claim the novel generates about its own creation. Who is the Marx of the Index, with his 'pernicious theory of history'? This may or may not be the real Marx; it may or may not be the reader's Marx; and indeed it may or may not be Gray's Marx, since authorial responsibility recedes continually behind a camouflage of different speakers.

If *Lanark* became an interactive computer game, there is every sign that players would be more likely to relish the ambiguities than seek straight courses. And as the future extends its intertextualities, copyright-holders and other complainants may well find that anyone or anything they want to sue for misappropriation will be able to echo Bob Dylan – It Aint Me Babe.

Edwin Morgan is a poet, critic and translator. Recent books include *Collected Poems* (Carcanet, 1990), *Hold Hands Among the Atoms* (Mariscat, 1991), *Cyrano de Bergerac* (verse translation of Rostand's play) (Carcanet, 1992), and *Sweeping Out the Dark* (Carcanet, 1994).

Concplags and Totplag: *Lanark* Exposed

Macdonald Daly

Hos ego versiculos feci, tulit alter honores – Virgil
Ficta voluptatis causa sint proxima versi – Horace

On 2 March 1757, Damiens the plagiarist was condemned "to make the *amende honorable* before the main door of the Church of Paris", where he was to be "taken and conveyed in a cart, wearing nothing but a shirt, holding a torch of burning wax weighing two pounds"; then,

> in the said cart, to the Place de Grève, where, on a scaffold that will be erected there, the flesh will be torn from his breasts, arms, thighs and calves with red-hot pincers, his right hand, holding the pen with which he committed the said plagiarism, burnt with sulphur, and, on those places where the flesh will be torn away, poured molten lead, boiling oil, burning resin, wax and sulphur melted together and then his body drawn and quartered by four horses and his limbs and body consumed by fire, reduced to ashes and his ashes thrown to the winds.[1]

For its abolition of this degree of punishment for this species of crime, Alasdair Gray, "author" of *Lanark*, stands as a direct beneficiary of the French Revolution.

I

The "Epilogue" to *Lanark*, a black hole of a chapter in which the narrative laws of conventional realism are gaily annihilated (the "Epilogue" itself, paradoxically, appearing, so far as the sequential numbering of pages can be taken as a measure, several chapters

1. *Pièces Originales et Procédures du Procès Fait à Robert-François Damiens*, III (Paris, 1757), pp. 372-4.

"before" the "end" of the novel), announces, at the head of an "Index of Plagiarisms" which materialises, seemingly *sui generis*, in a columnar marginality which squeezes the main body of the text into only two thirds of each page for its duration, that a great deal of the novel is, with varying degrees of concealment, thieved:

> There are three kinds of literary theft in this book:
> BLOCK PLAGIARISM, where someone else's work is printed as a distinct typographical unit, IMBEDDED PLAGIARISM, where stolen words are concealed within the body of the narrative, and DIFFUSE PLAGIARISM, where scenery, characters, actions or novel ideas have been stolen without the original words describing them. To save space these will be referred to hereafter as Blockplag, Implag, and Difplag. (*Lanark* 485)[2]

According to the novel's "Table of Contents" The "Epilogue" is "annotated by Sidney Workman", his commentary comprising, as well as the "Index of Plagiarisms", thirteen pedantic and distracting footnotes which signal, as well as their own gratuitousness, their equal derivation, along with the rest of the novel, from the previous textual practices of more distinguished forebears. Footnote 6 informs us that "from T. S. Eliot, Nabokov and Flann O'Brien" is stolen the idea of "a parade of irrelevant erudition through grotesquely inflated footnotes" (*Lanark* 490).

The bewildering effect of the entire "Epilogue" is achieved but also contained by indications that "Sidney Workman" is to be read as an *alter ego* of *Lanark*'s author, a persona adopted by Gray which enables him to debunk and undermine himself as part of a typically postmodern enterprise of textual deconstruction and iconoclasm. Sidney Workman thus bears a similar relationship to Gray as does Lanark the character to his author (a.k.a. the king and the conjuror) in their verbal confabulation in the main body of the text of the "Epilogue".[3] Thus, in footnotes 6, 7, 8 and 11, Workman is supremely contemptuous of the grandiloquence and Gongorism

---

2. All quotations from *Lanark: A Life in Four Books* (Edinburgh, Canongate, 1981) are followed throughout by the novel's short title and appropriate page number in parentheses.
3. This relationship itself is an inversion of the grumbling dependence of Dan Milligan on his author, Spike Milligan, in Milligan's novel *Puckoon* (1963). The fact that this literary larceny is not recorded in the "Index of Plagiarisms" betrays what we shall come to see as Gray's major diversionary tactic in *Lanark*, the hitherto undetected ploy of secreting major crimes by confessing to a multitude of minor ones. The critic must, therefore, not take the "Index" at its word, and should

of Gray's *magnum opus* (*Lanark* 489-90, 492, 493, 496).[4] But in footnote 13 Workman divulges details about the novel's production in the form of courteous acknowledgments to secretaries and friends which make it clear that he is to be seen merely as Gray in disguise (*Lanark* 499).

The reader's sense of the manageability of this profoundly paradoxical text rests, then, on a bedrock sense that a real author (Gray) is amusing us by ridiculing himself in a super-sophisticated and

---

bear in mind always that the triad of plagiarisms acknowledged in the "Index" is not comprehensive. There is also a great deal of CONCEALED PLAGIARISM, or Concplag. The degree of systematic Concplagging in *Lanark* will emerge in the course of analysis.

For the moment, however, quotation of one passage should be enough to demonstrate the lineage of *Lanark* from *Puckoon*. The following exchange is to be found on p. 9 of the Penguin edition of the latter (Harmondsworth, 1965):

> [Milligan] rolled his trousers kneewards revealing the like of two thin white hairy affairs of the leg variety. He eyed them with obvious dissatisfaction. After examining them he spoke out aloud. 'Holy God! Wot are dese den? Eh?' He look around for an answer. 'Wot are dey?' he repeated angrily.
> 'Legs.'
> 'Legs? LEGS? Whose legs?'
> 'Yours?'
> 'Mine'? And who are you?'
> 'The Author.'
> 'Author? Author? Did you write these legs?'
> 'Yes.'
> 'Well I don't like dem. I don't like 'em at all at all. I could ha' writted better legs meself. Did you write your legs?'
> 'No.'
> 'Ahhh. *Sooo*! You got someone else write your legs, someone who's a good leg writer and den you write dis pair of crappy old legs fer me, well mister, it's not good enough.'
> 'I'll try and develop them with the plot.'

Compare Lanark's discovery of his author (*Lanark* 481). Lanark's ability to bemuse his author by demonstrating his knowledge of matters unknown to the latter contrasts with Milligan, who always has to bow to Milligan's superior understanding.

4. Workman is thus presented as performing literally the function which Macherey ascribes to all critics in the thrall of the "normative fallacy": "Because it is powerless to examine the work on its own terms, unable to exert an influence on it, criticism resorts to a corroding resentment. In this sense, all criticism can be summed up as a value judgment in the margin of the book: 'could do better'." Pierre Macherey, *A Theory of Literary Production*, tr. by Geoffrey Wall (London, Routledge and Kegan Paul, 1978), p. 16.

contradictory manner by means of a recognisably fictional *alter ego*, Workman. If it could be demonstrated that there actually were a real person called Sidney Workman whose work did appear within the pages of *Lanark*, we would be unable to sustain our present understanding of the "Epilogue" and its function in the novel as a whole. Any misunderstanding as to Workman's fictive *doppelgänger* status would bring down the entire pack of textual cards. (One interprets the remark "The emperor has no clothes" differently, if it is spoken by the Emperor himself, than if it is uttered by a boy in the watching crowd.)

What, then, are we to do with *Lanark* when it can be demonstrated that Sidney Workman was, indeed, an historically real person? What if, moreover, it can be shown that the same Sidney Workman did not, in fact, write the "Index of Plagiarisms" and accompanying footnotes, but that these were, indeed, written by Alasdair Gray *as annotations to a manuscript called* Lanark, *written by Sidney Workman, which Gray ruthlessly appropriated and, in the most monumental act of literary forgery since the Ossian affair of the eighteenth century, passed off on an unsuspecting public as his own, giving Sidney Workman an ironically subsidiary role as mere glossographer?*[5] What if, in other words, the entire body of *Lanark*, with the exception of the "Epilogue", the "Prologue", some minor episodes and revisions and a few pretentious drawings, is not simply a composite of confessed Blockplags, Implags and Difplags, and unacknowledged Concplags, but the embodiment of that much more profound scandal, TOTAL PLAGIARISM, *Totplag*? The implications for our reading would, surely, be momentous and disturbing were it to be established beyond doubt that *Lanark* is indeed, in all essentials, a work of a Workman.

But this is not a matter for mere speculation. In the pages that follow I intend to offer evidence which renders this fact incontrovertible.

II

Sidney Workman was my maternal grandfather.

His own father, Antoine Ouvrier, was born into an Alsatian family of potash miners resident just north of Mulhouse since at

5. It is perhaps a prolonged troubled conscience which has made Gray assign precisely this role to himself in a recent work, *Poor Things: Episodes from the Early Life of Archibald McCandless, MD., Scottish Public Health Officer* (London, Bloomsbury. 1992), of which he is in fact the genuine author.

Antoine Ouvrier (1865-1939) in the 1930s

least the fifteenth century. In 1871, when Antoine was just six years old, Germany annexed Alsace and Lorraine. Many Alsatians fled to Belfort, the only part of the region preserved from Prussian imperial rule, and others who could do so took flight across the Vosges to find sanctuary in France. Later in life Antoine would recall how his uncle, a cobbler named Cicatrix, having deserted the French imperial army at Metz in September 1870, paid a fleeting visit home that month before enlisting in one of the workers' battalions that stormed the *Hotel de Ville* in Paris on hallowe'en of the same year. Cicatrix also reportedly took part in the demolition of Napoleon's victory column on the *Place Vendome* the following May, and died in full glory on a barricade a week before the collapse of the Commune. The day after the fall of Paris to Bismarck on 28 January 1871, by contrast, Antoine and his family woke up in Motherwell.

In the unpublished first volume of his unfinished autobiography, *From Mulhouse to Motherwell*,[6] Antoine explains that his mother's cousin had eloped with and later married a Scottish mining engineer, Sidney Buff, whom she had met in Strasbourg while on holiday in the summer of 1866. It was by means of this connection that the Ouvriers found refuge and a livelihood in Lanarkshire. For a few years Antoine's father worked in local mines, but then moved into textiles in Lesmahagow and, around 1890, advanced to the position of under-manager in a mill in Lanark. It was here that Antoine, now at the rather advanced bachelor age of twenty-five and with no settled ambition in life other than to be a poet (a vocation which caused his father endless expense and anxiety), met and fell in love with the daughter of a local widow, Oliphant Gouge. Antoine and Oliphant were married in 1893. Their first and only son was born on 28 June of the following year, and they named him Sidney, in honour of the man who had given shelter to the Ouvriers in the dark and early refugee days of Antoine's youth. Acknowledging at last his family commitments, Antoine accepted a job in the mill procured for him by his father. Although he had no talent for manufacturing and was unable to advance himself in it in any significant way, he was, by all accounts, perfectly happy in his domestic life, having few private interests beyond the well-being of his wife, the rearing of his son, and a passion for reading.

It is hardly surprising that Sidney Ouvrier should have come, in later life, to write a novel in which the same character appears with two different names. From his earliest lesson in French at school, when the Francophile dominie tortured him by translating his

6. MS in my possession.

surname for the rest of the boys, Sidney endured the schizophrenic experience of being registered as one person on official documents and constantly addressed by the much more disrespectful English equivalent in everyday blether.[7] He suffered a perpetual sense of social exposure before those who insisted on hailing him by the English version of his surname alone, and records in one early diary the advent of a terrible, cold hatred for his mother, when she, for the first time, used this appellation: "i wish i woz neer deep water i wid waid in and she wid watch me drown and she wid greet and id bee glad!"[8] Soon his father took to using the familiar term as well, but Sidney continued to blame his mother exclusively for the extinction of his French and lofty-sounding identity, and harboured an intensifying bitterness and apathy towards Oliphant Ouvrier, which was not mellowed even by her painful illness early in 1911, when he wrote, "This afternoon Mum was operated on for something to do with her liver. It seems that for the past year or two old Doctor Lake has been treating her for the wrong illness. I'm ashamed to notice that yesterday I forgot to record that she'd been taken into hospital. I must be a very cold selfish kind of person. If Mum died I honestly don't think I'd feel much about it."[9]

This is not the place to embark on a detailed biography of Ouvrier. That requirement may become a real one when his actual literary achievement is acknowledged, and it is the case for such

---

7. As with many passages in the novel, the detail of the evacuee Thaw telling his schoolmates "that 'wee' was French for 'yes'" (*Lanark* 132) takes on an added significance when the national descent of the real author is known: the notion of a psychological reconciliation between his French and Scottish identities is here inscribed. There is, consequently, a poignancy in Thaw's spirited defence of the learning of the French language and his subsequent forced abandonment of it under maternal and peer pressure in favour of "dead" Latin (*Lanark* 148-50), which the reader who believes Gray to be the author cannot begin to perceive.
8. Sidney Ouvrier, "My Daily Diary", primary school jotter, 28 August 1902 (in my possession). It is no coincidence that exactly the same date is found on the stone discovered by Duncan Thaw shortly before he attempts to, or does, drown himself (*Lanark* 353), or that the young Thaw envisages killing himself shortly after an altercation with his mother (*Lanark* 123).
9. Sidney Ouvrier, *Journal 1911*, 13 January 1911 (written in a Lanarkshire school science notebook, in my possession). The passage appears verbatim, with the name of the doctor being the one alteration, in Duncan Thaw's diary (*Lanark* 191), written similarly during his last year of schooling.

recognition which this essay aims to present. Suffice to say that, having performed with distinction in his final examinations, Ouvrier was able to proceed to the University of Glasgow, to read French and English Literature, largely thanks to the financial bounty which descended on the family following the untimely death of Oliphant Ouvrier in April 1911. Antoine Ouvrier had been most diligent in his life assurance arrangements.

III

Any brief account of Ouvrier's adult life runs the risk of giving the impression of a character out of Georges Perec.[10] The following brief account is based on the copious, although not chronologically comprehensive, journals which he left after his death.

He did not succeed in graduating from the University of Glasgow. The Great War opened just as he was preparing to enter his final year, and he signed up almost instantaneously. He was understandably caught by the double tidal wave of *entente* patriotism. The German occupation of Belgium, we should remember, would have struck many French observers as a repetition of the Prussian imperialism of 1871, and unsurprisingly he went with full paternal approval as well as, no doubt, the military example of his great uncle Cicatrix. He did not, however, see any real action, as his linguistic abilities meant that he was detained behind the front line as a liaison and translation officer servicing the British and French high commands. In this capacity he was present at the conclusion of the Versailles treaty on 28 June 1919, which returned Alsace and Lorraine to French hands. He was then demobilised. He claims not to have returned to Scotland mainly on account of a disaffection with his father, now turned a socialist and follower of John MacLean, over Antoine's participation in the famous "riot of George Square" of 31 January 1919. Sidney felt that his father's conduct was seditious and refused to communicate with him for more than a decade.

Exactly how Sidney Ouvrier got through the following thirteen years remains obscure. His extant correspondence from this time is sparse, he kept no journal throughout the twenties, and did not resume it until 1931. In his memoirs he is elusive and discreet about the entire period. It does, however, emerge that almost exactly at

---

10. I am thinking particularly of Rorschach in that hotchpotch of Implags, *Life: A User's Manual*, tr. by David Bellos (London, Collins Harvill, 1987).

Sidney Ouvrier (1893-1967)
with his mother, Oliphant, (1868-1911), in 1910.
The child has not been identified

the moment when (as Orwell was to record in 1940) "Paris was invaded by such a swarm of artists, writers, students, dilettanti, sight-seers, debauchees and plain idlers as the world has probably never seen",[11] Ouvrier left to retrace his origins to Mulhouse, where he seems to have remained, settled, married in 1923, and fathered a daughter (Martine Daly, *née* Ouvrier, the present writer's mother) in 1929. Precisely what Ouvrier did to maintain himself and his wife in the twenties is uncertain. The answer is perhaps very little, if his only child's recollections of coming to consciousness amid squalor, hunger, confusion, penury and misery are anything to go by. Ouvrier's domestic hopelessness was certainly grave if, as Martine attests, she was cooking, cleaning and sewing for him. But this may be unreliable testimony, given the vagaries of childhood recollection, or the possibility that Ouvrier may temporarily have gone to pieces after his wife's desertion in the early 1930s.

Thanks to the resumption of his journals we do know that in the early 1930s he wrote a novel, largely based on his War experiences. The novel appeared in 1932, under the imaginative title *La Guerre d'un Ouvrier* and the pseudonym Robert Walker.[12] According to Ouvrier, the one critic who reviewed it compared it to *Le Grand Meaulnes,* but this review has not been located. The novel was not much read, but it allowed Ouvrier into literary society. A few months later he founded a quarterly review which he entitled, rather bizarrely, *Les Préjudices.* It appeared twice and then folded. None of the authors published in it subsequently established themselves, and where Ouvrier got the money for the enterprise is a mystery. Martine recalls being dragooned as a three-year-old into stuffing envelopes with complimentary copies, which were then despatched to prospective subscribers. Though Ouvrier is very close with precise details on this point, it seems probable that it was a vanity-publishing enterprise. In any case, of all his pre-war projects it is the only one he does not describe as a total failure.

In late 1932 Ouvrier suddenly returned to Glasgow, reconciled to his father. This event happened to coincide with Ouvrier's discovery

---

11. George Orwell, "Inside the Whale", in *Inside the Whale and Other Essays* (Harmondsworth, Penguin, 1962), p. 9.
12. Robert Walker, *La Guerre d'une Ouvrier* (Paris, Les Éditions du Tonneau, 1932). It was of course, under the same pseudonym that Chapter 12 of *Lanark* first saw the light of day, as runner-up in the 1958 Observer short story competition. Ouvrier chose the surname because, apparently, it approximated to Mulhouse pronunciation of the English word 'worker'. No one seems to have noticed this felicitous irony.

Ouvriere Ouvrier (1901-?), nee Touslejours,
Sidney Ouvrier's absentee wife

that his father was now a rather affluent man, having in 1925, unknown to Sidney, patented a non-toxic screw-bolt for children's wooden toys, which were harmless if licked or sucked. The plasticisation of the toy industry in the 1950s has rendered this device obsolete, but between the registration of the patent and his death at the age of seventy-four in 1939, this screw-bolt earned Antoine Ouvrier over thirty thousand pounds. He continued with his mill work in Lanark as usual until his retirement in 1930, by which time sufficient revenues from his invention had amassed to allow him to purchase a spacious and splendid domicile in the Shawlands district of Glasgow. His confrontation with a granddaughter, in his closing years, was as unexpected and as welcome as his son's discovery of a possible inheritance.

Relieved of the necessity of daily toil, Antoine Ouvrier became committed to supporting financially his son's quest for the literary acclaim to which as a youth he had himself aspired. Sidney soon conceived a fiction on an epic scale. The primordial idea was a narrative whose movement, symbolically or otherwise, would encapsulate the massive difference between the pre-war and post-war worlds. The pre-war order would be figured in "a narrative of dissolution", embodied even at the level of the hero's surname: "Thaw: a melting from a solid, frozen, crystalline state; a descent from ice-perfect condition to fluid, swamping, anarchic *mélange*".[13] As the switch from English to French diction perhaps indicates, the result of the "descent" was deeply bound up with Ouvrier's personal experience of that dark, unrecorded post-war decade in Mulhouse. He made the decision early on to symbolise the central epochal contrast in a clash of narrative forms, the pre-war being represented in a realist and the post-war by a surrealist style. But shortly after his return from Germany in June 1933 the project became split into two separate novels. He began to write the first of these in earnest in that same year.

In its early development, this epic was one of long drawn-out composition rather than prodigious verbal substance. It is difficult to imagine that the 250-page fiction which resulted should take an entire fifteen years to finish. Even for a man of leisure the average rate of completion of one page every twenty-two days is stunning. But the next we know of the novel is the following rejection of it by the first publisher Ouvrier sent it to, the Glasgow firm of William McLennan and Co.:

---

13. Sidney Ouvrier, *Journal 1933*, 24 February 1933 (in my possession).

11 November 1948

Dear Mr Walker,
I write with reference to your recently submitted manuscript novel, *Duncan Thaw*. I am sorry to say that we are unable to proceed with publication. Last year we published a novel on a very similar theme, Mr J. F. Hendry's *Fernie Brae: A Scottish Childhood*. Indeed, I hope you will not take it amiss if I say that this is a far superior novel to your own with which, I am almost certain from the evidence of your own MS, you are familiar. (I note in passing that your place of residence is rather close to that in which Mr Hendry's novel opens.) I would venture so far, in fact, as to say that your own novel gives the impression of being a somewhat cursorily dashed off, at times even directly plagiarising, imitation of Mr Hendry's. On these grounds my advice is not to circulate it to other publishers, as we should certainly be forced to take legal action if any were so foolish or so undiscriminating as be persuaded to bring it into the light of day.

Yours faithfully
W. McLennan
Proprietor and Managing Director[14]

It was no doubt on receipt of this that Ouvrier decided to rethink the entire enterprise. He seems to have returned to his earlier conception of a bi-partite epic. It took him another eight and a half years to complete it.

Ouvrier finished *Lanark* in November 1957. He had taken so long to do so that, for the sake of preserving a sense of contemporaneity, he had been forced to reframe the timescale of the novel, which now related to the Second rather than the First World War. He left it to be typed by Martine and took a holiday, journeying through Switzerland to Frankfurt, then travelling on to Athens, Constantinople, Odessa and Alexandria. In early January 1958 he sailed to Gibraltar, where he had taken a house for three months, intending to visit an old army friend, Jock Brown. Brown had been in the Highland Light Infantry in Flanders, but was now working as a Toc H representative in Gibraltar, running an armed forces leave

---

14. The MS version of the novel to which this was a response has not survived. Ouvrier inserted the letter into his journal without comment, other than the question, "Who is J. F. Hendry?", which he pencilled at the bottom of the page. Although, as this proves, McLennan's terrible accusations were wholly unjust, Ouvrier seems to have taken his advice. There is certainly no trace of any further correspondence relating to *Duncan Thaw*.

hostel there.[15] The typescript arrived from Martine on 14 January 1958. A week later, Ouvrier wrote back to her, requesting that she enter a fresh typed copy of Chapter 12 of the novel in the *Observer* short story competition, which he had just seen advertised.[16]

A fortnight later he met Alasdair Gray.

IV

The scene, if not the crime, is described in Gray's own essay, "A Report to the Trustees of the Bellahouston Travelling Scholarship". This is a glum, prolix, exculpatory ramble, written in April 1959, in which Gray tries to satisfy the patient and aggrieved trustees as to why, their having offered him a Trust award to

> find a cheap place to live in southern Spain, paint there for as long as the money would allow, then travel home through Granada, Málaga, Madrid, Toledo, Barcelona and Paris, viewing on the way Moorish mosques, baroque cathedrals, plateresque palaces, the works of El Greco, Velázquez and Goya, with Bosch's *Garden of Earthly Delights*, Brueghel's *Triumph of Death*, and several other grand gaudy things which are supposed to compensate for the crimes of our civilization ... I eventually spent two days in Spain and saw nothing of interest.[17]

In the course of this laboured exercise in apologetics, Gray recounts how he landed, ill, in Gibraltar, then met, befriended, admired and was helped by Jock Brown. What he omits to record is that Jock Brown, ever solicitous for the social welfare of those in his charge, introduced him to Sidney Ouvrier. Ouvrier visited Gray in Jock Brown's hostel on several occasions, mainly to see how he was progressing with a mural, the *Triumph of Neptune*, with which,

---

15. The Toc H developed in France during the First World War, among British soldiers who wanted spiritual communion and found the official army priests too sectarian and not always near when things got tough. After the war it developed into a charitable organisation providing food, clothing and shelter to the needy, fighting loneliness and hate and encouraging Christian comradeship. The name derives from the obsolete telegraph code for T.H., initials of Talbot House, Poperinge, Belgium, the original headquarters of the society.
16. Postcard from Sidney Ouvrier to Martine Ouvrier, 21 January 1958 (in my possession).
17. Alasdair Gray, "A Report to the Trustees of the Bellahouston Travelling Scholarship", in James Kelman, Agnes Owens and Alasdair Gray, *Lean Tales* (London, Abacus, 1987), p. 181.

Gray proudly tells us, he spent some time decorating the walls of the hostel common room. When it emerged in conversation that Ouvrier had completed a novel, whose final draft he had just finished correcting, Gray managed to persuade him to lend it to him to read.

One day in early March 1958, Ouvrier received a distressing telegram from Martine, to the effect that there had been a fire in the study at the Shawlands house which had destroyed many of his papers, including the manuscript copy of *Lanark*. In a state of agitation, Ouvrier went to the hostel. There he was told by Jock Brown, who knew nothing of the novel, that he, Brown, had paid for a plane ticket to London for Gray and that he, Gray, had flown out the previous evening. Ouvrier, now in a condition of apoplectic anxiety (and, we should remember, in his sixty-fourth year), suffered a mental and physical collapse when he realised that Gray had taken the typescript of the novel with him.

It is possible that Gray departed with the novel purely as a consequence of hasty packing. If so, his report to the Bellahouston trustees, written just over a year later, reveal an early determination to capitalise on his mistake. He carefully inserts in the report descriptions of authorial activity designed to give the impression that he was at work on a novel before and during his foreign trip. But on careful reading these appear vague and decidedly ambiguous. Take the following account of how he apparently passed the time in a Gibraltar hospital before moving on to Jock Brown's hostel (i.e. before being introduced to Ouvrier, whose existence he at no point acknowledges):

> A few years ago I had begun work on a tragicomical novel and meant to write some more of it in Spain. In my luggage was a Cantablue Expanding Wallet, a portable cardboard filing cabinet shaped like an accordion and holding two complete chapters and the notebooks and diaries from which I meant to make the rest. I put this on my bedside locker and began working. I was slightly ashamed of this activity, which struck me as presumptuous because, like Scott Fitzgerald, I believed the novel was the strongest and supplest medium for conveying thought and emotion from one human being to another, which meant that a novelist needed to understand great states of feeling, and although twenty-three years old I had never known carnal love and feared I never would; banal because one or two friends had also started writing a novel, and the rest had thought of writing one. So when the nurses asked what I was doing I lied and told them I was writing this report.[18]

18. Gray, "A Report to the Trustees ...", p. 194.

In his time at Jock Brown's hostel, he later asseverates, "I wrote five chapters of my book".[19] Much more recently, with reinvigorated mendacity, he has stated that "I began to write the *Thaw* section of *Lanark*" in Summer 1953.[20]

Ouvrier never fully recovered from the blow of losing the corrected original of the typescript. He was three months in Gibraltar's King George V hospital before he regained enough strength to return to Glasgow. Martine, when she went to Gibraltar to be with him, found him in a monomaniac mental state over the disappearance of the novel whose tortuous composition had consumed the previous twenty-five years of his life (an overall rate of 16.3 days per page). She could not fully understand his concern, because the two carbon copies had not been touched by the fire, although her telegram hadn't said that they were safe. Despite her reassurances, even after their return to Shawlands, Ouvrier languished in a condition of mortal woundedness and inconsolable apathy. When Chapter 12 of the novel appeared in the Observer later that year, at just the moment when he may have managed to find a publisher for the entire work, he was apparently so aggrieved at being only the competition runner-up that he interred the two carbons in the safe and never mentioned them again. Martine Ouvrier left her father's home to marry Dalton Daly, a fibre glass factory machine operative, in 1959. The present writer, their only son, was born in 1963. Sidney Ouvrier died, aged seventy-two, on 2 March 1967.

The received wisdom about the compositional history of *Lanark* is a product of the calculating imagination of Alasdair Gray, foisted by him onto a gullible public and a critical establishment enslaved to the authority of authorhood, even where the latter is assumed rather than actual.[21] His account of the prolonged hold-ups in

---

19. Gray, "A Report to the Trustees ...", p. 204.
20. See Bruce Charlton, "Checklists and Unpublished Materials by Alasdair Gray", in *The Arts of Alasdair Gray*, ed. by Robert Crawford and Thom Nairn (Edinburgh, Edinburgh University Press, 1991), p. 199.
21. The hapless Bruce Charlton, for instance, is quite content to act as a conduit for such obvious unlikelihoods as the following: '*Lanark*'s most remote ancestor is the improbably [!! – M.D.] titled *Obbly Pobbly* from 1951, featuring as its semi-autobiographical protagonist "a potato-headed intellectual schoolboy ... [who would] go on a pilgrimage which would lead him out of the everyday drabness of post-war respectable working class Glasgow, through a fantasy pilgrimage, ending in an era of untrammelled artistic production". Bruce Charlton, "The Story So Far", in Crawford and Nairn, pp. 12-13.

The present author (1963-), with his mother,
Martine Daly (1929-), nee Ouvrier, in 1964

getting it published under his own name we have no cause to doubt.[22] Delay was in any case inevitable. Gray saw Chapter 12 of the novel published in the *Observer* in 1958, as the note on prior publication on the flyleaf of the published novel establishes. I picture Gray, throughout the 1960s, keeping one eye warily roving through publisher's catalogues while the other hopefully scanned the obituary columns.

In the meantime, it seems, he revised and embellished the expropriated typescript. Comparison of the published novel with Ouvrier's surviving carbons reveals that, in the main, Gray's textual fiddling was directed to giving the impression that Duncan Thaw was based on himself. This was not so very difficult, as it turned out, because Thaw was not a self-portrait of Ouvrier. Indeed, even in the original, Duncan Thaw was much more like Alasdair Gray than the urbane Sidney. Gray changed small particulars. In the early sections of the Thaw narrative he rewrote the details of Duncan's schooling to parallel his own, so that, for example, the educational establishment he attends is in Dennistoun, Glasgow, whereas Ouvrier's Thaw goes to school in Lanark. The "Prologue", a wholly extraneous short story of Gray's invention which he no doubt had lying about, was simply bunged in with no regard to its entirely distracting effect. Most cruelly, Gray composed an "Epilogue" in which the hero meets the author and outwits him by telling him things about his own verbal creation which the author does not know. Furthermore the real author, Sidney "Workman", is diminished to the scale of a peripheral functionary in the same "Epilogue" which is brazen enough, at one point, to obscurely confess the novel's wholly piratical status, its condition of being a Totplag:

> "Your survival as a character and mine as an author depend on us seducing a living soul into our printed world and trapping it here long enough for us to steal the imaginative energy which gives us life." (*Lanark* 485)

The origins of this sentence lie in the treachery at Gibraltar, as anyone acquainted with the history will recognise.

V

Before detailing the evidence which will unmask *Lanark* as a Totplag, some qualifying divarication as to the nature of Concplag

---

22. Transmitted by Gray through the slavishly faithful medium of Charlton. See the two preceding footnotes.

may be in order. Some modern theorists would deny the validity of the system of intellectual property rights on which the concept of plagiarism depends, but this is not a debate in which we need to become embroiled, as Gray himself, in the "Epilogue", is prepared both to invoke the concept and to indulge in the customary moralising associated with it ("A property is not always valuable because it is stolen from a rich man" [*Lanark* 490] – how true!). It may be objected, however, that not all Concplags – a term which can be applied to any verbal item "thieved without acknowledgement)" (*Lanark* 490)[23] – are Concplags. Some may simply be masquerading as Concplags, transparent to the weakest intellectual vision. And indeed, it has to be admitted that a certain kind of textual banditry is so manifestly impossible to conceal that one must have recourse to a more refined notion to explain it. Plagiarisms of this sort are obvious because they are promiscuous borrowings from documents with which sufficient members of an interpretive community will be familiar for it to be impossible for their debentured status to be misunderstood. This device may therefore be classified as OBVIOUS PLAGIARISM, or Obvplag.

The title face to Book Four of *Lanark* is a useful example of Obvplag. It Obvplags the title page of Hobbes's classic of political philosophy, *Leviathan* (1651), in a manner that requires no illustration. The obviousness of the Obvplag does not rest in the evident similarity of the contents of the illustrations, but in the widespread cultural recognition, the fame, of the Hobbesian icon. There would be little likelihood of Gray succeeding in passing this image off as his own. Technically speaking, he does not actually register the borrowing in the "Index of Plagiarisms". Under the entry for Hobbes he simply notes, "In a famous title page this state is shown threatening a whole earth with the symbols of warfare and religion" (*Lanark* 490). This should surely count as implicit acknowledgment.

The matter of undecidability between Concplag and Obvplag can be theoretically resolved, I am persuaded, by the introduction of a duplex system of categorisation of plagiarism consisting of ACKNOWLEDGED PLAGIARISM, or Ackplag, and UNACKNOWLEDGED PLAGIARISM, or Unackplag. By means of a

23. Ironically, this remark describes the author/king/conjuror's theft of a device from Milton. But it was Milton who defined plagiarism as copying without improving. Gray's one laudable achievement is the resurrection of this traditional understanding of plagiarism in contradistinction to the unsophisticated modern definition which sees plagiarism as merely a borrowing to which one does not admit.

diagram,[24] it is a simple matter to show how these two categories subsume all previously discussed forms of plagiarism with the exception of the universal Totplag:

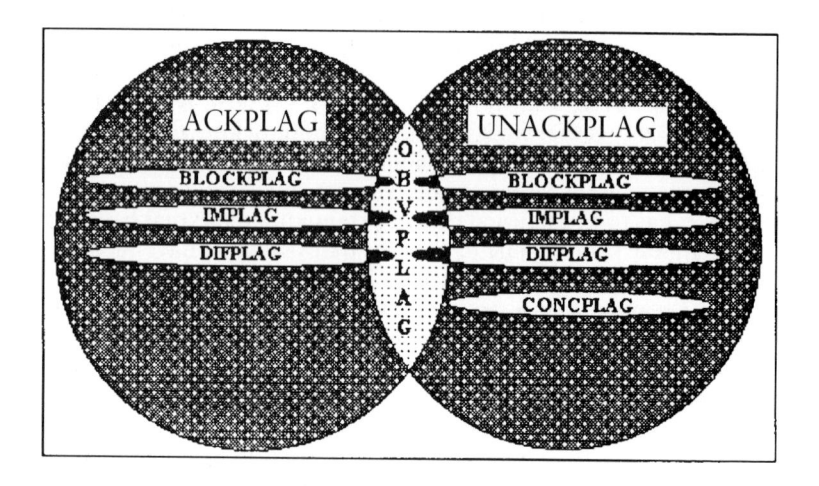

[Venn diagram showing two overlapping circles labeled ACKPLAG and UNACKPLAG. Both circles contain BLOCKPLAG, IMPLAG, and DIFPLAG. The UNACKPLAG circle additionally contains CONCPLAG. The overlapping region is labeled vertically OBVPLAG.]

In this representation two general forms of plagiarism, Ackplag and Unackplag, are shown, each consisting of the subsets Blockplag, Difplag and Implag. Obvplag is the grey area shared between Ackplag and Unackplag, and there may be categorical overlaps between Obvplag and Blockplag/Implag/Difplag. Concplag is a subset specific to the larger set Unackplag, and, for the purposes of this study, is not considered to overlap with Obvplag. The universal set, represented by the border of this diagram, may be taken to be Totplag.[25]

It should, theoretically speaking, be possible to assign each plagiarism in *Lanark* to a point on this diagram. Thus the title face to Book Four, arguably, would be situated in either of the doubly shaded areas in which Implag, Obvplag, Ackplag and Unackplag meet. Where, however, would we place, for example, the titlefaces to Books One, Two and Three? These are not Obvplags. If one were

24. Hereby Ackplagged from the English logician, John Venn (1834-1923).
25. Why, the reader may ask, are unacknowledged Blockplags, Implags and Difplags not subsumed within unacknowledged Concplags? Such a reader's extraordinary attention to detail may be commended, but is more properly to be suspected.

to present the title face to Book Four to a cross-section of moderately well-educated persons, it is likely that the frequency of identifications of its relation to Hobbes's *Leviathan* would be pretty high. This is not the case, however (taking the titlefaces in the order in which the reader encounters them), with that to Book Three (which is modelled on that to Sir Walter Raleigh *History of the World* [1641]), to Book One (Sir Francis Bacon's *Instauratio Magna* [1620]) or to Book Two (Andreas Vesalius' *De Humani Corporis Fabrica* [1543]). I have placed these pictorial reworkings before various distinguished Renaissance specialists without a glimmer of specific recognition. I did not even recognise them myself.[26] Unlike Hobbes, none of this trio of polymaths appears in the "Index of Plagiarisms". No one, then, could seriously make a case for these titlefaces being Ackplags. They are undoubtedly Concplags.[27]

A measure of the intensity of Gray's Concplagging can be gauged from analysis of the "Prologue", which, as has been noted, *is* Gray's own work. This was first published in the *Glasgow University Magazine* in 1974, "the so-called 'Prologue" being no prologue at all, but a separate short story", as a footnote in the "Epilogue" informs us (*Lanark* 499). The "Prologue", according to the novel's "Table of Contents", tells "how a nonentity was made oracular", and is narrated by the oracle, a wholly disembodied voice, "sexless and eager", which speaks "on an odd unemphatic note, as if its words could never be printed between quotation marks" (*Lanark* 104). Accordingly, the oracle's words are not rendered with the punctuational conventions used in writing to signal speech. Gray proceeds, in the "Prologue", to take this as a licence to use the work

26. For the identification of each I must acknowledge the endeavours of Valerie Durow, a postgraduate student under whose supervision I am currently working. I trust that she will offer corresponding acknowledgment of my brilliant intuition as to the role played by quantum theory in the narrative structure of *Lanark* in the thesis on which she is currently engaged. Impressive as its early drafts are, Durow's thesis is unlikely to be the last word on *Lanark*, as she prefers to labour under the illusion shared by most naïve readers, namely that the novel is the imaginative product of Alasdair Gray.
27. It is true that the first (Canongate) edition of the novel bears on the frontispiece the slogan "WITH ALLEGORICAL TITLEFACES IMITATING THE BEST PRECEDENTS". This was removed in subsequent editions. It may therefore be desirable to make the case for the titlefaces being acknowledged Implags, or Obvplags, in the Canongate edition, and Concplags in subsequent editions. But it is possible that many readers will come to find this method of categorisation unwieldy if it is employed with quite this degree of nicety.

of other writers without accreditation – in short, to Concplag mercilessly. It is possible to distinguish at least five major authors who are Concplagged in the "Prologue".

(1) *Karl Marx*. Much of the "Prologue" is an extended rewriting of classic passages from the great historical materialist's work. The oracle's story, in which a bleak accountant *cum* stockbroker tells how he came to lose his bodily existence, may be taken as a cautionary Marxist tale revealing the perils of attempting to put idealist philosophy into practice: "I have already mentioned my distrust of physical things. They are too remote from the mind. I chose to live by those numbers which are most purely a product of the mind and therefore influence it most strongly: in a word, money" (*Lanark* 108). In particular, although the oracle is hardly a Marxist, it has a quasi-Marxist understanding of the contradictions within what Marx called the universal equivalent form of value, namely money. Compare the following words of the oracle with Marx's thesis, in *Capital*, that "historically speaking, capital invariably first confronts landed property in the form of money":[28]

> It puzzles me that people who live by owning or managing big sums of money are commonly called materialistic, for finance is the most purely intellectual, the most sheerly spiritual of activities, being concerned less with material objects than with values. Of course finance needs objects, since money is the value of objects and could no more exist without them than mind can exist without body, but the objects come second. If you doubt this, think which you would rather own: fifty thousand pounds or a piece of land valued at fifty thousand pounds. The only people likely to prefer the land are financiers who know how to increase its value by renting or reselling, so either answer proves that money is preferable to things. (*Lanark* 108-9)[29]

Consider the above, to take just one additional germane example, with what Marx himself has to say in *Capital* about "the fetishism of the commodity" (the commodity in the case of the oracle being money):

> The commodity-form, and the value-relation of the products of labour within which it appears, have absolutely no connection with the physical nature of the commodity and the mate-

28. Karl Marx, *Capital: A Critique of Political Economy*, vol. 1, tr. by Ben Fowkes (Harmondsworth, Penguin, 1976), p. 247.
29. Lanark himself puts his finger on one of the contradictions in this: "You said money can no more exist without objects than mind without body. Yet you exist without a body." The oracle replies, "That puzzles me too" (*Lanark* 117).

rial relations arising out of this. It is nothing but the definite social relation between men themselves which assumes here, for them, the fantastic form of a relation between things ... To the producers, therefore, the social relations between their private labours appear as what they are, i.e. they do not appear as direct social relations between persons in their work, but rather as material relations between persons and social relations between things.[30]

The oracle's disappearance, or increasing abstraction as a consciousness from the physical world, is a narrative of the reified alienation which is the consequence of extreme commodity fetishism. To risk a paradox, it may be said that the oracle embodies this abstraction. Whether or not the oracle's progress can be said also to symbolise the process, at one time believed by socialists to be inevitable, of capitalism eventually evaporating under the pressure of its own internal contradictions, is an open question.

2) *Albert Einstein*. The oracle's apparent reversion to infancy, subsequent to adulthood, signified by his waking to find himself in a nursery uttering baby talk (*Lanark* 112), is a Concplag of Einstein's theory that a person travelling faster than the speed of light will get younger. It may owe a more immediate debt to an astronaut's encounter with a "Star-Child" on passing through a "Star-Gate" in a much-hyped contemporaneous science fiction feature film,[31] but this itself was just an earlier Concplag of Einstein.

(3) *T. S. Eliot*. The oracle is, in a sense, a literary artist. He tells a story. As such, the experience he recounts is obscurely related to Eliot's doctrine of artistic depersonalisation in his (in)famous essay of 1919, "Tradition and the Individual Talent": "the progress of an artist is a continual self-sacrifice, a continual extinction of personality".[32] Eliot goes on to liken the mind of the artist to a catalyst

30. Marx, pp. 165-6. Cf. also Marx's extensive comments about money and alienation in "Economic and Philosophical Manuscripts (1844)", in Karl Marx, *Early Writings*, tr. by Rodney Livingstone and Gregor Benton (Harmondsworth, Penguin, 1975), pp. 279-400, which are also Concplagged by the oracle. It is worth noting one other prophetic remark made by Marx in this regard, given that the oracle is in effect a man who becomes a commodity: "If commodities could speak, they would say this: our use-value may interest men, but it does not belong to us as objects. What does belong to us as objects, however, is our value" (*Capital*, vol. 1, p. 176).
31. For the book of the movie, see Arthur C. Clarke, *2001: A Space Odyssey* (London, Hutchinson, 1968).
32. T. S. Eliot, "Tradition and the Individual Talent", in *T. S. Eliot: Selected Prose*, ed. by John Hayward (London, Penguin, 1953), p. 26.

which remains inert and neutral in the chemical reaction which it effects: "the more perfect the artist, the more completely separate in him will be the man who suffers and the mind which creates".[33] Like Eliot's shred of platinum, the oracle has no sense of identity or relatedness to its environment: "I had become bodiless in a bodiless world. I existed as a series of thoughts amidst infinite greyness" (*Lanark* 111). It is not surprising to witness a writer whose primary talent resides in his failure to resist such easy puns on his own name being persuaded by the pernicious Eliotic description of the artist's mind as a kind of compost bin, "a receptacle for seizing and storing up numberless feelings, phrases, images, which remain there until all the particles which can unite to form a new compound are present together".[34] The regrettable feature of Gray's function in *Lanark*, however, is that only an infinitesimal number of the feelings, phrases and images the novel launches on the world are actually his own.

(4) *Roland Barthes.* "Writing is that neutral, composite, oblique space where our subject slips away, the negative where all identity is lost, starting with the very identity of the body writing."[35] The impact of Barthes's iconoclastic squib of 1968 on the "Prologue" is incontestable: "Later I sat on a swivel chair above fathoms of emptiness, grey emptiness all around except where, six feet to the right, a pencil moving on its point across an angled notepad showed where my secretary was taking down the words I dictated to her" (*Lanark* 111). It comes as no shock that Gray should wish to collaborate in the "removal of the Author"[36] in a novel whose real author he had already effaced in a manner we are soon to learn more about. One can understand perfectly his agreement with Barthes's pseudo-consensual pronouncement that "we know that a text is not a line of words releasing a single "theological" meaning (the "message" of the Author-God) but a multi-dimensional space in which a variety of writings, *none of them original*, blend and clash".[37] However, to have acknowledged a textual theft from a *French* writer would have been to come too close to reality for comfort. Hence Barthes is Concplagged and omitted from the "Index of Plagiarisms". It provokes no wonder that only one French writer (and that the most predictable) appears in the "Index" (*Lanark* 496).

33. Eliot, p. 27.
34. Eliot, p. 27.
35. Roland Barthes, "The Death of the Author", in *Image-Music-Text*, tr. by Stephen Heath (Glasgow, Fontana, 1977), p. 142.
36. Barthes, p. 147.
37. Barthes, p. 146. Emphasis added.

(5) *H. G. Wells*. It could be claimed that the relation of the "Prologue" to Wells's *The Invisible Man* (1897) is an Obvplag, particularly since the protagonist repeatedly manifests himself to Adye in chapter twenty-seven of that novel as no more than a voice. But, as with Marx and Eliot, Wells appears in the "Index of Plagiarisms" precisely to divert the reader's attention from this source by focusing it on texts or passages where the relationship is actually much more tenuous (*Lanark* 498, 494, 488 respectively). One cannot help but note, in this connection, the ironic perception in footnote 5 of the "Epilogue" to the effect that "the author's amazing virulence against Goethe is perhaps a smokescreen to distract attention from what he owes him" (*Lanark* 488).

VI

We must proceed to the sorry uncovering of the Totplag. The most significant enrolment made by the young Ouvrier at Glasgow University was in his first year, when he attended a course of lectures given by John Hepburn Millar. Millar was Professor of Constitutional Law and Constitutional History in the University of Edinburgh, but gave this particular series as a visiting lecturer in Scottish Literature at Glasgow in the academic year 1911-12.[38] It was thanks to this course that Ouvrier's abiding passion for Scottish writing of this period was ignited, and knowledge of its content is essential to an understanding of the sources behind major sections of the novel later to be published as *Lanark*.

Millar's lectures took the form, by and large, of an evaluative survey of the main prose writers of the two centuries: Drummond, Urquhart, Mackenzie, Kames, Blair, and so on. But the most material inclusion, so far as we are concerned, is his discussion of James Burnett, Lord Monboddo (1714-99). This writer is recorded in the "Index of Plagiarisms" of *Lanark*, where he is treated in scornful terms. For instance:

> He was a court of session judge, friend of King George and an erudite metaphysician with a faith in satyrs and mermaids, but has only been saved from oblivion by the animadversions against his theory of human descent from the apes in Boswell's *Life of Johnson*. (*Lanark* 494)

---

38. The lectures were published almost immediately in John Hepburn Millar, *Scottish Prose of the Seventeenth and Eighteenth Centuries* (Glasgow, James Maclehose and Sons, 1912).

No objective reader of Millar's discussion of Monboddo would come away with that impression of his abilities, and it is therefore doubtful that Sidney Ouvrier wrote these words. Millar does deal with the disagreement between Johnson and Monboddo, but in much less summary and partial terms than these, and has at least the grace to consider Monboddo's writings instead of relying on Johnson's contemptuous and reflexive dismissal of them. "It is beyond question," Millar tells us, "that Monboddo was a man of deep and extensive learning" whose knowledge of ancient tongues was remarkable and whose defence of Greek "is most refreshing and salutary doctrine for our own age, which has witnessed an insolent attack upon the cause of Greek at the English Universities, and its shameful betrayal in our own".[39] Praising Monboddo's principled refusal "to embellish his writing with meretricious ornament" (a resistance not so remarkable, one might add, in the inferior draughtsman whose Concplags form the various titlefaces to the published version of *Lanark*), Millar discusses his two major works, each of which appeared over a number of years: *Of the Origin and Progress of Language* (6 vols., 1773-92) and *Antient Metaphysics, or the Science of Universals* (6 vol, 1779-99). Of perhaps most moment for a consideration of the rôle played by Monboddo in *Lanark* are the following remarks:

> The *Metaphysics* winds up with a most interesting chapter on the condition of Scotland, in which Monboddo deplores rural depopulation and the swallowing up of small lairds by great. Though a zealot for the improvement of agriculture (and it is recorded that one night he went out with a lighted candle to take a look at a field of turnips), he insists that it ought not to be carried out at the expense of the farmers and cottars. "There are many in Scotland," he says, "who call themselves improvers, but who I think are rather *desolators* of the country. Their method is to take into possession several farms, which no doubt they improve by cultivation. But after they have done so they set them off all to one tenant, instead of perhaps five or six who possessed them before."[40]

It is manifest from this that the historical Monboddo's humane view of the society of his own time is virtually diametrically opposed to the fictional Monboddo's rapacious social policy in his own world, a consequence of pathological hostility towards "desperadoes" and "irresponsible intellectuals" who "seem anxious to break the world down into tiny republics of the prehistoric kind, where the voice of

---

39. Millar, pp. 220-2.
40. Millar, pp. 227-8, quoting from Monboddo's *Antient Metaphysics*.

the dull and cranky would sound as loud as the wise and skilful" (*Lanark* 54-6). The fictional Monboddo is therefore a product of artifice, a construct, a distortion, but is not recognised as such by the author of the "Index of Plagiarisms", who seems to believe that the historical Monboddo was actually as eccentric and dangerous as this representation. The "Index of Plagiarisms" and the novel thus appear to be at cross purposes, an indication that they were not composed by the same individual.

The individual who wrote the "Index of Plagiarisms" was certainly not Sidney Ouvrier. To begin with, there is the evidence of Ouvrier's own editions of the works of Monboddo cited by Millar. These were bequeathed to the present writer on the death of his grandfather in March 1967. If the extensive marginalia in Ouvrier's hand are anything to go by, all of the volumes were read with a thoroughness which few undergraduates of today could muster, and their rarity and expense suggest an interest in the author which a low evaluation would seem to preclude. Moreover, all of these marginal comments show either interest or approval on the part of the reader – none are negative. Ouvrier reading Monboddo is the opposite of Blake reading Sir Joshua Reynolds. On these grounds, it is impossible to see the annotator of Monboddo's works and the annotator of *Lanark* as one and the same man. But a curious and accidental piece of evidence clinches the case. This is a holograph letter inserted inside the front cover of volume three of Ouvrier's copy of Monboddo's *Antient Metaphysics*. For over twenty years after the bequest of this letter the present writer was unable to identify its author. Here is the text of the letter in full:

Dublin, 14 February

Dear Sid,
Herewith I return the Monboddo volume with warmest thanks for the loan of it. An extraordinary character, to be sure. I hope you haven't minded me holding on to it for so long. It's just that it provided me with some terrific notions for a book I've just finished. The only good thing about it is the plot and I've been wondering whether I could make a crazy play out of it. When you get to the end of this book you realize that my hero or main character (he's a heel and a killer) has been dead throughout the book and that all the queer ghastly things which have been happening to him are happening in a sort of hell which he earned for the killing. Towards the end of the book (before you know he's dead) he manages to get back to his own house where he used to live with another man who helped in the original murder. Although he's been away three days, this other fellow is twenty years older and dies of fright when he sees the other lad standing in the door. Then the two

> of them walk back along the road to the hell place and start thro' all the same terrible adventures again, the first fellow being surprised and frightened at everything just as he was the first time and as if he'd never been through it before. It is made clear that this sort of thing goes on for ever – and there you are. It is supposed to be very funny but I don't know about that either. I think the idea of a man being dead all the time is pretty new. When you are writing about the world of the dead – and the damned where none of the rules and laws (not even the law of gravity) holds good, there is any amount of scope for back-chat and funny cracks.
>
> B.O'N

It was not until 1988, when the present author, in the course of tracking Gray's fabrications to their lair, was pursuing the trivialising allusions which litter the "Epilogue", that the identity of "B. O'N." became clear. Footnote 6 of the "Epilogue" wishes to persuade us that the novel is a monumental and multiple Difplag: "The index proves that *Lanark* is erected upon an infantile foundation of Victorian nursery tales, though the final shape derives from English language fiction printed between the '40s and '60s of the present century. The hero's biography after death occurs in Wyndham-Lewis's trilogy *The Human Age*, Flann O'Brien's *The Third Policeman* and Golding's *Pincher Martin*" (*Lanark* 489). On looking into the O'Brien novel, first published posthumously in September 1967, I discovered a "Publisher's Note" appended to the book, which states, "On St Valentine's day, 1940, the author wrote to William Saroyan about this novel, as follows", and proceeds to reproduce, *verbatim*, the entirety of the above quoted letter, with the exception of its first four sentences, which are replaced with the single sentence, "I've just finished another book."[41] Thus I discovered that "B. O'N.' was, of course, Brian O'Nolan, the Irishman who wrote under the pseudonym of "Flann O'Brien". It became clear that O'Nolan, writing to Saroyan and Ouvrier on the same day about the same matter, did what many busy correspondents do for the sake of temporal economy, and wrote substantially the same letter to two unacquainted recipients, modifying the opening of his letter to Ouvrier only on account of the Monboddo volume he was returning therewith.

We need not dwell on the personal relationship between O'Nolan and Ouvrier. There is in any case very little detail. According to Ouvrier's diaries they met only twice, on consecutive evenings

---

41. "Publisher's Note" to Flann O'Brien, *The Third Policeman* (Picador, 1974), p. 173.

(22 and 23 May 1933), in the same bar in Köln, Germany, where Ouvrier had gone to examine the cathedral as early research for the novel which was to become *Lanark*. (He almost instantly abandoned Köln as the model for his cathedral because it was "too big".[42]) Ouvrier records that O'Nolan, then only just more than half Ouvrier's age, introduced himself by claiming to be studying at Köln University. Ouvrier was impressed by O'Nolan's ostensible erudition to the extent that he loaned him the Monboddo volume which he had been reading when O'Nolan accosted him. They exchanged addresses and agreed to meet the next evening, at which time O'Nolan would return the volume. When Ouvrier returned to the bar on the following night O'Nolan was drunk, had failed to bring the book, and almost immediately launched into what Ouvrier took to be a pro-German tirade. Ouvrier, whose personal family history had been so shadowed by German military aggression, lost patience with the young Irishman, threw a glass of beer over him, and left. Only later did he remember that he had not recovered the Monboddo volume. When he returned to Scotland in June he wrote to O'Nolan's Dublin address, but received no reply.[43] In his diaries he records writing to the same address on at least eight occasions in the next twelve months, each time to no avail, at the end of which he gave up, never expecting to retrieve the prized Monboddo. His astonishment at receiving the book out of the blue six years later was acute.[44] But understandably, he never replied to O'Nolan's letter.

As it stands, this is the kind of literary *minutiae* which deserves a half column in *Notes and Queries*. Why is it important? Crucially, the evidence establishes that *Lanark* was not and could not have

---

42. Sidney Ouvrier, *Journal 1933*, 24 May 1933 (quarto notebook, in my possession).
43. It seems, in fact, that O'Nolan remained in Germany until June 1934, and thus may not have received any of Ouvrier's letters. But his 'German interlude', rather like his ambiguous feelings for the Nazis, remains essentially unelucidated. The obscurity is only deepened in Peter Costello and Peter van de Kamp, *Flann O'Brien: An Illustrated Biography* (London, Bloomsbury, 1987), pp. 45-50, whose attempts to discover more about this period than O'Nolan himself later recorded run into a brick wall: they too can find no objective evidence of any enrolment at Köln University, and even June 1934 as the termination date of his sojourn, they tell us, is uncertain. They are forgivably unaware, also, of the meeting of these two nascent literary giants, and of O'Nolan's consequent debt to Ouvrier.
44. The diary entry for 16 February 1940 is a contrary verbal explosion of bliss and fury.

been in any way indebted to *The Third Policeman*. Indeed, to understand the relationship, one is required really to reverse its terms: that is to say, The *Third Policeman*, in its portrayal of the mad experimentalist de Selby, presents by means of bogus scholarship a caricature of Monboddo, which would have been impossible without the learnedness and aid of the real author of *Lanark*. This can be quite specifically established. The first extended passage on de Selby in *The Third Policeman* announces the influence patently enough to any Monboddoist:

> De Selby has some interesting things to say on the subject of houses. A row of houses he regards as a row of necessary evils. The softening and degeneration of the human race he attributes to its progressive predilection for interiors and waning interest in the art of going out and staying there. This in turn he sees as the result of the rise of such pursuits as reading, chess-playing, drinking, marriage and the like, few of which can be satisfactorily conducted in the open. Elsewhere he defines a house as "a large coffin", "a warren", and "a box". Evidently his main objection was to the confinement of a roof and four walls.[45]

Anyone who knows Monboddo's *Antient Metaphysics*, and particularly the third volume which O'Nolan held onto for almost seven years, will deduce from this that he studied it rather carefully. Millar's summary of *Antient Metaphysics* makes this clear enough:

> The chapters on Man are probably the most interesting in the book. It is there that we get the author's most characteristic views. He is a great advocate of the open air. So are we all nowadays, but we do not carry our enthusiasms to his lengths, and object to houses and clothes altogether. As for the use of fire, it "only serves to aggravate the mischief of houses and clothes".[46]

Readers of *The Third Policeman* will not fail to notice here, additionally, the provenance of de Selby's regret at "industrial activities involving coal-tar by-products".[47] De Selby's doctrine of "hydraulic elysium" ("water is rarely absent from any wholly satisfactory situation") is, furthermore, positively Monboddoesque: as Millar tells us, "Monboddo is a great believer in water for external as well as internal use. He would like to see public baths erected in the

---

45. O'Brien, p. 19.
46. Millar, p. 226, referring to Monboddo's *Antient Metaphysics*, vol. III, pp. 80, 92.
47. O'Brien, p. 101.

Highlands for the benefit of the inhabitants, who never change their shirts, once they put them on, till they are reduced to rags."[48]

We know that, after a rejection of *The Third Policeman* by Longman in 1940 O'Nolan was so stung that he "made up tales of losing it at a pub, on a drive through Donegal ... The great lost novel was a secret, something that remained unknown to all save his closest friends."[49] There is no question, then, of Ouvrier having ever read it. It was not published until September 1967. Ouvrier had already died in March of the same year. It may be objected that there is enough in O'Nolan's letter to Ouvrier to give him the idea of incorporating the "hero's biography after death" notion into *Lanark*, as well as borrowing the "hero, ignorant of his past, in a subfuse [sic] modern Hell, also from Flann O'Brien" (*Lanark* 490). This may be a tenable argument, but it does not address the issue at hand, namely the authorship of the "Index of Plagiarisms" and associated footnotes. The "Index of Plagiarisms" (*Lanak* 495) and the footnotes mention "Flann O'Brien" and "*The Third Policeman*", but it would have been impossible for Ouvrier to have done so. Ouvrier had never heard of either. He knew Brian O'Nolan only under that name. O'Nolan's letter to him, although giving an outline of the plot of his novel, did not inform him of the title. Ouvrier died before *The Third Policeman* saw the light of day. Nothing more is required to demonstrate the impossibility of the "Index of Plagiarisms" and footnotes being the products of Ouvrier's endeavour.

In the face of its internally contradictory evidence, it is impossible to resist the conclusion which the "Epilogue" insists that we partly deny: namely, that the "Index of Plagiarisms" and footnotes were in fact written by Alasdair Gray. Their purpose is to reveal that *Lanark* is a patina of forgivable (forgivable because confessed) plagiarisms. Such a confession is intended, no doubt, to lead the ordinary reader to admire the spectacle of a literary artist at last "coming clean" about his own vast pretension; even, perhaps, to wonder at the consummate artistry and irony of "employing" a fictional "real" worker (Workman) to this end. But, for anyone in possession of the evidence withheld from "the ordinary reader", Gray's *Lanark* has, as Walter Benjamin might have said, an origin which s/he cannot contemplate without horror.[50] The proper reac-

---

48. Cf. O'Brien, pp. 126-8, and Millar, p. 227.
49. Costello and van de Kamp, p. 64.
50. On re-reading, I see that this sentence in itself is nothing more than a politically corrected Implag. There is no "might" about it. Benjamin actually did say this. See his "Theses on the Philosophy of History", in *Illuminations*, ed. by Hannah Arendt, tr. by Harry Zohn (Glasgow,

tion to Gray's admission of widescale textual pilfering ought to be the same as that with which we greet a politician's disclosure of an error of judgment: we should search for the greater evil eclipsed by the divulged lesser. Blockplags, Implags and Difplags are purloinments of a trifling, juvenile, but ultimately tolerable character. But to admit them as part of a strategy to conceal the graver atrocities of Concplag and Totplag is hardly vindicable. It is the duty of literary scholarship to tear asunder the veils that prevent recognition of such duplicity.

VII

In quieter moments, when my spleen gives way to a more philosophical disposition – often following the consumption of a medicinal draught, mind-expanding substance or realist novel – I find my whirling thoughts coming to a centre in the question of what the words would be, were he by my side, that my admirable old *grand-père* would utter in summation of the unhappy history it has been my sorry and profitless duty here to recount. The words that I hear are not any of his own, but those of a great poet and contemporary, who was also incidentally a notorious practitioner of plagiarism, and whose lines I shall therefore reproduce without accreditation, as they may not even be his own:

> After such knowledge, what forgiveness? Think now
> History has many cunning passages, contrived corridors
> And issues, deceives with whispering ambitions,
> Guides us by vanities. Think now
> She gives when our attention is distracted

Fontana, 1973), p. 258, where he is describing the cultural consequences of the domination of the working by the ruling class – by way of a Bellonic metaphor – in words that equally well depict the usurpation of Ouvrier which Gray exultantly enacts: "Whoever has emerged victorious participates to this day in the triumphal procession in which the present rulers step over those who are lying prostrate. According to traditional practice, the spoils are carried along in the procession. They are called cultural treasures, and a historical materialist views them with cautious detachment. For without exception the cultural treasures he surveys have an origin which he cannot contemplate without horror. They owe their existence not only to the efforts of those who have created them, but also to the anonymous toil of their contemporaries. There is no document of civilization which is not at the same time a document of barbarism."

And what she gives, gives with such supple confusions
That the giving famishes the craving. Gives too late
What's not believed in, or if still believed,
In memory only, reconsidered passion. Gives too soon
Into weak hands, what's thought can be dispensed with
Till the refusal propagates a fear. Think
Neither fear nor courage saves us. Unnatural vices
Are fathered by our heroism. Virtues
Are forced upon us by our impudent crimes.
These tears are shaken from the wrath-bearing tree.

Macdonald Daly is Lecturer in Modern Literature at the University of Nottingham. His *Engels on Video*, a book of short stories written with Ellis Sharp, has just been published by Zoilus Press.

6 October 1994

Edinburgh Review
22 George Square
Edinburgh   EH8 9LF

Sir,

   I have received MacDonald Daly's essay *Lanark Exposed*, which claims that my first novel was written by his maternal grandfather, Sidney Ouvrier. You obviously want to know if I will use the law to prevent its publication. Cheer up. *Lanark Exposed* shows the effect of more than one of my fictions on a nit-picking academic whose brain has been addled by a deranged form of ancestor worship. To exhibit his delusions in a law court would be like trying to cure a bad case of leprosy by whipping the leper. I will not do it. The Edinburgh Review may "expose" *Lanark* without risking a penny.

   In a footnote to his thesis Mr. Daly says he will not make public a scrap of evidence which supports it because "Gray's litigiousness, as his much publicised action over the staging of one of his plays in the 1980s showed, is not worth provoking." If he publicly accused me of murder, while explaining he had better withhold the proof because it was not worthwhile interesting the police, then neither the police, nor the intelligent public, nor myself could take him seriously. Mr. Daly (fortunately for himself) has nothing but falsehood in common with the director of plays I took to court in 1987. The latter accepted my play *The Fall of Kelvin Walker* for production, changed the words without consulting me, staged it without inviting me to see it, yet advertised it under my name. I closed his theatre to stop the promotion of a mutilated text. The text of *Lanark* is immune to Mr Daly's fantasies. Had he the power he would publish it without my Epilogue, would change the author's name, probably attach his insanely detailed "exposure" as an introduction, and of course grab my royalties. Since he will never wield such power I can smile at him, not unkindly.

         Yrs truly,

         Alasdair Gray

            Alasdair Gray

Two Poems

Thom Nairn

Untouched by Corruption
(Boris Pasternak: 1890-1960)

And death stood there, like an official,
Between the headstones in the grove,
And stared at me as though to gauge
The right dimensions of the grave.

(Boris Pasternak, 'August'
Selected Poems pp. 135-136)

Past shadows in strange halls,
Passing friends and strangers,
Not so distant
Darkening dreams of familiars.

This one's faced as rough as turf,
Stalking the New Town,
Mean as a wall with teeth to kill.

He's there, as,
Grey-lean and streaked as a ferret,
The old harridan presides
Over another lunch
Of wine at Cafe Biarritz.

Far from still or content,
Pasternak's shadow passes,
Soundless from his corner table:
Silhouetted-gaunt, the jaw dark,
Hard eyes still wandering other worlds,
The places the poems draw from,

Pulled as meticulously as gleaming teeth,
Hard. Tight. Shiny.
But discursive,

Elusive and travelling
With that same coldness,
Tough roughness and precision
The face holds out.
But smirking and quietly calculating,
He steps out from this old world,

(Pencil in yellow teeth, notebook in hip-pocket,
Mangled Levis leaving dust stains
On immaculate flooring),

Steps into a new world and
Onto the edge of someone
Else's Revolution.

Noting the date,
He opens both eyes wide,
Gets down to the business of
Scribbling another strange world into
Some kind of shape.

Sky – Burial

1
Your back was animal lithe and warm
In the night, though you slept deep,
Its power and force reached through me.
The low quiet touch of my fingers
Crackling in the night
      From the prickling, the frightening,
         Of invisible fur.

Turning deep, breathing, moving over to
The night and the wind
Sweeping trees with missed punches,
Rain pounding for welcoming earth
And finding too often hard glass
To waste and shatter
Life and immaculate structure,
The cold stone sucks deep too,
Its children are new forms
From its own disintegration,
Reintegration. The stone takes time
To find its own space and time, shape and home.
'There are no ruined stones'.

2
Your silence, stillness, warmth,
    (Your back a white ghost
    In the back of my closed eyes,
    And, opening,
    You glow in the twisted half-shadows,
    Dark roots closing and
    Light swelling relentless at that
    Glass and the fragile cloth
    And its cold and damp implicit edge
    From the rain and the wind),
Your prickling, frightening, invisible fur.
Bristling at the world and all it can throw.
This can be way far back, somewhere forward.

3
And an old dog growls and howls
In the night near my window,
A friend, I know him, a prowler,
A ghost and traveller
Who lives in a different place
Of caves and islands:
    Shadows of cloud
        Moving like lean, dark fish
            On a shallow edge of depths.
Hawks and buzzards
    Weighing the balance, in balance,
    Of the nothing that's not there
    And the nothing that is
    Or might be.
Diving at shadows in a clear moon
With a high wind
Maybe should be undertaken lightly

To realise the brash panic
Of illusion
In icy water
Wild as an animal,
To run with the land,
    With the water
    Under the dawn
    With open eyes
    And fight
    To rise.

4
And working, working on secret signals,
    (The prickling, the frightening),
New codes and codas
For when, for a time, faces may be gone,
    (The wind sweeping trees with missed punches),
For a next world around,
    (Roots closing and light swelling),
And working hard on this,
Working closer into a place
This may be already.
    (A friend, I know him, a prowler),
Dead in a new place

We haven't registered yet.
    (Icy water, wild as an animal),
Talks of coldness,
A sharp bird in the night:
    Something like silence
        Has never left.

5
My black, long coat hangs on a nail
Like a bat on the wall,
Tired as the moon must be.

The night and the dark and the wind,
Ghosts and travellers, caves, islands,
The night growls, I whisper to my candle.

Touch the long lean coil of your spine,
The lean long blonde of the hair rising.
Old coal crackles
In a low warm glow,
    Still kicks off the dawn.
    This is the good place,
    Wrapped around with stone,
    With blankets
        Candle and fire.
    The prickling, the frightening
        Of invisible fur.
Working on new signals in silence,
Diving at shadows in a clear moon,
For when, for a time, faces may be gone.

(I must acknowledge allusion, theft and very free translation from the work of Wallace Stevens, Hugh MacDiarmid and Eugenio Montale).

Thom Nairn was born in Perthshire in 1955. He is co-editor of *Cencrastus*, and his poetry and criticism have been published widely in magazines and anthologies. His first collection of poems, *The Sand Garden*, appeared in 1994. He is currently working on a new book of poems, *Sky Burial*, and a prose/poetry collection, *Animal Heads*.

TALUS

Journal of Creative Writing & Inter-Cultural Studies

TALUS appears twice a year,
& publishes new poetry, fiction & drama,
as well as essays investigating inter-cultural materials,
area studies, & suitable artwork.

Past issues have included work by:
*Amiri Baraka, Eric Mottram, Bill Griffiths, Anne Waldman
Clayton Eshleman, Allen Ginsberg, Joel Oppenheimer
Robert Kelly, Ronald Sukenick, Denise Levertov
Ishmael Reed, Bob Cobbing, Jerome Rothenberg
Allen Fisher, Roseanne Wasserman
Tom Raworth, Barbara Guest*

Price per issue:

Individuals	£5.00	$10.00
Institutions	£10.00	$20.00

Annual Subscription:

Individuals	£10.00	$20.00
Institutions	£20.00	$40.00

Some back issues are still available at reduced rates

Second class postage is included.
British subscribers please make cheques payable to **TALUS**.
Other subscribers should pay by £ Sterling,
$ Dollar Travellers Cheques, or International Money Order.

Please write to:

TALUS
Department of English
King's College
Strand
LONDON WC2R 2LS

REVIEWS

BERTHOLD SCHOENE: Andrew Grieg,
Western Swing

MURDO MACDONALD: Timothy Neat,
Part Seen, Part Imagined

LISA BABINEC: Colin Manlove,
Scottish Fantasy Literature

MARIO RELICH: Allan Massie, *The Ragged Lion*

ANDREW GRIEG: Duncan McLean, *Blackden*

WILLY MALEY: Jacques Derida, *Specters of Marx*

ELIZABETH BURNS: New Poetry

Western Swing: Adventures with the Heretical Buddha
Andrew Greig
Bloodaxe Books 1994
ISBN 1 85224 268 X pbk £7.95

In this half-dramatic, half-narrative 'longpoem', a sequel to *Men on Ice*, Greig transports his readers from Glencoe to Fife with intermittent stops at places as various and eclectic as Kathmandu, Cambridge, Dublin, the High Atlas Mountains, Marrakech and the ancient Scottish kingdom of Dalriada. His protagonist, indifferently called 'I', strikes us as a Scottish J. Alfred Prufrock of the 1990s, who is just as much afraid, as determined to face up to the post-Christian, even post-existentialist human condition, and to explore the 'overwhelming question' of what his life is actually all about.

In the aftermath of 'yet another grotty scheme' of the heart, Greig's hero wakes to find himself 'alone,/ bereft and empty as a sheath/whose blade is gone'. His personality has completely disintegrated, his self lies shattered – literally. Ken, his mind, has absconded to pursue an academic career in Cambridge; Stella, his heart, has committed herself to a hospital where she regularly overdoses on Tedium; while Brock, his body, is badly hungover and clearly incapable of emerging from his squalor and booze-induced mental stupor toward a single straight thought or action. If it weren't for the encouragement of HB, the Heretical Buddha, a trickster-like demigod or superego who plays the part of both guardian and guide, 'I' would probably not even consider embarking on the quest 'for better beer and synthesis' which inspires the elegant and pleasantly melodious free-verse rhythm of Greig's *Western Swing*.

The longpoem is clearly inspired by the famous poetic sequences of Hugh MacDiarmid, T. S. Eliot and Ezra Pound, particularly *A Drunk Man Looks at the Thistle*, *The Waste Land* and *The Cantos*. Greig openly acknowledges this intertextual indebtedness in five appended pages of notes, in themselves an imitation of Eliot's or even Alasdair Gray's deliberate idiosyncrasies. However, Greig's poem is a far more daring and ambitious enterprise than that of any of his precursors. It aspires to weld, rather than merely juxtapose, samples from sources as diverse as Robert Henryson's *Testament of Cresseid* on the one hand and song lyrics by Lou Reed, David Bowie, John Lennon and Talking Heads on the other. The aim is a seamless, rather than self-consciously fragmentary, text that attempts to equal in both scope and imagination 'the plurality (literary, linguistic, artistic and social) of a culture and a generation'.

Due to the fragmentation of the protagonist into discrete individual personae, who stand for different constituents of the human self, *Western Swing* is loaded with allegorical meaning. This suggests parallels with two contemporary Scottish allegories: George Mackay Brown's *Time in a Red Coat* and Iain Banks' *The Bridge*. Both Brock in *Western Swing* and the Primitive Swordsman in *The Bridge* speak 'barbaric' Scots. Like the narrative movement in *Western Swing*, the quest of the archetypal princess in Brown's book takes us to several foreign countries before it finds resolution in Scotland. Banks's novel explores the multilayered complexity of the human consciousness before eventually reuniting the different narrative strands when the hero's identity emerges intact from a coma. The same desire for oneness pervades Greig's poem: 'The shards of my psyche/are come together again [...] and finally they slept as One.' These three books share a pursuit of synthetic closure in the creation of a myth of the self and, in consequence, their apparent imperviousness to the inevitable aporetic pitfalls of postmodernist literature.

The central figure of *Western Swing* is both a man determined to re-establish his identity as an intact individual human being, and the country of Scotland as a whole eager to re-assemble its multifarious parts and acknowledge its intrinsic plurality: '[...] the many voices of my land/hissed like drizzle on the tent/as I lay listening/for the ordering within...'. The Dual Blade, the central object of the quest, is 'a healing blade', indicative of Greig's wish that the dissection of the Scottish self in compliance with absurd theoretical models like that of an innate 'Caledonian antisyzygy', and the compartmentalisation of the Scottish nation into Highlanders and Lowlanders, Catholics and Protestants, traditionalists and progressives as well as Gaelic-speakers, Scots-speakers and English-speakers, may please soon come to an end. It is high time to ring out this century of division. Those who still have 'nothing in their hands except/the very ordinary knives of death' are greeted with 'Nurse! Clear these clowns outa here,/their century is ending.'

As with Christopher Marlowe's *Doctor Faustus*, the central sections of Greig's *Western Swing* are problematic. The actual adventures of Stella, Ken, Brock, 'I' and HB frequently appear as mere digressions from the book's main concern. Moreover, these sections are far less spell-binding in their poetic realisation than the first and last parts of the book, with the exception of masterpieces like 'A Munelicht Flittin (run through the MacDiarmidtron)' and 'Stella after the Monkey-Man'. Good old-fashioned prose might in many instances have been a better choice than a poetic narrative that is too sketchy to be truly informative, and too desultory in its metric and stanzaic structure to be artistically convincing.

The middle parts of *Western Swing* also suffer from Greig's perfunctory and rather facetious description of an encounter between his Scottish 'tourists' and a gang of Arabic terrorists. To the reader's embarrassment, the Scots escape unharmed because they are neither American nor British but Scottish, thus capable of conjuring up a sense of solidarity between members of 'stateless' nations whose fight for political independence is supposedly comparable, if not – as suggested here – a common cause. Equally tenuous is Greig's allusion to parallels between the world views and living conditions of Moroccan mountain villagers, almost entirely untouched by twentieth-century progress, and Scottish tourists of the 1990s. Due to their hereditary 'peasant's mentality', Greig's Scots not only get away with the intrusive curiosity and naive cosmopolitanism that is so characteristic of Western tourism, they turn out to be born diplomats who actively contribute to world peace and international understanding. It is also unfortunate that his quest for unity of self introduces Greig's hero to nothing more exciting than the rigid role patterns of a blissful kailyard domesticity. In the end we are left with the clichéd image of a Scottish male stereotype. A forty-year-old father-to-be, contentedly resigned to the complete uneventfulness of his future existence, muses by the fireside about his own little private happiness of having found the perfectly complementary wife. When he first met her 'in a quiet street in Fife', she was wearing a silver panama hat with a black band that strikingly matched his own hat, black with a silver band. It was love at first sight.

Rather than flawed or even remotely unsuccessful, Greig's *Western Swing* strikes me as simply much too short for what it is trying to achieve. If only it *were* 'thick enough to crush a crustacean'. It is without doubt a very interesting attempt, and does make a thoroughly enjoyable read. The 'Prologue' and 'Endscript' constitute two of the most memorably compelling celebrations of the questing human spirit and its vulnerability in the whole of Scottish poetry.

Berthold Schoene

Part Seen, Part Imagined
Timothy Neat
Canongate Publishing 1994
ISBN 0 86241 366 4 £25 hb

Timothy Neat's *Part Seen, Part Imagined: Meaning and Symbolism in the Work of Charles Rennie Mackintosh and Margaret Macdonald* is perhaps the most interesting commentary to be published about Mackintosh and his circle since Thomas Howarth's pioneering *Charles Rennie Mackintosh and the Modern Movement* in 1952. Forty years on, Howarth's book is still a quarry for the curious researcher, and to return to it is to cast off the stereotypes that have tended to bind 'The Four' in the intervening years.

One of the most durable of these is that Mackintosh is best understood as a proto-modernist whose work leads inexorably to the abstractions and simplifications of the machine ethic, held to define art produced between about 1900 and about 1950. Re-reading Howarth reminds us that while such a view is not entirely wrong (indeed Mackintosh was one of the first to use the word 'modernism' with respect to art) it misses a great many points. One way of beginning to explore these missed points is to note the significance that is accorded by Howarth to the Celtic revival in the work of these Glasgow artists. It is somewhat ironic to note Howarth's words: 'Undoubtedly one of the most potent stimuli in the evolution of the Glasgow style, and one that has been generally overlooked, was the incipient Celtic revival in Scotland.' This general oversight has continued for almost half a century, but at last, with Timothy Neat's book, the Celtic revival takes its place at the heart of the work of The Four. Neat concentrates on the work of Mackintosh and Margaret Macdonald, and here the other great strength of his book emerges, for he emphasises the collaborative evolution of their style. Neat's account of the total intellectual and emotional engagement between these two people provides a convincing context for both the quality and the integrated nature of the art which was forthcoming.

Macdonald's significance in her own right has, of course, become increasingly clear over the last few years, not least as a result of the 'Glasgow Girls' exhibition and book. In *Part Seen, Part Imagined* Neat develops some of the thoughts he put forward in his contribution to that earlier work. The central point is that whether one turns to a work of architecture such as Mackintosh's Glasgow School of Art, or to a panel such as Macdonald's *Opera of the Seas*, one can fully appreciate neither unless one appreciates the thinking behind them as symbolist. A fundamental part of this symbolist thinking is Celtic revival thinking. The other crucial symbolist element for Neat is the Rosicrucian philosophy (which, most clearly through W. B. Yeats, has a direct connection to Celtic revivalism). This is a fascinating argument, well put and well explored; if at times Neat's enthusiasm pushes it further than is probable, that is a small price to pay. Neat's involvement with his subject in turn enthuses the reader. He is the antithesis of the dry historian (and the odd dry historian may feel threatened by this), introducing a document which is a creative and relevant interaction with the work, in which the works, and lives, of Mackintosh and Macdonald live again for us.

What Timothy Neat has done in this book is to half-open a door which Thomas Howarth opened a crack. Yet, paradoxically, it is by returning to Howarth that we get the clue as to how the door can be opened fully. Howarth does great service by linking the Celtic revival as manifested in Glasgow with that of Edinburgh, the former in the persons of The Four and their associates, the latter in the group which gathered around Patrick Geddes. This explicit linkage between the Geddes group and the Mackintosh group is a lost but crucial piece of Scottish cultural history, which is slowly beginning to find recognition. It gives context to the fact that it was Geddes who intervened on Mackintosh's behalf when, due to his interest in drawing and his 'foreign' accent he was arrested as a spy in the English county of Suffolk at the beginning of the First World War. It also gives context to the recent discovery that Geddes commissioned plans for some of his Indian projects from Mackintosh. Neat is not unaware of this link, but he does not pursue it. Nevertheless a tantalising hint of the further possibilities in this direction is given in the following passage:

> The Celtic flavour of The Four was strong in its will towards a rhythmical abstraction, in its use of multi-evocative and apparently indecipherable imagery. They all carried their 'Macs' with pride. The only signed book known to have been owned by Margaret Macdonald is MacPherson's heroic eighteenth-century fiction, *Ossian*. Both Mackintosh and Macnair worked as young men on the reconstruction of St Columba's Cathedral on Iona, where the book of Kells was created. Mackintosh's father was brought up in Morayshire, where the Gaelic language would have been a natural reality of everyday life in his childhood ... it was he

who, as very keen gardener, developed in the young and slightly sickly Charles an undying love of flowers. It was, however, the very British John Ruskin who revealed to Mackintosh the architectural potentiality of plant and flower symbolism. Ruskin's vision and advocacy was precise: 'we cannot all have our gardens now, nor pleasant fields to meditate in at evening time. Then the function of our architecture is, as far as it may be, to replace these; to tell us about Nature; to possess us with memories of her quietness ... full of delicate imagery of the flowers we can no longer gather.' [*The Stones of Venice*, I. ch. xxx.]

One wonders if the *Ossian* which Margaret Macdonald owned was the 1896 centenary edition introduced and edited by William Sharp, and published by Patrick Geddes and Colleagues at the Outlook Tower in Edinburgh. It is tempting to assume this, but whether it was this edition or not, the Ossianic link is made. Similarly, the fact that in his *Masques of Learning* Geddes attached such importance to the restoration of Iona Cathedral; that Fiona Macleod (William Sharp) wrote about Iona; that another of Geddes's colleagues, Victor Branford, wrote a biography of Columba; that both Mackintosh and McNair worked on the restoration of the cathedral, speaks volumes. As does the fact that the edition of *Ossian* mentioned above has a title page Celtic-interlace decoration, probably by John Duncan, Helen Hay, or Helen Baxter, which takes its inspiration from the Book of Kells.

There is still a tendency to underestimate the quality of the art produced by these and other members of the group of artists around Geddes. This may be partly because the most often repeated comment about Geddes's magazine *The Evergreen* is a negative but memorable one by H. G. Wells: 'Bad from cover to cover, and even the covers are bad.' This is clever enough, but it can hardly be taken as serious criticism. In this context it's interesting to find Timothy Neat noting (p. 176) that Mackintosh had similar problems with Wells, and completely rejected his views on art (Wells saw art as being a kind of delightful, spare-time decoration to the serious business of life, by which he meant science, war, commerce etc). Thus much more relevant than Wells in any attempt to assess the contribution of the artists around Geddes is the fact that the year after the first *Evergreen* was published two of the artists, John Duncan and Robert Burns, had had their works reproduced in the definitive *Of the Decorative Illustration of Books, Old and New*, by Walter Crane, published in London by George Bell in 1896. Helping Crane select for this book was none other than Gleeson White, the influential editor of *The Studio*, the magazine which helped to bring both Aubrey Beardsley and The Glasgow Four to prominence. If one is to begin to be interested in the contribution of the likes of John Duncan, Helen Hay and Robert Burns, it is with the considered assessment of Gleeson White and Walter Crane (or indeed Thomas Howarth) that one must start, not with the scientism of H. G. Wells.

Neat's further references to Mackintosh's awareness of Gaelic, and the importance to him of his father introducing him to gardening, have a quite uncanny correspondence to Geddes's childhood experiences. The influence of Ruskin on both is another point of contact, and here one could develop the argument that the 'very British' Ruskin is to all intents and purposes part of the Scottish intellectual tradition, as his two earliest biographers, Collingwood and Harrison, point out. A heritage shared by Ruskin, Mackintosh and Geddes is of some considerable interest.

It's not my intention to suggest that Timothy Neat should have covered these points in his book. The point is that by writing this book, he has helped to clear the way for a new approach, not only to Mackintosh and Macdonald, but to the intellectual and artistic culture of late-nineteenth-century Scotland as a whole. Scottish history has been routinely excluded and misrepresented by 'British' histories, but this late-nineteenth-century period has suffered more than most. The light that Timothy Neat has shed is to be greatly welcomed.

Murdo Macdonald

Scottish Fantasy Literature: A Critical Survey
Colin Manlove
Canongate Academic 1994
ISBN 1 898 410208 £16.99 hb

As I stood browsing in James Thin's, I felt a ripple of excitement as my eyes touched upon Colin Manlove's new book, *Scottish Fantasy Literature: A Critical Survey*. My spirits rose as I read the list of authors it was to cover: James Hogg, Thomas Carlyle, George MacDonald, Margaret Oliphant, Robert Louis Stevenson, J. M. Barrie, Alasdair Gray, and Margaret Elphinstone among others; in short, a star-studded cast of Scottish fantasy writers.

My spirits were dampened somewhat as I read the flyleaf: 'At last Scottish literary criticism's long-held bias towards realism finds a counter-balance in this, the first major study of Scottish fantasy' which establishes 'the existence of a strong yet largely unrecognised genre in Scottish writing'. Correct me if I'm wrong, but isn't the bias in Scottish literary studies clearly towards fantasy, and isn't it true that the fantasy genre from oral tales of the supernatural to the writings of MacDonald, Stevenson, Gray, and Elphinstone has been well-established and prevailed as an object of academic study for a very long time? To be sure, no scholarly text has yet solely focused on fantasy in the Scottish literary tradition, but many a critical article or excerpt from surveys, edited collections, and texts on selected authors proudly heralds the long tradition of fantasy in Scottish literature. Perhaps I am making too much of Canongate Academic's inaccurate claim, so let's return to the text itself.

As I continued to leaf through the book, I came to a plate section with portraits and photographs of the individual authors. A nice idea to present readers with visual images of each writer. To my surprise and consternation, the illustrations were not left to speak for themselves; rather, Manlove draws conclusions about each author's character from the features of the face and position of the body in the snapshot. Of Alasdair Gray

Manlove writes, 'a coolly interrogative Gray, whose narrow lips and strong nose, together with the sheer hairiness of aspect, sufficiently suggest the academic manqué who has outdone all academics', and on Margaret Elphinstone he describes the 'mixture of warmth and shyness in the features ... countered in the exact and piercing eyes'. The very presence of comments such as these are laughable, especially within the context of a book of literary criticism, and leads me to ask whether Manlove thinks of himself as a literary critic or a physiognomist.

Illustrations and my personal distaste for physiognomy aside, there are a number of problems with Manlove's study. Much of the analysis rests on anecdote and description and often includes curtailed generalisations about individual stories and novels. For instance, on Andrew Lang's *The Princess Nobody: A Tale of Fairy Land*, *Prince Prigio*, and *Prince Ricardo of Pantouflia, being the Adventures of Prince Prigio's Son*, Manlove notes, '[t]he emphasis is light, comic and above all on wit: indeed it is Prince Prigio's problem that he is made too clever by half by one of his fairy godmothers, and must learn to tone it down'; likewise, on George Mackay Brown's story 'Sealskin' he comments, 'in "Sealskin" he describes the unhappy marriage of a seal-woman to a fisherman, and how she finally leaves him and escapes back to her kind in the sea'. Manlove does not differentiate between children and adult fantasy, discussing MacDonald's *At the Back of the North Wind*, *The Princess and the Goblin*, and *The Princess and Curdie*, Lang's *The Gold of Fairnilee*, and C. S. Lewis's *The Chronicles of Narnia* alongside James Hogg's *The Private Memoirs and Confessions of a Justified Sinner* and Alasdair Gray's *Lanark* without ever considering the different motivations or preconceived audiences behind fantasy literature for either children or adults. Manlove's interpretation hinges on his own subjective impressions, and his book for the most part displays a lack of critical awareness both in terms of critical theory and previous critical analyses of Scottish fantasy literature by a variety of literary scholars.

If the flaws listed above were the only flaws in the study, my initial disappointment might have waned. However, as I continued to read the book, my disappointment magnified as Manlove frequently offered appalling misreadings of authors in highly prejudicial terms. For instance, he contends that William Sharp, 'Fiona Macleod', 'was sexually dimorphic, but for him that dimorphism related to areas of the mind rather than to compulsions of the body' and 'it is ironic that the "swimminess" he so felt to be a part of the feminine is not reflected in many women writers'. He asserts that in Margaret Oliphant's story 'The Open Door' the ghost is that of a youth who haunts the scene of his mother's long-past death, too foolish and weak-witted to realise that, as the minister who finally releases him tells him, her soul has long since gone to heaven', only to contradict this reading on the following page with 'the spirit in "The Open Door" is refusing the true open door, that of heaven'. He believes '*Lanark* has one feature in common with many other Scottish fantasies: the hero is in some sense a freak' while most English fantasies 'deal with "perfectly normal" individuals'.

More problematic, though, Manlove appears to be lost in a gender time-warp. He suggests that in all of Margaret Elphinstone's works 'we find the steady pressure of a feminist view' as well as 'that simple, tentative, delicate quality of woman that [she] puts over rather less as plain description than as a programme for living'. He goes on to conclude that since nearly all her novels and stories put 'women and women's values' at the centre, the 'result is a certain one-sidedness, and one which over long distances, as in the novels, can be stifling'. At this point I must ask that over the long distance, who doesn't find the urban and emotional despair in *Lanark* stifling? Finally, Manlove's concluding remarks highlight the central role of women in Scottish fantasy literature even in Hogg's *Confessions* 'where the "masculine" brother is killed and the effeminate one dominates the story', in Brown's *Magnus* which 'gives us a gentle, "womanly" man as hero, and in Margaret Elphinstone who 'is overtly feminist, to the point where her women take on some "male" heroic characteristics'. I can only throw my hands up in horror at the use of such explosive and outdated stereotypes which promote dangerously vague and abstract notions that cannot be called anything but myopic. Sentiments such as these do nothing to enhance our understanding of Scottish fantasy literature and reveal a disturbing separateness from debates connected to feminism and gender studies which have become central to Scottish literary studies.

My criticisms of the book do not mean to suggest that his study has nothing to offer. Quite the contrary, for the book does on occasion advance constructive and detailed analysis of individual texts; namely, of the philosophy of clothes in Carlyle's *Sartor Resartus*, of patterns which MacDonald weaves in *Phantastes*, of the inability to escape from one's self in Stevenson's *Jekyll and Hyde*, and of the emphasis of the unconscious in David Lindsay's *A Voyage to Arcturus*. Nevertheless, all too often Manlove tantalizes us with provocative one-liners which he then fails to develop. A case in point comes from Oliphant's story 'The Library Window' of which Manlove argues that for the young female protagonist 'it is clearly implied that her vision of this figure could be a sexual projection, and yet at the same time it is also much more than that'. The questions which remain are patent: why and how is the young protagonist's vision sexual and what, exactly, is implied by 'much more than that'? These questions, and many others evoked by equally elliptic commentary, continue to encroach as we move further into Manlove's study.

On finishing *Scottish Fantasy Literature* the reader is left with a number of unanswered questions and an overwhelming desire for clarity. What's more, because Manlove's argument reads more like a series of articles on individual works, he fails to deliver a cohesive interpretation of an entire literary tradition. This consistent failure to contextualise authors and texts or to discuss the different motives and types of fantasy which emerge across the centuries is bound to leave readers wondering where the

Scottish fantasy tradition derives from, how it all fits together, and what the long-standing and comprehensive use of fantasy devices says about Scottish literature and Scotland as a whole. In the end, rather than the 'first major study' we are promised at the outset, we are left with yet another perfunctory survey of Scottish literature sadly deficient in literary criticism.

Lisa Babinec

The Ragged Lion
Allan Massie
Hutchinson 1994
ISBN 0 09 177412 8 £15.99

It is foolish to encourage people to expect mottoes and such like Decoraments. You have no credit for success in finding them and there is a disgrace in wanting them. It is like being in the habit of shewing feats of strength which you at length gain no praise by accomplishing while there is some shame occurs in failure.
Sir Walter Scott, *Journal*
(24 March 1826)

The Ragged Lion, despite many favourable reviews, is likely to disappoint those curious about Sir Walter Scott, and irritate others familiar with 'The Great Unknown'. Supposedly a recently 'discovered' autobiographical memoir, it is certainly readable, even entertaining, but it falls far short, perhaps inevitably, of Scott's genuine autobiographical writings. Massie's sources include the great man's own short 'Memoir', used by Lockhart to form the first chapter in his biography of 'the Author of *Waverley*', and Scott's rather more considerable *Journal*. Much more of Scott's private side is revealed in the *Journal* than in the 'Memoir'.

Unfortunately for Massie, Scott's *Journal* has been in the public domain for quite a long time, and its artistry is of such a high order that although Lockhart could plunder from it, a novelist doing so seems rather less justifiable. Almost anticipating such spoil-sport criticism, Massie's 'Introduction', in which he describes how he came across the 'lost' manuscript (in a manner tediously similar to how the lost 'autobiography' of *Augustus* was found) makes this bold assertion: 'Certain passages resemble parts of the *Journal* very closely – often indeed almost word for word; others bear an equally striking resemblance to sentences or paragraphs in Lockhart's biography. It could therefore be a fabrication made chiefly from these sources'. The conspiracy with the reader here is that he or she should allow the novelist to have his cake and eat it. *The Ragged Lion*, nevertheless, reads too much like 'a fabrication made chiefly from these sources'.

The 'Afterword', purportedly by Sir Walter Scott's son, pretty much gives the game away in this extract:

> For my part, I incline to the possibility that the whole manuscript was composed during the last year of his life, and mostly during his sojourn in Italy; but it was contrived in such a manner as to appear otherwise, and to be a disconnected, yet roughly chronological, record of what occupied his mind in the last five or six years of his life. If this is so, it will be properly regarded, I believe, as a remarkable feat of intellectual

and imaginative effort to have been performed by one as sorely afflicted as he was in these unhappy months.

It is up to the reader to decide whether *The Ragged Lion* itself can be considered 'a remarkable feat of intellectual and imaginative effort' on Massie's part.

While what Massie's Scott calls a 'ragged memoir' looks back at his entire life, even if selectively, the original *Journal* is more coherent. It records much of crucial importance about Scott's final years, when he wrote heroically against the clock to avoid bankruptcy, and stoically endured the death of his wife after a long illness. David Hewitt, editor of the very useful *Scott on Himself*, has rightly said about the *Journal*, 'there is no greater or moving diary in English'. It testifies not only to Scott's acute powers of observation, but also his ability to recreate living moments and to face his own anxieties in unflinching manner.

Here is an excerpt about Castlereagh and Stanhope, both friends who had committed suicide:

> He is gone, and my friend Stanhope also, whose kindness this town so strongly recalls. It is remarkable they were the only persons of sense and credibility who both attested supernatural appearances on their own evidence, and both died in the same melancholy manner. I shall always tremble when any friend of mine becomes visionary. (1 Nov. 1826)

Such a passage reveals a very tough-minded Scott, suspicious of 'supernatural solicitings', however much he uses them in his fiction, but it appears to provide the hint for Massie's Scott, who is rather more soft-centred, self-absorbed, and even drily academic in the following passage:

> Now – when I have learned to know better the wayward motions of my own mind, when that energy which formerly surged forth and led me into the realms of imaginative creation, seems turned in on itself, when I work with difficulty and dream dreams that disturb me, I have a better understanding of poor Castlereagh's terrors. For it seems likely to me now that they were the expression of that duality of which I have written; that in his disordered terror he gave vent to that Double whose existence he had denied, suppressed, drowned in a flood of activity, and which now revenged itself on him in his weakness. For in my weakness, between waking and sleeping, I have been afflicted by like fancies and images – though taking a different form from his, equally horrible and alarming.

Here, Scott speaks more like Karl Miller in his book on *Doubles* (in Scottish and English fiction) than the great writer in his twilight months haunted by guilt. The chapter in which these musings occur is entitled 'Of Death and Dreams', but there is something too pat and ersatz about Massie's Scott in this mood.

More generally, Massie's Scott is heavily compromised by his own view of the novelist as a kind of cultural, eminently Scottish, yet also unionist and cosmopolitan, role-model. That Massie believes such a role-model is urgently needed in Scotland today can be gauged from an observation in his recent book on *Edinburgh*: 'Scottish intellectual life has no characteristic impetus of its own, but exists as a paler copy of life being lived more intensely elsewhere'. The same stricture can, ironically, be applied to how *The Ragged Lion* 'palely copies' Scott's *Journal*.

One living moment recorded in Scott's *Journal* describes his meeting with John James Audubon, the American ornithologist famed for his drawings of birds:

> Visit from Mr. Audubon, who brings some of his birds. The drawings are of the first order – the attitudes of the birds of the most animated character, and the situations appropriate; one of a snake attacking a bird's nest, while the birds (the parents) peck at the reptile's eyes – they usually, in the long run, destroy him, says the naturalist. The feathers of these gay little sylphs, most of them from the Southern States, are most brilliant, and are represented with what, were it (not) connected with so much spirit in the attitude, I would call a laborious degree of execution. This extreme correctness is of the utmost consequence to the naturalist, (but) as I think (having no knowledge of *virtu*), rather gives a stiffness to the drawings. (24 Jan. 1827)

Here, Scott makes Audubon's drawings come dramatically to life, revealing at the same time why he does not find them of high artistic merit. He could appreciate the scientific accuracy with which Audubon depicted birds, but felt the drawings lacked that spark of life he called *virtu*.

Similarly, *The Ragged Lion* is certainly admirable for the way it sustains the illusion of Scott revealing his most private thoughts to the reader, but Massie's achievement is more a case of 'virtual reality' than the *virtu* Scott demanded from any kind of artist.

Mario Relich

Blackden
Duncan McLean
Secker 1994
ISBN 0 436 27632 1 £9.99 pb

What kind of writer was I going to be? A story teller. What kind of storyteller? An honest storyteller. I mean, one who isn't trying to make a case, or impose in any way, who has no bias, who tries to let people and places reveal themselves as they are. (Duncan McLean)

A writer will tend to assume a reader who reads as carefully as the writer writes – but not many do. Despite the banner of 'Realism' and the apparent simplicity and lightness of the story, *Blackden* is very much a work of literary art that deserves and repays close, attentive reading.

Its true antecedents are not the Doric scene but writers like Kelman, Flaubert, Chekhov and Hemingway. It has the same scrupulousness, subtlety and ordering, for all the apparent 'naturalness' of the story. Like these writers, Duncan McLean has arrived at a narrative tone that is his own, at one with the story and the telling and the teller – an achievement which makes *Blackden*, for this writer at least, a true delight.

Though most of the *Blackden* reviews are positive, there is something muted in their enthusiasm. Even the best lack that suitable 'soundbite' to adorn the cover of the author's future novels (the next three are already planned). Reviewing is often a form of hurried and poorly-paid journalism masquerading as literary criticism, but the glaring mis-readings of *Blackden* are revealing.

Carl MacDougall in the *Herald*, though largely accurate and insightful, notes that the novel 'is mostly set in the present tense'. It isn't. Patrick Hunter's wander around Blackden is entirely in the past tense, conveyed with an immediacy which makes the narrative *feel* present. The *Independent on Sunday* review refers to 'the book's nationalism – almost deafening in opening pages packed with Scots vernacular'. The opening pages are certainly a *tour de force* of rural Scots, and a conscious tip of the cap towards Lewis Grassic Gibbon. But Nationalism? The only nationalist politics is the variety offered by Patrick's aunt, provoking one of the protagonist's most memorable rejoinders: 'I'd like the Scottish Nationalists more if they didn't have the word Nationalist in their title... Or Scottish... I reckon they should call it the Land and Water and Trees and Rain and Buildings Party. That way nobody gets left out...' Towards the end of the novel, he comes back to his aunt and tells her he definitely won't be attending the local Party meeting.

Particularly revealing here is the reviewer's equation of the use of words from a particular area with nationalism, deafening or otherwise. This anticipates the dismissal of James Kelman's Booker speech, a lucid defence of any culture's right to be heard, as 'Scottish Nationalism'. It is interesting that the same metropolitan establishment wouldn't think to label a writer using 'Standard English' as an English nationalist.

Even more myopically, reviews in *The Times* and *Elle* refer to 'teenage protagonists [living] on slummy estates in Scotland where drunkenness, violence, hopelessness and boredom are rife', and 'a raw slice of urban Scottish life'. This is enough to make one choke on a bannock. *Blackden* takes place entirely in a rural village with no estates, slummy or otherwise. There is drink taken (though hardly any by Patrick); degrees of frustration and potential aggression; but what is striking about the novel is the way in which it breaks with these distorting stereotypes of Scottish writing. These stereotypes have become powerful because they permit the laziness of tired labels like 'gritty urban realism'. Such terminology limits both writers and readers. Ironically, Kelman's literary integrity has made it possible for careless equations such as Scottish = Urban = 'Gritty' (or S.U.G. for short) to gain currency. So we find Scottish writing at the very moment of its highest achievement being backed into a new kailyard. The danger here is a real one, coming from within and without. Scottish writers may find their imaginations internally colonised by S.U.G., while editors, publishers and readers can sideline anything that does not meet their expectations of The Scottish Novel.

Blackden is to be valued because it takes the chance of breaking with these expectations. *Bucket of Tongues*, brutish, 'unflinching' and Kelman-esque, deserved its success: part of the bafflement and disappointment of those reviews is that the novel is not in the same vein. Defying such strong expectations takes considerable artistic courage.

Blackden is not just in a different vein, it's in a different arm. There is a striking generosity and affection emanating from the writer, from Patrick, from the relationships between the characters. As Young Hero, Patrick lacks the ego, narcissism and sense of personal superiority which characterises his counterparts in *Catcher in the Rye* and *Portrait of the Artist*. The reviews, though, kept referring to Patrick as 'alienated'. Again, this is lazy reading. It is essential to the Young Hero to feel apart, angry, misunderstood. But Patrick is uncertain, not angry. He has warm relationships with his aunt and grandfather, and a wary unspoken tenderness with his mother. He is deeply aware of, and respectful to, what he comes from. He gets on easily and well with practically everyone he meets. It is the very warmth and support he finds in his life in Blackden that makes it so hard for him to contemplate leaving. If not paradise, it is in its own way a tender trap. It is comforting and *known*.

Patrick's problem is not that he defines himself as different; it is rather that he can't define himself at all – which seems a more truthful account of the condition of being nineteen. The question of definition or identity is a theme which runs subtly through *Blackden* like an underground river, and only second or third readings reveal it. The author has suggested as a key to the book a quotation from Sartre: *We only become what we are by the deep-seated and radical refusal of that which others have made us*. Like Kelman, Duncan McLean is as much an existentialist as a realist, and the social reality in his work is selected and organised towards those concerns.

Throughout the two days of his whirl around Blackden, Patrick is offered a selection of causes, identities and self-definitions. His aunt offers political commitment. The minister offers him religion. He is offered one future as an auctioneer, another as a copywriter and general dogsbody in a project to market tea-towels of Great Scottish Battlefields, with a view to a postcard series of The Sun Sets on the Great Scottish Industries, by the entrepreneur Mr Brindle (who is not, as the reviewers assumed, English, but actually Scottish – from 'Queeniesomething'). He is offered roles as Local Lad in Pub, Town Clown, or Rebel. None of these will do, and all are refused – not violently, or with certainty, but almost regretfully.

The theme of identity laps around the feet of other characters. Pointedly, people are changed or defined by their work. Bill Murray, the breezy, confident auctioneer with the energetic patter, is dissociated from Bill Murray the possibly cuckolded husband. Then there is 'Shona Findlay the chef, and Shona Findlay the human being, and they hate each other's guts'. This blends Marx-Engels alienated labour with Sartre's 'inauthenticity' in a way which arises naturally from the story.

Far from being a simple 'slice of life', *Blackden* is patterned, shaped and selected throughout. Patrick's apparently random progress around his village involves meeting all the principal characters twice, and though each meeting is different, the sense of revolving around a small place is reinforced. The narrative is organised around three set-pieces emblematic of rural life: the roup, the dance, and the midnight curling-match. These are apparently straightforwardly depicted events with symbolic resonances: the roup, for example, involves the end of a working farm, the buildings bought by the incomer Brindle, and the tack and gear sold off to the locals. This is a sell-off and a sell-out: part of that ineluctable process of change in which Patrick, meditating on his forebears and his future in the peace of an old bothy, is symbolically caught.

Like Kelman's, McLean's form of 'realism' is anything but artless. It is expressed with a casualness and self-effacement which can seem like inconsequentiality, but this is part of the point, since McLean's 'realism' deliberately eschews the major dramatic event. All the novel's possible flashpoints never ignite. There is no fight. Patrick doesn't burn anything down, or get off with anyone. McLean's is a Flaubertian realism – keeping the author's bias and opinions out of the story is a moral and aesthetic principle. Here we have warmth, security and affection alongside loss, frustration and claustrophobia. We also have, despite reviewers' 'bristling with swear words', a low Fuck Per Page count. The F.P.P. reflects the way people actually speak in a place like Blackden. The lads swear in laddish situations; Shona swears like a trooper under pressure in the hotel kitchen, then not at all when she is out of it. Young Patrick doesn't swear in narration, only in dialogue. The aim is not to distort according to personal vision nor forge a linguistic purity, but simply to show language and people as they are: inconsistent.

This quiet, stubborn insistence on *what is* is a Kelman principle which here produces a very un-Kelman result. *Blackden* produces a picture of another, decentralised Scotland, one as real and and contemporary as the urban dispossessed picture of S.U.G. The novels of Iain Banks, Alan Warner and Robert Alan Jamieson feel like moves in the same direction. Iain Crichton Smith has been quietly producing such fiction for years; my own *Electric Brae* was an attempt to show that S.U.G., with its soaring F.P.P., was only part of the picture.

Yet I still hear it being written and taught and accepted that contemporary Scottish writing is urban, angry, guilt-ridden, refuses joy, cannot deal with women or love, sex or the middle-class. Perhaps at one time that was true. Now, increasingly, it is not. As Kelman's Children begin to go their own ways, our literature begins again to reflect our culture – multiple, mongrel, constantly changing, inviting but defying identification – heading, like Patrick in *Blackden,* we're not sure where.

And we keep reading and writing and living to find out.

Andrew Greig

Specters of Marx: The State of the Debt, the Work of Mourning, and the New International
Jacques Derrida (translated by Peggy Kamof)
Routledge
ISBN 0 41591 045 5 £11.99 pb

It was a consummation devoutly to be wished. Derrida's first sustained engagement with Marx has been long awaited. Many would say it is long overdue. Derrida anticipates this response: 'Already I hear people saying: "You picked a good time to salute Marx!" Or else: "It's about time!" "Why so late?" I believe in the political virtue of the contretemps.'

Derrida believes in the virtue of being untimely. It is the spirit of revolution. In fact, he believes in ghosts, and one of the ghosts he believes in is Marx. Marx is dead. We know this, but Derrida constantly reminds us of this fact, as if we had not really taken it in, as though we were in denial. Marx is dead, but not dead enough. The work of mourning continues. Moreover, the 'refuteniks' still have some exorcising to do. Because Marx is coming back. And this time there's more than one.

A spectre is haunting Europe, the spectre of communism. In 1848, and still in 1995. Then as a ghost to come, now as a ghost from the past, but one which could come again. Derrida, listening to the rattling of chains in that first manifestation in *The Manifesto of the Communist Party*, insists that 'one can never distinguish between the future-to-come and the coming-back of a specter.' Both *Living Marxism* and *Marxism Today* are titles that conjure Marx into a perpetual present.

Derrida takes the pulse of Marx and pronounces him dead, not in order to crow over his grave, but to release us from the tyranny of 'today', of a daily bread of politics that domesticates difference and refuses the possibility of a day like no other. Call it a day for Marxism. Forget *living* Marxism, or Marxism *today*. We can evoke Marx in another way. *Specters of Marx* – what a great title for a new journal!

According to Derrida: 'It will always be a fault not to read and reread and discuss Marx'. There is 'no future without Marx, without the memory and the inheritance of Marx.' Reading Derrida, one has a sense of *déjà vu*. Hegel's famous claim, repeated by Marx, that all events in history occur twice, first as tragedy then as farce, is shaken up by Derrida. Where Marx thought that it was possible to ward off the possibility of parody, through proletarian revolution, the notion of 'anachrony' is central to Derrida's understanding of time, more complex than Marx's Hegelian tragicomedy in two acts. Derrida is into survivals and revivals in a big way. Communism is out of time. So what's new? It was out of time a century and a half ago. We've been here before. Derrida turns Hamlet's remark that 'the time is out of joint' into a political theory that offers hope, and the prospect of an unforeseen eruption. The cycle of tragedy and farce can always be broken.

There is a risk implicit in paying attention to Marx now that 'communism is dead'. The risk, as Derrida puts it, 'is that one will try to play Marx off against Marxism so as to neutralize, or at any rate muffle the political imperative'. Turning Marx into a 'classic' will earth his revolutionary energy. Derrida is eager 'to avoid the neutralizing anaesthesia of a new theoreticism', the idea that Marx can be read safely as a philosopher in the wake of communism, now that we are no longer afraid of 'a ghost that goes on speaking.' Derrida wants to welcome Marx as a disruptive outsider: 'Marx remains an immigrant ... a glorious, sacred, accursed but still clandestine immigrant as he was all his life ... One should not rush to make the clandestine immigrant an illegal alien, or, what always risks coming down to the same thing, to domesticate him. To neutralise him through naturalization'.

Are those who pronounce communism dead signing a death certificate or issuing a death warrant? Derrida interprets for the dead: 'In short, it is often a matter of pretending to certify death there where the death certificate is still the performative of an act of war or the impotent gesticulation, the restless dream, of an execution.' Fear of the dead is pervasive. There is always the danger of political levitation, of an uprising. Derrida parts company from a recent French tradition that wants to claim Marx as a philosopher, or to strip his thought of its messianic import: 'Not only must one not renounce the emancipatory desire, it is necessary to insist on it more than ever.' Derrida refuses any distinction between Marx's philosophical and political writings. He refuses, too, the division of Marx into late and early, between the Marx of the Paris Manuscripts and the Marx of *Capital*. All Marx is late Marx, because Marx is late. He is the late Marx. He has ceased to be. But all Marx is also early Marx. Marx is untimely. More untimely than is suggested by the cataloguing information on this text, where it is filed under '1. Marx, Karl, 1818-1883. 2. Communism. 3. Post-communism.' That third classification belongs, in Derrida's view to the realm of wishful thinking. We all know the apocryphal tale of Mao being asked what he thought of the French Revolution and replying that it was too early to say.

Derrida proposes a new *hauntology* against the prevailing ontology. For Derrida, 'Haunting belongs to the structure of every hegemony.' We are all heirs of Marx, and we are all haunted by Marx. His is the medium in which we move. Like Hamlet, we are following a ghost, the ghost of a dead father, but 'what seems to be out in front, the future, comes back in advance: from the past, from the back.' Marx himself was something of a ghostbuster, Derrida reminds us: 'Marx does not like ghosts any more than his adversaries do. He does not want to believe in them. But he thinks of nothing else. He believes rather in what is supposed to distinguish them from actual reality, living effectivity. He believes he can oppose them, like life to death, like vain appearances of the simulacrum to real presence. He believes enough in the dividing line of this opposition to want to denounce, chase away, or exorcise the specters but by means of critical analysis and not by some counter-magic. But how to distinguish between the analysis that denounces magic and the counter-magic that it still risks being?'

What Derrida wants to deconstruct is the opposition between the real and unreal, matter and spirit, natural and supernatural. He is not calling for a return to idealism, but for a broader, more inclusive and rigorously all-embracing materialism, one that will incorporate ghosts. Deconstruction is a radicalisation of Marxism insofar as it widens the net of materialism. Derrida is the perfect host, for whom there can be no uninvited guest at the table: 'This hostility to ghosts, a terrified hostility that sometimes fends off terror with a burst of laughter, is perhaps what Marx will always have had in common with his adversaries... He will have tried to conjure (away) the ghosts *like* the conspirators of old Europe on whom the *Manifesto* declares war.' Another familiar tenet of deconstruction – you become like the thing you attack.

Derrida dwells on what he considers an untenable distinction between 'use value' and 'exchange value'. It is impossible to reconstitute the mindbending, not to mention 'table-turning' argument here, but Derrida's 'conclusion', if one can speak of conclusions for deconstruction, is that exchange value is not anterior or exterior to use value. Exchange value haunts use value.

Specters of Marx is dedicated to Chris Hani, who shared Marx's passion for Shakespeare, and 'whose assassins', Derrida recalls, 'were out to get a communist'. There is a politics of dedication which refuses to give up the dead, or to give up on the dead. For Derrida, 'there is nothing outside the text', making 'para' and 'post' problematic prefixes. Our attempts to rule certain things out of court, or out of date, are doomed to failure. The paranormal is inside the generalized social text. It has to be taken into account.

Derrida is in a unique position: 'There has never been a scholar who really, and as scholar, deals with ghosts. A traditional scholar does not believe in ghosts – nor all that could be called the virtual space of spectrality'. But Derrida is no traditional scholar. This is a book that won't be read in a hurry. It requires infinite patience, a rare commodity in our sound-bite culture. Yet, paradoxically, there's plenty of time for Derrida, and for Marx, all the time in the world. Marx may be dead, but Derrida gives him a ghost of chance. Against Marx's distinction between phrase and content in the eleventh Thesis on Feuerbach – 'The philosophers have only *interpreted* the world in various ways; the point, however, is to *change* it' – Derrida posits an 'interpretation that transforms what it interprets.' A slow process, but well worth the work it entails.

Willy Maley

Selected Poems
Carol Ann Duffy
Penguin, 1994
ISBN 0 14 058735 7 pbk £5.99

One Road
Angus Peter Campbell
Fountain Publishing, 1994
ISBN 0 9520010 1 2 £7.95
(Available from: Sabhal Mòr Ostaig, Sleat, Isle of Skye)

Sheet Mettle
Drew Milne
Alfred David Editions, 1994
ISBN 1 874433 00 3 £6.50
(Available from: 3a Palace Road, London SW2 3DY)

'Why do you / keep me in that black box? I can ask questions too, / you know.' So speaks the ventriloquist's dummy in Carol Ann Duffy's poem 'Dummy', in a sense representing all the other previously mute creatures whom Duffy, in her monologues, sets free from the 'black box' of silence where they've always been kept, allowing them a voice. Bored schoolkids, Aesop's wife, a thief, a murderer, a tabloid writer, even the dolphins kept in a tank ('And now we are no longer blessed, for the world / will not deepen to dream in'): Duffy gets inside the skins, and minds, of others, to let them tell the story of their lives.

Each of her four collections represented here (together with work from the forthcoming *The World's Wife*) are peopled as thickly as fiction with characters, and Duffy slips effortlessly into the first person voice, whether it's one speaking out of contemporary Britain, where 'The economy booms / like cannon far out at sea', or from history – the widow of Lazarus, for example, or the American Indian who has 'sold Manhattan' ('I wonder if the ground has anything to say...').

Duffy uses these voices as a way of exploring what's going on beneath the perceived surface, most obviously perhaps in 'Model Village', where characters intersperse the picture-book description with *Under Milk Wood*-like monologues. There's often a submerged eroticism lurking too, as in 'Correspondents': 'Beneath my dress, my breasts / swell for your lips... This secret life is Gulliver, / held down by strings of pleasantries'. This sense of duplicity, of double lives, often extends to the characters deceiving themselves, or not quite knowing who they are, as in 'Liar', about a woman who invents stories of her life. But as Duffy writes, allowing no distance, and implicating the reader, 'She lived like you do, a dozen slack rope-ends / in each dream hand, tugging uselessly on memory / or hope. Frayed.'

Amongst all these voices there's little sense of the poet herself, other than as ventriloquist, allowing her 'dummies' to speak. But by the end of her third book, *The Other Country*, the poems are becoming more personal: the 'I' is now sometimes Duffy herself. Here, and in her most recent book *Mean Time*, she begins to probe questions of 'other countries', of exile and loss. She writes of her own childhood exile from Scotland, remembering how an accent is suddenly 'wrong', how '*I want our own country*, I said'. And another poem about that lost accent, 'The way my mother speaks', traces the strange ways in which language, as well as landscape, changes as the poet moves from north to south.

The old language, the tongue of

'the other country' gets lost, along with memories of childhood ('the vanishing scents and colours like a melting balloon'). In 'Moments of Grace', 'Memory's a caged bird won't fly', and, similarly, 'A thin skin lies on the language', which only 'moments of grace', the 'blessing' of love, can lift, giving the poet vibrancy again. But it's in another poem, 'Away and See', that this fragile optimism in the face of loss comes through most strongly: 'Away and see the things that words give a name to' writes Duffy, exuding a wonderful sense of the enthusiastic curiosity that sends her delving, with such remarkable poetic skill, into the fascination of other people's lives, as well as the lost country of her own past.

For Angus Peter Campbell, coming from South Uist and now living on Skye, the themes of loss, exile and the fragility of language are also familiar ones. His second collection, *One Road*, with poems in both Gaelic and English, records a way of life and explores its history.

At his best, Campbell produces poems with a simplicity that speaks volumes, as in 'Sgailaraidh': 'The men / at sea. / The world of coloured flags and / the world of women, / creels on wide backs.', or in the brief poem 'Now', quoted in full:

> Today, Blàbheinn looks like my father,
> the first sprinkling of winter snow
> and a tiny wisp of white cloud
> brushing across his gentle forehead.

In poems like these, however brief, there's a feeling of universality, so that in 'In the sink', for example, Campbell sees the whole world in the image of his mother, 'grey and bowed', washing dishes: 'The universe is filled with great stories / that have, finally, filtered down to this sink...' This universality, the relating of the world of the islands to elsewhere, can occasionally sound forced and self-conscious, as where, in linking the 'one road' that joins the Islands and a lowland housing scheme, Campbell drops the words 'and Czechoslovakia' into his poem, as though to make some political point, but here it seems glib and falls flat. Elsewhere, though, the image of the 'one road' works well: in a poem on colonialism, for example, where Uist schoolboys giggle at the Eskimo language their schoolbook tells them is peculiar, or in the lovely lullaby which has Fidel Castro's mother singing to her child in Gaelic.

However, though there are a good many of these perfectly-crafted lyrics among the hundred poems in the book, too often Campbell seems over-wordy, carrying a poem on beyond what it needs. The tiny poem 'At Your Granny's', for example ('...your Granny, fae Dundee: / on Saturdays, after Doctor Who, / giving you egg and chips, and a thick slice of half-loaf. / Then home, counting the Christmas trees on the way.') seems with its last line to conjure up the anticipation of Christmas far more evocatively than the much longer 'Counting the Christmas Trees' which draws the memory out, and adds too much of the voice of the knowing adult to that of the excited child.

Like this one, many of the poems seem to ramble, and often seem a broth, a jumbled mix of memory and anecdote, with chunks of prose, bits of the Bible, and fragments of other peoples' poems thrown into the mix. There can be an endearing freshness to this, a sense of the poet being at your side, telling you tales and throwing in asides as he goes, with a kind of Whitmanesque enthusiasm and desire to include everything. But too often there's a lack of rhythm, a feeling that the words have not been shaped or structured, so that the poetry seems more like fragmented prose. The apparent lack of editing – either on the part of Campbell, or of his publishers – is a pity, as it seems that some of the poems could have tightened up to better effect.

One Road seems, therefore, rather an uneven book, that might have been better for being somewhat shorter and more thoroughly edited, so that the excellent lyric poems are not drowned out by the noise of longer, less considered ones.

After Campbell's formlessness, Drew Milne's strict verse forms come as a sharp contrast. Like Campbell's, his poems are something of a soup, gathering eclectic fragments along the way. Milne's ingredients, though, are very different: while Campbell's are as earthy and accessible as home-grown vegetables, Milne's are more like esoteric spices, ground to perfection. His references are wide-ranging and multi-lingual, his puns (beginning with the title) all-pervasive.

There's a richness of language, a delight in it, that's beguiling, and Milne has written elsewhere of the importance of the play of poetic language, how it comes out of the 'wounds of a divided body we call communication'. He also speaks of 'thinking with one's ears', seeming to imply that the sound of language is pre-eminent, and in his poems it appears that language, as an abstract force, can be allowed to dominate over meaning. For his work is often cryptic, maze-like in its intricacy, withholding meaning like a treasure that can only to be found once all the clues have been deciphered.

So his self-proclaimed politics are therefore more or less buried in the interstices of these dense and complex poems, belying the simplicity of the cover drawing which makes a neat comment on the attitude of government to the endlessly dispensable 'pool of unemployed'.

Though most of the poems don't wear their political hearts on their sleeves, the final sequence 'Foul Papers' is a potent comment on the reality of living in a free market economy. Each section begins with the word 'Clamour', and though it's hardly a war cry, it does offer some memorable phrases: 'A young man died / of chicken pox and one party rule', while in the city, where 'bull / is the name of the game in soft gold' and 'the grey suit sticks to each skin', the dealers are oblivious to the 'handless baby clusters' they have indirectly created. Similarly in 'A Garden of Tears', which begins 'It's a long way from love to the state we're in', there are ruminations on the arms trade, 'the milky way of defence costs', the fact that 'we fear no more the heat of the trident'.

Compared, though, to the voices of ordinary people so perceptively represented by Duffy, these seem remote and intellectualized comments on society, so that Milne's purported beliefs and his subtly layered forms sit oddly together. There are a few brief, demotic lines in Scots which work well, suggesting that this might be a voice to be explored further, but Milne's love of English, its sounds and rhymes and curious double meanings, shines through these poems, and phrases leap from the page – 'the cream lined plum', 'the velvet crumble of voice', and, in one of the sonnets in 'A Garden of Tears', the loveliness of lines like

> ...this eldritch sadness stills the warm felt of breath
> across whose cheek, and in tears, the curfew dries
> as hope is salted round the lips in Gaza...

But though the sounds and surfaces may be beautiful, the meaning is often obtuse and often buried deep. Reading Milne's poems is like trying to picture someone else's dream, to get inside another's mind – and unlike Duffy, who acts as a kind of translator, slipping between the minds of her characters and those of her readers, Milne offers little in the way of a phrase book, a common tongue.

Elizabeth Burns

theatre SCOTLAND

Scotland's essential quarterly theatre magazine. Every issue includes a contemporary Scottish playscript, star-name interviews and lively debate, all lavishly illustrated with photographs from Scotland's most exciting young photographers.

On sale at theatre box offices and book shops for only £3 or a *discount subscription rate* with this advert for only £10.

Make cheques payable to
THEATRE SCOTLAND
and send to:
**Theatre Scotland (Box ER)
9a Annandale Street, Edinburgh
EH7 4AW**

or phone with Credit Card details:
031 556 3255

SHORTLEET

INSTITUTE OF IRISH STUDIES
QUEEN'S UNIVERSITY, BELFAST

Ulster 1641: Aspects of the Rising
Edited by Brian Mac Cuarta SJ
ISBN 085389 491 4 hb £15

A comprehensive exploration of the breakdown in Ulster society between natives and settlers, along ethnic and religious lines.

Dictionary of Ulster Biography
Kate Newmann
ISBN 085389 478 7 pb £9.50

A celebration of extraordinary lives, the dictionary includes the men and women who have belonged to Ulster and who have achieved in some significant way.

Nationalism and Unionism
Conflict in Ireland in the late 19th and early 20th centuries
Edited by Peter Collins
ISBN 085389 495 7 pb £9.50

Ten essays, written with both the academic and the general reader in mind, cover all the major aspects of this seminal period of Irish history.

'Life that is Exile':
Daniel Corkery and the Search for Irish Ireland
Patrick Maume
ISBN 085389 492 2 hb £16.50

The first full study of Corkery, drawing on much new material including his private papers.

Irish Review
A forum for critical and creative writing in English and Irish
Two issues per year; annual subscription £12/$30 including postage
Issue 15 (February 1994) focusses on the politics and culture of Northern Ireland in the wake of the Downing Street Declaration.

The Irish Diaspora: A Primer
Donald Harman Akenson
ISBN 085389 499 x hb £22.50

For the first time the Irish Diaspora is dealt with as a single world-wide phenomenon.

8 FITZWILLIAM STREET, BELFAST BT9 6AW
TEL/FAX: (0232) 439238

Shortleet will include brief notices of books, magazines and journals of possible interest, some of which may have received scant publicity elsewhere. Not all will be recent publications. Send review copies/advance information to the editors, Edinburgh Review, 22 George Square, Edinburgh EH8 9LF.

Scanning the Forth Road Bridge
Robin Bell
Peterloo Poets, 2 Kelly Gardens, Calstock, Cornwall PL18 9SA
ISBN 871471 46 H 48pp £5.95

Bell's poetry has a broad subject base, expressed in language-as-spoken, but carefully crafted so that even rhyme is unobtrusive. Here and there other voices break in: poetry takes the spotlight as in the title poem 'a handy mnemonic for metrical forms in which iambic trains, trochaic trains, dactylic trains etc cross the Forth Bridge in their various rhythms'. Others are set in the author's native Perthshire, warm rememberings of family and friends, or are treatments of strangeness and dislocation, like his celebrations of James 'Balloon' Tytler, the 18th century eccentric, and John Two Salmon, a native American touring the Paris exhibition.

Klytemnestra's Bairns
Bill Dunlop
diehard, 3 Spittal Street, Edinburgh EH3 9DY
ISBN 0 946230 21 8 55 pp. £4.50

The text of Dunlop's Scots translation of Aeschylus's *Oresteia* cycle, as performed on Calton Hill during the Edinburgh Festival last year. 'This version imagines a possible response to a request from a financially constrained Athens for an accessible reworking of the text, making use of local varieties of language' and it is accessible Scots, easily read without the aid of a 'howdumbdeid' heid.

Providence II
Poems and photographs by Ian Stephen
The Windfall Press, Hedmark, 42 Gress, Isle of Lewis PA86 0NB
ISBN 1 874167 01 H 95 pp. £10.95 pb.

This beautifully produced volume of Stephen's highly individual work is drawn from the world he lives and works in – the seas, winds, tides, shorelines of Lewis, where he makes his living as a Coastguard Officer. Stephen's poetry, insistent like the swell of the ocean, spins graceful stories of sea-faring island folk, their work and sense of place, in verse forms created out of carefully controlled internal dynamics. This is complemented by around thirty fine colour photographs of things maritime and a foreword outlining the poet's lifelong relationship to his subjects. All royalties from this edition go to Friends of the Earth.

Dan
Kenneth C. Steven
Scottish Cultural Press, PO Box 106, Aberdeen AB9 8ZE
ISBN 1 898218 07 2 160pp.
£5.95 pb

In *Dan* Kenneth Steven tells the lifestory of his eponymous protagonist retrospectively, as the old Perthshire hill-farmer rises from his death bed for a final walk around his land. Every step presses on memories reaching back through a century of war and migration, and the episodes that have shaped him spring to life. The old ways which Dan represents are under threat and Steven, whose home is in Highland Perthshire, seeks to celebrate them in this, his second novel. The rural world is portrayed not as a net to escape from, but one to mend, in a prose style heavy with poetry and reminiscent of Neil Gunn's mystic wanderings through the borderland between Gaelic and English culture. A gently elegaic antidote to the harsher urban school of contemporary Scottish fiction.

Life for Each
Daisy Zamora, trans. Dinah Livingstone
Katabasis, 10 St. Martins Close, London NW1 0HR
ISBN 0 904872 22 H 70 pp.
£5.95 pb

Zamora was a Sandinista combatant and was behind the clandestine Radio Sandino which broadcast the call for insurrection in 1979. Now a professor of literature at the central American University in Managua, this is the first appearance of her work in English. Dinah Livingstone, herself an accomplished poet, presents her translations alongside the originals. This is poetry born out of personal and political struggle, painful to read yet all the more inspiring for that.

Muse in Torment: The Psychopathology of Creative Writing
Alex Mezey
The Book Guild Ltd., 25 High Street, Lewes, Sussex
ISBN 0 86332 925 X 328 pp.
£12.95 hb

A lengthy study examining 'the contribution that mental disorder can make to literature'. Dr Mezey, who has a private psychiatric practice in Harley Street, digs deep into the minds of the great writers, using their fiction, letters and autobiographies as source material. Sick minds? Mezey's conclusion is that 'among the greatest writers and poets there is the most disturbing collection of neuroses, obsessions and perversions'. But before you reach for the pistol, hear his final words: 'Mental pathology, or its absence, can never be the criterion against which the worth of a work of art, or of an idea, can be judged'. In the words of Jaspers, 'The spirit stands above the antithesis of health and disease'. Whew! Not easy reading for the creative writer, but a profoundly worthwhile work.

The Beetle House
David Crystal
Clocktower Press, 27 Alfred Street, Stromness KW16 3DF
ISBN 1 873767 04 8 28pp £2.50

Another in Clocktower's highly collectable series of pamphlets, which have showcased the emerging talents of Alison Kermack, Irvine Welsh and Alan Warner among others. Northumberland-born David Crystal, who now edits DOG magazine in London, writes sometimes poignant, sometimes funny downbeat poems which sketch the outlines of half-lives glimpsed among the detritus of the 90's, like in his *Jarrow Elvis* where 'Gracelands is hungry. Stereo smashed/ the last suit in the pawn shop window'. In *The Beetle House*, though disappointment hovers over dreams, Crystal's poetry is resigned to coursing through reality.

Footsteps of the Goddess
Margaret Gillies Brown
Akros Publications, 18 Warrender Pk. Terrace, Edinburgh EH9 1EF
ISBN 086142 019 5 59pp.

Margaret Gillies Brown's sixth volume of verse marks the relaunch of Duncan Glen's Akros, such a force in Scottish poetry a generation ago. In this collection, inspired by Virgil's *Georgics*, MGB excels in lyric renderings of country life where closely observed detail spurs correspondent thought, so that landscape and mindscape become one. Forms and tones vary, between patterned and free verse, English and Scots, the philosophical and the humourous, but throughout her words are reassuringly calm and hopeful, a still centre in the *fin de siecle* typhoon.

Chapman No 78–79: Ian Hamilton Finlay
Editor Alec Finlay
4 Broughton Place, Edinburgh EH1 3AX
ISBN 0 906772 61 3 208pp.
£5.95 pb

A double issue of 'Scotland's premier literary magazine' devoted to the life and work of Ian Hamilton Finlay, and guest-edited by his son, this is a fascinating miscellany of Finlay-related pieces. Contributions to the cornucopia include memoirs of IHF's crucial role in the radical Scottish poetry scene of the early sixties by Gael Turnbull, Duncan Glen, and Michael Hamish Glen; an appreciation of his early poems by David Black; reviews and examples of his correspondence with international poets; essays on his work by, among others, the editor, Mary Ann Caws, John Haldane, Timothy Neat and Angus Calder. Sandwiched between these are eighteen pages of IHF's poem-sculptures, plus a number of short testimonials on the inspirational value of a visit to Little Sparta by writers such as Ian Stephen and Tessa Ransford. An outstanding issue, essential to all those who want to tune to the IHF wavelength.

Fellow Readers: notes on multi-plied language
Robin Kinross
Hyphen Press, 51 Grafton Road, London NW5 3DX
ISBN 0 907259 07 3 32 pp. £4.50 pb

An intriguing essay on contemporary debates in typography and graphic design, arguing against those who regard linguistic theory after Sausurre as justifying the creation of 'complex, hard-to-decipher work [which] does not, as the proponents of deconstruction argue, give freedom of interpretation to readers. Rather it creates a high-sounding alibi for an old habit of desingers: to impose their will onto users of their products'. Instead, Kinross emphasises the social role of typography, where 'multiplied text and images provide a common ground'.

Children in Society: a libertarian critique
Stephen Cullen
Freedom Press, 84b Whitechapel High Street, London E1 7QX
ISBN 0900384 62 H 43pp. £1.20

Cullen criticises the effects of the once traditional 'strict routine' on a child's development, and attempts to define those areas of contemporary life which most curtail the realisation of a child's freely-arrived-at needs, such as the influence of 'mass-consumption society'. The imposition of adult priorities 'refuses to treat children as having equal status and rights as any adult' and condemns them to a life of conforming, of being moulded to the plans of others and of learning to manipulate in turn. A wise and earnest discussion of essential issues.

Writings Against Power and Death
Alex Comfort, ed. David Goodway
Freedom Press, 84b Whitechapel High Street, London E1 7QX
ISBN 0900384 71 9 168pp. £5.00

A collection of all Comfort's anarchist writings, including his most definitive individual statement *Peace and Obedience* and his classic contribution to anarchist thought *Authority and Deliquency*. Now best known as the author of *The Joy of Sex*, Comfort was a prodigy whose career stretched broadly, as novelist, poet, critic, medical doctor and pioeer biologist. In this volume, David Goodway provides a substantial study of Comfort's life and work in an introduction which places his anarchism in the context of all his other activities.

Cutting Teeth 1
ed. Carl MacDougall, Graham McKenzie, Collette Coen, Jim Craig.
c/o Castlemilk Library, 100 Castlemilk Drive, Glasgow G45 9TN £1.99 45pp.

New A4 format magazine arising out of writer's group activity and the Castlemilk writer's residency first held by Dilys Rose and now by co-editor Carl MacDougall. From the brief editorial it seems that the magazine exists to provide an outlet for local writers, but the startling day-glo pink cover boasts an array of established talent including Agnes Owens, Duncan McLean, Graham Fulton and Janet Paisley. There's much more inside, where *Cutting Teeth* is equally as bold in its layout, sometimes giving short single poems a full page, so creating mini posters.

Northern Lights
ed. Marian McCraith
Lancaster House, 255 Lancaster Road, Morecambe LA4 5TJ
ISBN 0 9523154 0 8 149pp.
£6.99 pb

Northern Lights provides 'a platform for talented new writers from the north of England', twenty short stories from twenty 'unique voices'. Editor Marian McCraith admits to a retrospective realisation that many of the stories share certain themes: 'the main character is an outsider, alienated from their situation and yearning to belong in some way – to a community, a family or one other person'. She doesn't see this as a weakness, but the dominant '(s)he said/(s)he said' form can weary the reader. While none of the stories are less than interesting, a little experimental writing, or more idiosyncratic approaches to the short story form along the lines of David Almond's poetic *The Man with the Ladder*, would have helped enliven the collection as a whole.

Talus No. 8
ed. Marzia Balzani, Hanne Bramness, Stephen Want, Shamoon Zamir
c/o Department of English, King's College, Strand, London WC2R 2LS
ISSN 0951 628X 213pp. £5/$10

Issued bi-annually, Talus 'is intended as a meeting place for writers from many countries and will publish new poetry, drama and fiction, as well as essays investigating inter-cultural materials and area studies'. No. 8 includes a short interview with Phillip Glass, a superb translation of sixty one stanzas by Tunisian Abdelwahab Meddeb, *Tomb of Ibn Arabi*, and a substantial essay *Ta'Wil & Henry Corbin: the legacy for Radical American Poetics* by Eric Mottram. An attractively-produced eclectic journal, refusing to be pigeon-holed as simply 'academic'.

Metropolitan No. 2 new urban writing
ed. Elizabeth Baines, Ailsa Cox
19 Victoria Avenue, Manchester M20 2GY
ISSN 1350 3227 48pp. £2.50

A4 magazine from Manchester, here publishing fiction by new or less than well known writers, other than Moy McCrory and Glen Patterson whose essay 'on cities and fiction' is the only non-fiction piece included. Without losing sense of a house-style, work included displays a good variety of voices and the youthful 'street' feel suggests that Metropolitan has a bright future, though it might usefully stretch to include some sharp-end poetry in forthcoming issues.

Casscando Issue 4
the national student literary magazine
ed. Lisa Boardman, Emily Ormond
Cascando Press, PO Box 1499, London SW10 9TZ
ISSN 0966 7628 107pp. £4.50

The fourth issue of this super-glossy showcase for student talent includes a memoir of Derek Jarman, interviews with Sean Hughes and John Hegley and a translation from the Polish of Andrzej Stasiuk, as well as poetry, fiction and reviews. A useful focus for the literary minded generally, the editorial smacks of rage-against-exclusivity. The *New Generation* poetry promotion comes in for heavy shelling, suggesting that the iconoclastic fury is such that the hype-blimps are exploded even as they rise: 'Where's the bravery in art vanished to? Thirty-somethings are not usually the target audience of Radio 1 FM, which was persuaded to read a New Generation poem a day for a week. Perhaps this is where bravery has got them'. And bravo to all that...

Light's List of Literary Magazines
John Light
Photon Press, 29 Longfield Road, Tring, Herts. HP23 4DG
ISBN 1 897968 01 9 70p

A listing of around 350 small-press magazines in what looks like *samizdhat* form. Many could be found in a writer's yearbook, but some of the lesser known titles fascinate – it's worth 70p to know that there is a 'Vocal Poetry Tabloid' called *Pomes* published in York, or indeed where to send your 'pagan poetry' (*Moonstone*), your polemic (*Massacre*), your 'Arthurian poetry (yes, you guessed, *The Round Table*); and, for that piece you can't quite make up your mind about, try *Xizquil* in New Mexico, who are interested only in 'strange fiction'.

Trafika: An International Literary Review
ed. Michael Lee, Alfredo Sánchez, Jeffrey Young
Janouského 14, 170 00 Prague 7, Czech Republic
224pp Single copies $10, subscription $35

Produced quarterly in Prague entirely in English, *Trafika* has four issues extant at the time of writing. Early numbers featured such as Miroslav Holub, Arnost Lustig, Josef Svorecḱy, Bo Carpelan and Joyce Carol Oates. No. 4 presents an interview with Paul Bowles; a discussion between Mia Couto (Mozambique) and José Eduardo Agualusa (Angola) on post-colonial experience; short fiction from John Barth and Kristien Hemmerechts (Belgium); poetry by Denis Johnson, Douglas O'Connor (USA) and Edoardo Albinati (Italy); and first-time English publication of work by András Csedy (Hungary), Lars Jakobsen (Sweden), Xiao Kaiyu (China), Luis Leante (Spain), Elena Sazanovich (Russia) and Klaus Johannes Thies (Germany). The editors are keen to establish contacts in Scotland and invite submissions. Guidelines are available from *Edinburgh Review* on request.

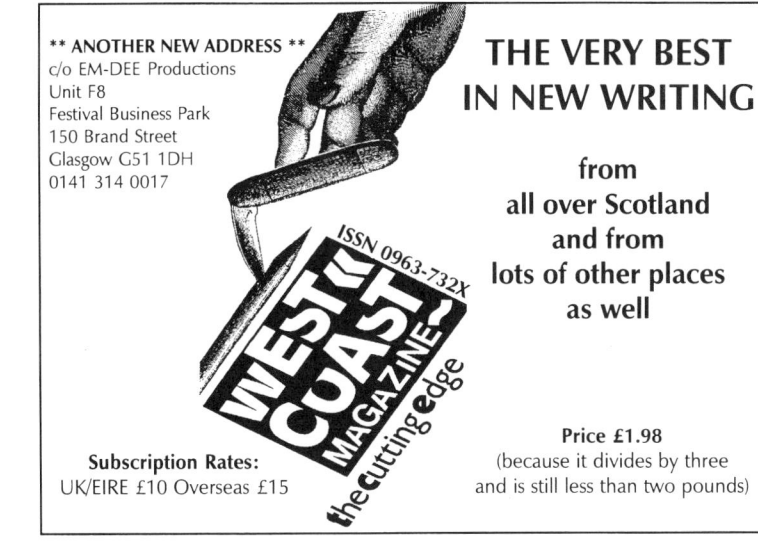

** ANOTHER NEW ADDRESS **
c/o EM-DEE Productions
Unit F8
Festival Business Park
150 Brand Street
Glasgow G51 1DH
0141 314 0017

THE VERY BEST IN NEW WRITING

from
all over Scotland
and from
lots of other places
as well

ISSN 0963-732X

WEST COAST MAGAZINE
the cutting edge

Subscription Rates:
UK/EIRE £10 Overseas £15

Price £1.98
(because it divides by three
and is still less than two pounds)

Edinburgh Review

SUBSCRIPTION RATES (2 Issues)

Individuals		**Institutions**	
UK and EC	£12	UK and EC	£22
Overseas	£13.50	Overseas	£24
N. America	$23.50	N. America	$44

Postage
Surface postage included in the subscription.
Please add £5 or $10 for airmail delivery.

HOW TO ORDER

Return this form to:
Subscriptions
EDINBURGH UNIVERSITY PRESS LTD
22 George Square
Edinburgh EH8 9LF
Tel: 0131 650 6207
Fax: 0131 662 0053

Please send me a 2 issue subscription to *Edinburgh Review*.

NAME _____

ADDRESS _____

_____

POSTCODE _____

☐ I enclose cheque/money order
(please make cheques payable to
Edinburgh University Press Ltd)

☐ Please debit £
to my VISA/Mastercard
Account number _____

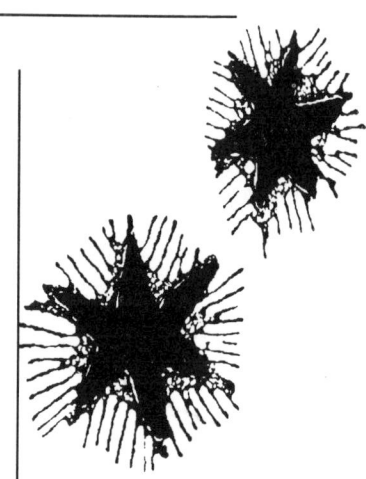

Expiry date _____

Under its new editorship this acclaimed literary and cultural review will continue to publish a wide range of original and topical material with a new emphasis on the literary by both new and established writers. Lively, controversial and eclectic, Edinburgh Review is the only forum which positively asserts the rich diversity of Scottish arts and culture while attending to international literary and cultural events. New poetry and short stories rub shoulders with philosophical musings, interviews and book reviews in 'Scotland's foremost intellectual/literary magazine.'
Scotland on Sunday.